Imagining

Imagining the Congo

The International Relations of Identity

Kevin C. Dunn

IMAGINING THE CONGO
Copyright © Kevin C. Dunn, 2003.
All rights reserved. No part of this book may be used or reproduced in any manner whatsoever without written permission except in the case of brief quotations embodied in critical articles or reviews.

First published 2003 by
PALGRAVE MACMILLAN™
175 Fifth Avenue, New York, N.Y. 10010 and
Houndmills, Basingstoke, Hampshire, England RG21 6XS.
Companies and representatives throughout the world.
Transferred to digital printing 2005
PALGRAVE MACMILLAN is the global academic imprint of the Palgrave Macmillan division of St. Martin's Press, LLC and of Palgrave Macmillan Ltd.
Macmillan® is a registered trademark in the United States, United Kingdom and other countries. Palgrave is a registered trademark in the European Union and other countries.

ISBN 1-4039-6159-X hardback
ISBN 1-4039-6160-3 paperback

Library of Congress Cataloging-in-Publication Data

Dunn, Kevin C., 1967-
  Imagining the Congo : the international relations of identity / by Kevin C. Dunn.
    p. cm.
  Includes bibliographical references (p.) and index.
  ISBN 1-4039-6159-X—ISBN 1-4039-6160-3 (pbk)
    1. Congo (Democratic Republic)—Relations—Foreign countries. 2. Congo (Democratic Republic)—Foreign public opinion. 3. Congo (Democratic Republic)—Politics and government. 4. Congo (Democratic Republic)—Colonial influence.
I. Title.
DT653.3.D86 2003
967.51-dc21

A catalogue record for this book is available from the British Library.

Design by Autobookcomp.

First edition: May 2003
10 9 8 7 6 5 4 3 2 1

Printed in the United States of America.

For

Mattie C. Fallowfield

and

Anna G. Creadick

Contents

Acknowledgments	ix
List of Acronyms	xi
One. Introduction: Identity and International Relations in the "Heart of Darkness"	1
Two. Inventing the Congo: Henry Morton Stanley, Leopold II, and the "Red Rubber" Scandal	21
Three. Congo as Chaos, Lumumba as *Diable*: Independence and the 1960 Crisis	61
Four. From Congo to Zaïre: Mobutu's Production of an "Authentic" National Identity	105
Five. Cancer, Kabila, and the Congo: Central Africa at the End of the Twentieth Century	139
Six. Taking Inventory	171
Notes	183
Works cited	197
Index	215

Acknowledgments

A number of events transpired while I wrote this book. When I began, the Congo was called Zaïre and its dictator, Mobutu Sese Seko, was relatively healthy and seemingly firmly in control. Now, several years later, Zaïre is again the Congo, and Mobutu has been dethroned and buried, as has his successor. These changes are a greater reflection of the quickness of events in central Africa than of the slowness of my typing skills. In the several years that it has taken me to research and write this book, the list of people and institutions I am indebted to has grown. Undoubtedly, this list will only capture the tip of the iceberg of the innumerable people who have helped me along the way. Any omissions are deeply regretted at the outset.

At the institutional level, the research for this project was partly funded by a grant from the Belgian American Education Foundation (BAEF). Thanks to the BAEF, the Unité de science politique et de relations internationales (SPRI) and Institut d'Etudes du Developpement at the Université Catholique de Louvain, the Departement sociale en culturele anthropologie at the Katholieke Universiteit Leuven, the Institut Africain in Tervuren, Mbarara University of Science and Technology, and Boston University's African Studies Center and political science department. To the staff and personnel of each institution, I owe my deepest thanks. Thanks also go to the faculty and students of Boston University, Hartwick College, and Hobart and William Smith Colleges, and to the editors of *Millennium*. A shorter version of chapter four appeared in *Millennium*, 30(2), 2001.

I am deeply indebted to the various teachers who have helped educate me about Africa over the years, particularly Edouard Bustin, Timothy Shaw, and J. Harris Proctor. Thanks also to Sheila Smith, James Der Derian, James Pritchett, and David Mayers for their feedback on the manuscript at its earliest stages. I have also been fortunate that Daniel Bach, David Blaney, T. J. Boisseau, Patrick Chabal, Roxanne Lynn Doty, Siba Grovogui, Naeem Inayatullah, and René Lemarchand lent their time and energy to read this work (in parts or its entirety). I am deeply grateful to them all for their insights, criticisms, and support.

Jody Gardner, Nathan Coscia, Jack Vickrey, and Chris Welch tried to keep me in tune along the way, which was never an easy task. Several people provided invaluable support and inspiration over the years, most notably Morten Bøås, T. J. Boisseau, Gabriel Callealta, John F. Clark, Chuck Crews, Filip De Boeck, Marc Decrollier, Frédéric and Cécile Delepierre, Liliane de Muynck, Patricia Goff, Jean Hay, Alex Hayden, Haco Hoang, Kirk Hoppe, Jean-Pierre Jacquemin, Anne Kirk, Jules Marchal, Marianne Marchand, Pamela Mbabazi, Jane Parpart, Larry Swatuk, Dominque Thelen, Mary Vanderlaan, Jean-Luc Vellut, Gauthier de Villers, Cynthia Weber, Kate White, and Jean-Claude Willame. Thanks also to my parents, Bill and Diane Dunn, and my extended families: the Dunns, Holts, Creadicks, and Shermans. Special loving gratitude to the next generation: Charlotte, Alex, Erica, and Jasper Dunn and Isaiah, Kade, and Avery Holt. I am indebted to my colleagues at Hobart and William Smith, who have been supportive while I finished this book, especially Cedric K. Johnson, Craig Rimmerman, David Ost, Jodi Dean, Manisha Desai, Paul Passavant, Virginia Tilley, and Richard Salter. Thanks also to the cartoonists, newspapers, and institutions who let me reproduce their work throughout this book. At Palgrave Press, I am especially indebted to the fabulous Ella Pearce and the dashing Nathan Gemignani. Most of all, thanks to Anna Creadick and Jasper C. Dunn. Anna remains my greatest inspiration, editor, intellectual colleague, fan, friend, and partner.

List of Acronyms

ABAKO	Alliance des Bakongo
AFDL	Alliance des Forces Démocratiques pour la Libération du Congo
CEHC	Comité d'Etudes du Haut-Congo
CIA	Central Intelligence Agency
CNDD	National Council for the Defense of Democracy
CRA	Congo Reform Association
DRC	Democratic Republic of the Congo
FAR	Forces Armées Rwandaises
FAZ	Forces Armées Zaïroises
FDD	Front for the Defense of Democracy
FNLA	Frente Nacional de Libertação de Angola
FRODEBU	Front Démocratique du Burundi
IAA	International African Association
IAC	International Association of the Congo
MLC	Mouvement pour la Libération du Congo
MNC	Mouvement National Congolais
MPLA	Movimento Popular de Libertação de Angola
MPR	Mouvement Populaire de Révolution
OAU	Organization of African Unity
RCD	Rassemblement Congolais pour la Démocratie
RPF	Rwandan Patriotic Front
SPLA	Sudan People's Liberation Army
UNITA	Uniao Nacional para a Independência Total de Angola
UPDF	Ugandan People's Defence Forces

Chapter One

Introduction: Identity and International Relations in the "Heart of Darkness"

On the afternoon of January 16, 2001, Congolese President Laurent-Désiré Kabila was sitting in his office. Kabila had been president of the Democratic Republic of the Congo for less than four tumultuous years. Earlier that day, President Kabila had refused to eat his lunch because of reports that it was poisoned. Forty-five minutes later, Rachidi Kasereka, a young member of his personal bodyguard, reportedly walked in and fired several bullets into his body at close range. Kasereka fled the scene but was apprehended and executed on the spot by the president's chief of staff, Eddy Kappend. Kabila was flown to Zimbabwe for treatment but was officially declared dead on January 18.[1]

Kabila's assassination came almost forty years to the day after the assassination of the Congo's first independent leader, Prime Minister Patrice Lumumba. In both cases, much mystery and speculation surrounds the assassinations; namely, who was really behind each murder. In the case of Kabila, one of the most thorough inquiries to date suggests that the assassin was motivated by disenchantment among the military, particularly former "child soldiers" from the eastern part of the country (Smith 2001). However, there are many questions regarding the possible involvement of participants from the south of the country and possible direct involvement by the government of Angola (Turner 2001). A complete explanation is unlikely to ever emerge.

At the time of both men's respective assassinations, the Congo was partly occupied against their wishes by foreign troops. In the case of Kabila, the entire eastern half of the country he presided over was occupied by Ugandan, Rwandan, and Burundian troops and the various Congolese rebel forces with whom they had aligned themselves. In the other half of the Congo, Kabila was only able to enjoy control through the presence of troops from Zimbabwe, Angola, and Namibia. During Kabila's four years in office, the Congo had been carved up by various neighboring forces and it resources were looted by these occupying forces, as well as by Kabila and his own entourage. While many questions still remain unanswered about Kabila's assassination, it is likely that his murder had as much or more to do with external factors than with internal Congolese dynamics. In fact, Kabila's own rise to power was largely due to the machinations of external regional actors, particularly the regimes of Rwanda and Uganda. During the 1960s, Kabila was a minor revolutionary operating in eastern Congo, particularly in the provinces of Kivu and North Katanga. During this time, a Cuban expeditionary force led by Ché Guevera briefly joined Kabila's rebels, garnering it a fleeting claim to fame (Gálvez 1999). However, by 1967, Kabila and some of his remaining supporters withdrew into the mountains of South Kivu and created a minor fiefdom in the region, featuring collective agriculture, rudimentary Marxist-Leninist reeducation, extortion and exploitation, and mineral smuggling. By the late 1970s and early 1980s, Kabila had become a successful trader and smuggler in East Africa, maintaining homes in Dar-es-Salaam and Kampala, where he reportedly encountered Yoweri Museveni, the future leader of Uganda. Museveni and former Tanzanian President Julius Nyerere would later introduce Kabila to Paul Kagame, the future leader of Rwanda. These connections proved fortuitous for Kabila when the Ugandan and Rwandan regimes began looking for a Congolese face to place on their intervention to overthrow the thirty-year-old dictatorship of Mobutu Sese Seko, who had renamed the Congo "Zaïre."[2]

Why Mobutu was overthrown is related largely to earlier events that occurred in neighboring Rwanda. In 1994, in the wake of the assassination of Rwandan President Habyarimana and Burundian President Ntaryamira, a hundred-day killing spree resulted in the murder of around 800,000 Rwandans, the overthrow of the Rwandan government by Paul Kagame's Rwandan Patriotic Front (RPF), and the exodus of over 2 million Rwandans to refugee camps inside Zaïre. These refugees were a mix of civilians, Interahamwe (the militia largely held responsible for the genocide), and members of the defeated Rwandan army (Forces Armées Rwandaises, FAR). The refugee camps quickly became controlled by the Interahamwe and FAR. Over the next two years, these groups (with the blessing of Mobutu's central government and regional strongmen) reorganized and rearmed. Soon, they began launching attacks from the camps into neighboring Rwanda and against the Banyamulenge community in South Kivu. After their requests for assistance were ignored by the international community, the Rwandan government and local Banyamulenge decided to take matters into their own hands by attacking their attackers through the organization of a rebellion. Orchestrated and assisted by the RPF regime in Kigali, the rebels quickly moved from south to north, gaining control of the 300 miles of Zaïre's eastern frontier. The refugee camps were attacked and disassembled. As the rebellion quickly gained strength and land, Laurent-Désiré Kabila was tapped to become the Congolese leader of the rebels united under the label Alliance des Forces Démocratiques pour la Libération du Congo (AFDL).

As the rebels moved westward, they were joined by other anti-Mobutists. Their external supporters included the regimes in Rwanda, Uganda, and Burundi (and some logistical support from the United States). As the rebels moved toward the capital, Kinshasa, Angolan government troops poured across the border to assist them in the overthrow of Mobutu. By May 17, 1997, Kinshasa had fallen and Mobutu and his entourage had fled. Soon afterward, Kabila proclaimed himself the new president, renamed the country the Democratic Republic of the Congo (DRC), reintroduced the flag and the currency unit originally adopted at independence, banned political parties, and began to consolidate his power.

Initially, Kabila's strategy for survival was to rely heavily upon regional and international support. Of particular importance was his dependence on Rwanda, Uganda, and Angola. However, in order to strengthen his domestic hand, he soon broke with his Rwandan and Ugandan backers. On August 2, 1998, a new rebellion broke out in the eastern part of the country, exactly where the original rebellion had occurred. It quickly became apparent that the rebellion was being directed by the regimes in Uganda, Rwanda, and (to a lesser extent) Burundi, seeking to depose the man they had imposed a year earlier. Kabila's regime was rescued by the governments of Angola, Zimbabwe, Namibia, and, to a more limited extent, Sudan and Chad. After several months of fighting, it appeared a military solution was untenable for either side. Negotiations began, but by the summer of 1999, the rebel front had splintered into three groups backed by different foreign sponsors, and fighting had broken out between the Rwandan and Ugandan contingents occupying different portions of the Congo. Despite the signing of a ceasefire, the conflict continues with the country effectively divided in half. Ugandan and Rwandan troops and their Congolese allies occupy the east. In the west, the Kinshasa government is sustained largely by the presence of thousands of Zimbabwean,

Angolan, and (to a much lesser extent) Namibian soldiers. With the ground war at a standstill, Laurent-Désiré Kabila was gunned down by one of his own bodyguards. In the immediate aftermath of the assassination, Joseph Kabila, the army chief of staff and the murdered president's twenty-nine-year-old son, was appointed the new president of the Congo.

The exact cost of the war that began in 1998 is unclear, but a *New York Times* article from February 2000 estimated that at least 100,000 combatants, refugees and civilians have been killed since it began (*New York Times,* 6 February 2000, 8). Given the events of the 1990s—two Congolese rebellions, the 1994 Rwandan genocide, and a seemingly intractable civil wars in Burundi—many observers have asserted that the region is inherently chaotic and that there is nothing Western powers can do about it (see Kaplan 1996; *Jeune Afrique,* 20 November 1996; *New York Times,* 17 March 1997; *Time,* 15 March 1999; *Newsweek,* 15 March 1999). For many in the U.S. and European media, the complex political dynamics of the civil war are incomprehensible, because they are seemingly outside the logic of established state-centric approaches to international relations: Angolans fight Angolans in western Congo while Rwandans fight Rwandans in the east.

A year after Kabila's assassination, an American nightly news program on ABC ran a series of "in-depth" reports on the war in the Congo. The title they gave the series was "Heart of Darkness." The reports by ABC, which aired during the week of January 21–25, 2002, were intended to shed "light" into this region in order to make sense and provide a sense of order to what was portrayed as inherently chaotic and anarchic. The title was extremely telling because it re-employed a century-old label originally given to the Congo by Joseph Conrad in his famous novel of the same name. The ongoing conflict, ABC News reports intonated, was further evidence that this central African country was a land of violence, chaos, and avarice, perhaps beyond the comprehension of Western audiences.

By employing the established trope of the "Heart of Darkness," ABC News inadvertently highlighted two central themes of this work. First, Western understandings of the Congo, even in the twenty-first century, rely heavily upon earlier representations generated by Westerners. This has led to an interesting paradox: While Westerners are generally uninformed about Congolese history and politics, they feel they know it well because of the powerful images of it encountered everyday. As historian David Newbury puts it: "[Central Africa] is a region not well known in the west, but one nonetheless enveloped in a century of powerful imagery—ranging from the 'Heart of Darkness' to the 'Noble

Savage'" (Newbury 1998, 76). The images that shape Western understandings of the Congo are numerous and come from such sources as *Heart of Darkness*; Tarzan; *National Geographic*; media reports on the Ebola virus, AIDS, famine, or continuing "tribal" violence; and countless cinematic and fictional portrayals of the Congo and its inhabitants. At the time of the 1998 rebellion, Barbara Kingsolver's novel *The Poisonwood Bible* was published. This best-selling novel, set in the Congo during 1960, is a story of a self-involved American missionary who takes his wife and four young daughters to save Congolese souls in the "heart" of Africa. The nonfictional events of 1960 that provide the novel's backdrop include the granting of Congo's independence by Belgium, the breakdown of the newly independent state structures, direct intervention by the United States and Belgium, and the overthrow and murder of Patrice Lumumba, the Congo's prime minister. The novel's protagonists are unable to understand the dynamics or implications of these events within their Western-defined worldviews because their perceptions of the Congo and Congolese are firmly rooted in colonially scripted images of African backwardness and primitivism. Likewise, many Western observers in the twenty-first century still conceptualize events in the Congo by employing colonial images and hundred-year-old racial stereotypes and by privileging Western definitions of the state, sovereignty, and security. As Kingsolver's novel illustrates, how one imagines the Congo frames how one understands the events there. Considering the Congo inherently chaotic and irrational, for example, guarantees that the events that occur there will lack political rationale. By re-employing the label "Heart of Darkness," ABC News attempted to make the events in central Africa comprehensible to their viewers by drawing on a tradition that frames that part of the world through a lens of primitivism, backwardness, and irrationality.

But the use of the "Heart of Darkness" label by ABC News illustrated a second and more important point that this work seeks to explore: These representations have political consequences. That is to say, discourses and imagery on the Congo's identity have directly influenced political policies toward the Congo. To put it succinctly, representing the Congo as a primitive, chaotic "heart of darkness" has made certain things happen in the political world. For example, Henry Morton Stanley, an American writer turned explorer, violently conquered and colonized the region in the name of Belgian King Leopold II, in part because he believed he was bringing "order" to a chaotic space. Seeing the inhabitants as primitive savages allowed Stanley and other colonizing agents to exact brutality against them. Such actions would have been unthinkable if the inhabitants had been imagined in other ways. By persistently employing images of the Congo as chaotic, backward, and uncivilized/uncivilizable, external actors like Stanley have worked to forcefully replace existing sociopolitical practices and systems of knowledge with Western-scripted notions of sovereignty, modernity, and development. Alternative and competing images of the Congo have frequently been produced, only to be closed off and/or stamped out. In some cases, this erasure/imposition has been done directly, as was the case in the 1960s when the United States and Belgium intervened militarily in the Congo and plotted to have its democratically elected leader assassinated after they defined Congolese independence as "chaotic" and the prime minister as a communist-leaning troublemaker. At other times, external actors have acted indirectly, as Western governments did through their installation and promotion of Mobutu Sese Seko's repressive dictatorship. In each case, the ways in which the Congo was imagined legitimated certain political actions. The long-term implications of these discourses and actions are now evident. The extent to which the people within the Congo now find their country violently fragmented, preyed upon by external actors, and marginalized by international inattention can be directly traced back to historical constructions of their identity. Those past imaginings have cumulatively helped make the current situation possible.

Reports like the ABC News series on the "Heart of Darkness" have not only been produced to explain the current conditions in the Congo but have greatly contributed to the *production* of the current events they purport to explain. By labeling their series of reports "Heart of Darkness," ABC News unwittingly underscored the fact that this and other tropes have formed the basic grammar and vocabulary of the discourses on Congolese identity, a discourse fundamental to Western understandings of itself and the African Other, a discourse that has helped produce conditions of the present. I use the term "discourse" here in a specific way, referring to "the conventions for establishing meaning, designating the true from the false, empowering certain speakers and writers and disqualifying others" (Quinby 1994, xv). Once we recognize the persistence and fluidity of these discourses, Western policies and media coverage of contemporary events can be seen as extensions of older and, to a certain degree, detrimental traditions and practices.

To understand the Congo's current condition, one needs an examination of the Congo's origins and the forces that have produced and defined it. Such a history of the present is what Michel Foucault refers to as a genealogical approach, providing a "form of history which can account for the constitution of knowledges, discourses, domains of objects, etc., without having to make reference to a subject which is either transcendental in relation to the field of events or runs in its empty sameness throughout the course of history" (Foucault 1980, 117). In the words of political scientist David Campbell, such a genealogical approach "seeks to trace how such rituals of power arose, took shape, gained importance, and effected politics. In short, this mode of analysis asks how certain terms and concepts have historically functioned within discourse" (Campbell 1992, 5). Understanding the events in the Congo today requires an examination of how the Congo has been imagined over time: exploring how the Congo has been defined, by whom, and to what ends. I speak of the "imagining" of the Congo's identity to draw attention to the constructed and contested nature of identity. In this project, I am interested in historicizing and contextualizing the construction of the Congo's identity in order to analyze its political implications. For that reason, this work focuses on four pivotal historical periods of identity production for the Congo: the colonial "invention" of the Congo at the end of the nineteenth century, its decolonization in 1960, its reinvention as "Zaïre" during the 1970s, and the "return" of the Congo at the end of the twentieth century. During each of these four periods, the identity of the Congo was being contested, with numerous forces attempting to produce and attach meanings to its territory and people. These forces have sought to create regimes of "truth" about the Congo by defining and inscribing its identity.

The Congo, Identity, and International Relations

The "Congo" did not enter the European collective imagination until 1482, when a Portuguese ship piloted by Diego Cão landed on the western shores of Africa near the mouth of a great river and encountered a group of Africans who had organized themselves into the Kingdom of Kongo. Over the next four centuries, various European groups attempted to venture up the river. All failed to reach beyond the cataracts of the river, with the British Captain Tuckey reaching the farthest in 1816. However, European interest in the interior was not particularly strong given that the resources that interested them— slaves, ivory, and other trade goods—were brought to the coast for them by African traders (Slade 1962, 20). With the collapse of the Kingdom of Kongo, the decline of the Portuguese empire, and the failure to travel further into the interior, the territory surrounding the Congo River remained peripheral to the Western imagination until European imperial powers engaged in a "scramble for Africa" at the end of the nineteenth century.

At the 1884–85 Berlin Conference, the European imperial powers formally agreed among themselves upon the physical delineations of their African possessions. King Leopold II of Belgium claimed sovereignty over the region around the Congo River basin, effectively inventing the political space known as the "Congo." The resulting political entity, like other colonially defined African states, was the creation of Western minds and not the result of African sociopolitical dynamics. As a colonial creation, the Congo serves as a representative case study for interrogating the discourses that invented and assimilated the African continent into the modern international state system. However, several factors make the Congo unique. First, the Congo was colonized at the end of the nineteenth century after most of Africa had already been "claimed" by European states. Furthermore, the Congo was regarded as the possession of an individual, Leopold II, not a European state. For these two reasons, the dynamics of colonization were distinctly different from other colonized areas. While other European powers had been engaged in their colonial projects for quite some time, Leopold II and his colonial agents had only a few years to establish their imperial control. Moreover, Leopold II's colonial project was able to borrow heavily from other, pre-existing European models. For those reasons, the mechanisms of colonial expansion and coercive control were condensed and are more easily discernible.

The Congo is also unique because, since its creation, the Congo has become overly textualized; it has been a discursive space onto which numerous actors—internally and externally—have projected characteristics, images, and meanings in their attempt to define and delineate the identity of the Congo. For many, the Congo has been regarded as the "heart of Africa," making it a symbolic stand-in for sub-Saharan Africa. Together with the "Safari Africa" of East Africa and "Apartheid Africa" of South Africa, the Congo has often been used as a conceptual marker in Western demarcations of "Africa." However, the meaning of that symbolic value has evolved over time, with varied political implications attached. For example, at the end of the nineteenth century, the Congo symbolized the promise of a free trade paradise in the minds of most Westerners. A decade later, it had become a symbol of Leopold II's greed and brutality. In the 1960s, for many Western observers, the Congo symbolized the inherent inability of Africans to rule themselves. In the 1970s, Mobutu attempted to reshape the Congo (Zaïre) into a symbol of Third World nationalism. By the end of the twentieth century, however, it was once again used to symbolize the failures of a post-colonial Africa plagued by civil war, corrupt governments, health crises, and dire poverty. It had once again become known as the "Heart of Darkness."

Throughout the past century, the Congo has also been important as a site for international competition between European colonial powers, cold war superpowers, and regional forces. Very few African states have endured as much external involvement in its affairs as has the Congo. These incursions have been possible primarily because of the ways in which the Congo has been perceived by external forces. Intervention in the Congo has been intimately tied to the Congo's identity, particularly in external actors' attempts to control the definition of the Congo and its sovereignty. As international relations theorist Cynthia Weber has noted:

> states are "written" effects of attempts to exert effective control over representation, both political and symbolic. If a state is unable politically or symbolically to represent its people, then it risks losing its source of sovereign authority . . . If, for example, a state experiencing domestic turmoil can no longer write its "people," then another sovereign state may claim to speak for the sovereign authority within this divided state (Weber 1995, 28).

In the case of the Congo, external actors have frequently attempted to characterize the country as divided, chaotic, and lacking the ability of self-articulation, which in turn has allowed external actors to speak for it.

The focus of this work is on the production and contestation of the Congo's identity. The concept of identity has become an important feature of recent international relations (IR) scholarship, where increased recognition has been given to how identity shapes the hierarchy of social positions of power, influences how actors are perceived and treated by others, and affects how actors view and understand the world around them (Zalewski and Enloe 1995). Identity is intimately linked to political acts; it is bound up with the "selves" and "others" who act in the political world. However, much of the recent work on identity in IR seems to reproduce an older trend in the discipline: the marginalization of Africa and African experiences. This marginalization furthers the Western-centrism of the discipline, much to its own detriment. For example, a large part of a state's identity involves the authorship of its sovereignty and stateness. Focusing on non-African examples tends to reify Western conceptualizations of both. However, recent scholarship in African studies has shown how sovereignty and the state have been defined and employed in myriad ways that challenge the "universality" of Western approaches and assumptions (Clapham 1996; Grovogui 1996; Villalón and Huxtable 1998; Dunn and Shaw 2001). The small degree of IR scholarship on Africa and identity, while tremendously important, has either run the risk of overemphasizing external hegemonic actors without addressing African agency or resistance (see Strang 1996 and, to a lesser extent, Doty 1996), or focused exclusively on the production of African "imagined communities" without sufficient attention to international contexts (see Mudimbe 1997). This study moves beyond approaches that overemphasize either external hegemons or internal agency to explore the contested nature of identity production, consumption, and resistance.

Identity is the product of multiple and competing discourses, which construct unstable, multiple, fluctuating, and fragmented senses of the Self and Other. The identity of the Congo, like all identities within the international realm, is socially constructed, conditional and lodged in contingencies that are historically specific, intersubjective, and discursively produced (see Hall 1995, 1996). As British sociologist/cultural theorist Stuart Hall has argued, the "subject is produced 'as an effect' through and within discourse, within specific discursive formations, and has no existence, and certainly no transcendental continuity or identity from one subject position to another" (Hall 1996, 10).[3] A useful key to understanding identity is to recognize that identities are constructed through discursive narratives. It is through discursive narratives that we make sense of the world around us and our place(s) within it. However, these narratives are rarely of our own making. Moreover, there are multiple narratives and they shift across time and space, largely through political struggle and the distribution of power. Thus, the history of the "Congo" in international relations is largely the history of the struggles over the discursive narratives and representations of identity. This work will analyze the production and contestation of these discursive narratives by exploring the specific historical/institutional sites of identity production, the specific enunciative strategies used, and the specific modalities of power at play.

It should be stressed at the outset that by focusing on discourses, I am not treating discourses as simply words or ideas but also as the actions and practices that enact the idea, that make it "real." Discourses construct the narratives that constitute our social identities and give meaning to the world around us. That is to say, discourses structure and delineate reality, making it knowable. Too often critics make the false assumption that discursive approaches deny the "reality" of the subject being discussed. Quite the contrary: Subjects are "real" only through discourse.[4] The concept of discourse has an explanatory role since social interaction can only be explained in relation to its discursive context. Unlike other IR approaches that focus on *structure* (either in a neorealist or Marxian sense), a discursive approach rejects the idea of an organizing center that arrests and grounds the play of meaning. As such, a discourse informs rather than guides social interaction by influencing the cognitive scripts, categories, and rationalities that are indispensable for social action (Torfing 1999, 81–82). Structural IR approaches mistakenly privilege prescriptive norms of conduct and specific resource allocations—both of which are discursively constructed.

A discursive analysis approach examines the discourses that construct the subject—in this case, the "Congo." Over the past century, the Congo's identity has been discursively constructed in different ways, by different actors, within different historical contexts. Yet, it is important to keep in mind that, while discourses shape power, power also shapes discourse and that power, like discourses, is never totally centralized. The primary goal of this project is to explore the relationship between discourse and power as they relate to the Congo. This is not to suggest that only the discursive is important for understanding the history of the Congo and international relations. Indeed, much work has focused on the economic practices of various actors. For example, Adam Hochschild's *King Leopold's Ghost* focuses exclusively on the Belgian king's greed while David Gibb's *The Political Economy of Third World Intervention* (1991) argues that neocolonial economic interests determined the West's relationship with Mobutu's Zaïre for several decades. These and similar works are important and valuable contributions, but they focus exclusively on material practices while completely ignoring the discursive. In reality, the material and the discursive are inherently intertwined because it is unsustainable to maintain a distinction between practice and discourse. Exclusive focus on material practices mistakenly assumes that interests, agendas, motivations, and identities are all inherently given. Yet, all of these elements are discursively articulated and produced. This present work focuses on the discursive, though not at the expense of the material, in order to better situate and explain material practices.

Material practices in international relations and discourses on the Congo are intimately related in large part because discourses enable external actors to "know" the Congo and to act upon what they "know." Certain paths of action become possible within distinct discourses, while other paths are "unthinkable." This approach has important implications with regard to social action and agency. It rejects approaches such as (neo)Realism and (neo)Liberalism, which argue that actors are motivated by inherent (universal) interests, rational means-ends preferences, or internalized norms and values. Rather, I argue that social action and agency result because people are guided to act in certain ways and not others by their sense of *Self* and *Other,* as defined at that particular place and time. Agency can only be understood by recognizing the various discursive narratives in which actors find themselves. I accept cultural theorist Judith Butler's position that identity and agency are both effects, not preexisting conditions of being (Butler 1990, 142–49). Thus, as IR theorist Roxanne Doty has pointed out, the question of agency becomes one of how "practices of representation create meaning and identities and thereby create the very possibility for agency" (Doty 1996, 168). This approach resituates power in history away from a focus on subject *positioning* (as reflected in the theories of [neo]Realism, [neo]Liberalism, and Marxism) to one of subject *production.*

In Doty's work on "imperial encounters" between the North and South, she argues that representation does not uncover "truth" and "knowledge" but rather the "regimes of 'truth' and 'knowledge' . . . through which we have come to 'know' the world and its inhabitants and [which] have enabled and justified certain practices and policies" (1996, 2, 3). Likewise, representations of the Congo have established regimes of "truth" and "knowledge," particularly a "reality" in which practices such as domination, exploitation, and brutality have been enabled—both by external actors and indigenous Africans. The process of imagining the Congo involves attempts to fix the meaning of the "Congo" and to establish its positional relationship vis à vis other actors. The policies taken by external actors toward the Congo—from colonization to conquest, exploitation to intervention—have all been enabled by these actors' successive discourses on its identity. Perhaps most important of all, these imaginings have, cumulatively, allowed the current state of affairs in the Congo to develop.

While the Congo's identity has always been discursively constructed, similar rhetoric used to define the Congo has been used in different ways at different times. The imagery of the Congo gets reproduced in changing ways across different historical contexts, which are themselves informed by other discourses. The result is that the same rhetorical trope can engender different political dynamics. For example, within the discourses of colonialism, the image of the Congo as chaotic allowed Westerners to violently pacify it for the "betterment" of the inhabitants and themselves. To the U.S. government operating within a cold war context, a chaotic Congo represented a communist threat, thus necessitating the violent removal of a leader they rhetorically constructed as illegitimate (Lumumba), as well as support for a leader they defined as being able to bring order to the chaos (Mobutu). In the current post–cold war context, the same constructed image of inherent Congolese chaos has resulted in the non-involvement of Western governments in the complex regional wars and genocides that arose in the 1990s. Because narratives and discourses shift over time and space, it is important to historicize and contextualize the analytical relationality of identity in international relations. For that reason, this work focuses on historicizing the relational settings of Congolese identity. While categorical or essentialist approaches to identity assume that identities are fixed, the approach I employ (re)introduces time, space, and analytical relationality.

Relatedly, identity discourses are interpreted differently by different audiences. Actors do not incorporate narratives and discourses in a direct way. Rather, they are mediated through the vast spectrum of social and political relations that constitute our social world. Cultural studies theorists have shown that audiences often resist discourse or read/consume images in ways that might have been unintended by their producers. The foundational work on this subject has been done by Stuart Hall (Hall 1980, 128–138). Hall conceives of any communication process as "produced and sustained through the articulation of linked but distinctive moments—production, circulation, distribution/ consumption, reproduction" (128). The production of discourses— rhetoric, representations, and actions—are "encoded" with meanings based in specific frameworks of knowledge. When these discourses are consumed and reproduced, their meanings are "decoded" through the framework of knowledge held by the consumer. As Hall notes, the "codes of encoding and decoding may not be perfectly symmetrical" (1980, 131). This point is significant to remember, because it suggests that meanings of the discourses on the Congo's identity were not always "decoded" exactly as they were intended or consistently by all audiences. Identity discourses are consumed in different ways, by different groups, and in different historical contexts.

Moreover, a historical examination of the Congo's identity illustrates that not all actors are able to access discursive space equally. Discourses on the Congo's identity become accepted over time, in large part through the acts of articulation, circulation, and repetition. Yet, discursive *authorship* of the Congo has not been equal. For example, during the colonization and conquest of the Congo at the end of the nineteenth century, authorship of the Congo's identity was primarily controlled by Westerners—namely Henry Morton Stanley, Leopold II, and his colonizing agents. The colonized Africans were largely unable to access discursive space to articulate or circulate alternative discourses on their own identity. They had neither their own written texts nor access to Western languages, print technologies, media, or speaker circuits through which to challenge the colonizing discourses. This is reflective in large part to the asymmetrical encounters between the Europeans and Africans—what Doty refers to as an "imperial encounter" (1996, 3), where the former has enjoyed hegemonic power. Hegemony here can be understood in a Gramscian sense, where the dominant discourses and narratives of the world accumulate the symbolic power to map or classify the world for others.[5]

A useful way of understanding the historic contestation over identity narratives and discourses can be found in the "long conversation" concept of historical anthropologists Jean and John Comaroff (1991). In their work on the colonial contact between the Tswana peoples of South Africa and British Christian missionaries, the Comaroff's define the "long conversation" as "the actions and interactions that laid the bases of an intelligible colonial discourse" (Comaroff and Comaroff 1991, 199). They argue that there were two faces to this conversation between colonizer and colonized: what was talked *about* and the struggle to gain mastery over the *terms* of the encounter. A similar long conversation has taken place over the identity of the Congo, where multiple actors have come together to contest the meaning of that identity and the terms in which it is expressed. However, there is a third dimension to the long conversation overlooked by the Comaroffs. I refer to the struggle over finding and creating an acceptable position or space within the conversation. Specifically, this refers to the ability to access "discursive space"— acceptable space within which to engage in the conversation. Delineating and policing discursive space has been an important element in the imagining of the Congo. At times, international discursive space has been actively closed off to competing discourses, particularly those produced by Congolese. For example, during the 1960s, Western governments intervened directly to deny not only the seating of Patrice Lumumba's United Nations delegation but also his access to the radio station in his country's capital.

One of the implications of this unequal access is that politically and economically dispossessed actors search for other ways to articulate discourses on their identity. Frequently, violence functions as a discursive tool. For example, when denied the space to articulate resistance, dissidents in the eastern part of the Congo took up arms against the Belgian colonizers at the end of the nineteenth century, against Western governments and their imposed Congolese leaders during the 1960s, and again, against the regime of Mobutu at the end of the twentieth century. While each armed expression occurred in its own specific historical context, what unites these events is the use of violence as a tool for the discursively dispossessed and disenfranchised. Throughout this project, therefore, I examine why certain voices are "heard," and others not, in the long conversation of imagining the Congo.

In the case of the Congo, there has been a slow increase in the number of discursive voices engaged in this long conversation over the past one hundred years. At the time of colonization, discursive authorship was primarily held by a handful of Westerners. At the time of decolonization, the number of discursive voices came not only from Belgium but from the United States, Soviet Union, United Nations, numerous Third World nations, and the Congo itself. By the end of the twentieth century, the number of competing discourses had grown tremendously. In large part, this long-term shift was due to the development of new media and technologies such as radio, television, cell phones, and the Internet, as well as new international platforms such as the United Nations and Organization of African Unity (OAU), through which alternative discourses could be articulated and circulated.

Despite this multiplicity of representations, certain earlier rhetorical images have had tremendous staying power and influence. At the beginning of the twenty-first century, the rhetoric produced by Stanley, Leopold II, and other colonizing agents continues to be reproduced and re-employed in Western discourses on the Congo. The "Heart of Darkness" metaphor and imagery of Congolese primitivism continues to crop up in Western discourses on the Congo and in political dialogue on the current civil war, and continues to affect what actions can and cannot be taken. This repetition reflects not only the lingering effects of past discourses but also the difficulties faced in introducing new and competing discourses on the Congo's identity. Almost a century after Joseph Conrad coined the phrase "Heart of Darkness" to characterize Belgian colonial rule in central Africa, ABC News re-employed the trope to characterize a complex regional struggle for power and resources. By using the phrase, ABC News obscured more than it illuminated, and the phrase continues to carry important political currency that should not be overlooked or underestimated.

Methodology and Outline of Chapters

Much of the research for this work was conducted in the United States and Belgium and during several trips to the Great Lakes region. Because of the active armed conflict during the writing of this work, extensive research in the Congo itself was not feasible. This is highly regrettable because more work needs to be done on the numerous local identity discourses and resistance activities. The contention of this work is that the Congo's identity has been authored largely by external actors to the overall detriment of the people on the ground. Many Congolese voices will be examined throughout this work, but I look forward to future research on local-level Congolese identity constitution and contestation to fill many of the gaps in this work.

The empirical data for this book necessarily comes from a broad array of sources, many of which may be considered outside the scope of traditional political science analysis. While the majority of sources utilized in this study come from the "political" realm of governmental reports, speeches, and documents, I also draw from journalism, travel literature, academic treatises, fiction, film, museum displays, art, images, maps, and other "alternative" texts. These texts often provide the most vivid and potent examples of the techniques by which Third World subjects have been negated, a point political scientist Craig Murphy has made in his review of Doty's *Imperial Encounters* (Murphy 1997, 1003). For many outside observers, including politicians, these are the sources that have provided the primary framework within which the Congo has been made "knowable." As historian David Newbury (1998) pointed out, many Westerners are intellectually uninformed about the Congo but are so inundated by stereotypical images that they feel they have a defined cognitive framework. Clear examples of this include the use of popular press reports as "evidence" in Congressional debates on the 1960 crisis by U.S. Senators such as Styles Bridges, Olin Johnston, and Paul Dague (see *Congressional Record*, 12 August 1960, 16281; 17 August 1960, 16641; and 16 February 1961, A955), and the continued employment of Joseph Conrad's "Heart of Darkness" metaphor by ABC News and *Newsweek* magazine (31 March 1997). Novels such as *Heart of Darkness*, films such as *Congo*, and cartoons such as *Tintin in the Congo* constitute the basic discursive structure through which many Westerners view the Congo even today. As political scientist Kennan Ferguson has noted, "To determine the American understanding of Africa, for example, most academics study canonical texts of foreign policy like state department bulletins or administration policy statements. These are not unimportant sources, but ... [pop singer] Paul Simon is ... a far more important American-international diplomat than whoever happens to be the American representative to the United Nations at a particular time, because he has far more control over representations of 'Africaness'" (Ferguson 1996, 180–181).

Most importantly, the increasing number of authors on Congo's identity has meant that their discourses have been expressed in a new multiplicity of sources, so that one must cast the net more broadly. Over time, attempts to craft alternative or challenging images produced multiple sources, some effective, others not. For example, the discourses produced by colonial agents can be found largely in their writings, speeches, and publications. However, at the end of the twentieth century, discursive authorship of the Congo's identity was being articulated and circulated in a myriad of forms: in the international and regional media, on the floors of the UN and OAU, in pamphlets and fliers passed around at political meetings across the globe, in government pronouncements from Western and African capitals, in best-selling novels, in fictional and documentary films, in the "bush" of the Congolese jungle, and at numerous Internet websites. Obviously, some of these voices were reproduced and circulated more than others, giving them a greater degree of "weight." In order to measure the complexities of this overall discursive production, this book has required engagement with a wide and diverse spectrum of sources.

It should be stressed at the outset that this project is not an exhaustive history of Congolese contact with the "outside world." Nor is it an in-depth study of the Congo's political systems. There are numerous excellent works already done on those subjects, many of which will be discussed throughout this work. This present work is a genealogy of the Congo and, as such, does not tell us the whole story of the Congo's past. Nothing does, in and of itself. Nonetheless, focusing on four specific and pivotal historic moments throws valuable light on the politics of identity in international relations, and on the often brutal encounter between the Congo and the Western world. Furthermore, it offers insights into similar processes that were and are at play in other parts of the colonized/postcolonial worlds. The following chapters of this project relate to the four historical periods under examination.

Chapter two examines the invention of the Congo—as the "Congo Free State"—within the Belgian colonial project. Specifically, I examine the discourses produced by Henry Morton Stanley, King Leopold II, and various colonial agents at the end of the nineteenth century. These actors delineated the territorial entity of what became known as the Congo. By simultaneously inventing this entity and denying its sovereignty, these actors violently dismissed existing political and social structures. These colonial actors also created a "knowable" Congolese subject in the collective minds of Westerners. By representing the Africans as inhuman, inferior, and childlike, Leopold II and his colonial agents were able to embark on the dual campaigns of military pacification and economic exploitation of the region. Colonial agents used coercion and extreme violence in their quest to acquire wild rubber. As international attention turned to Leopold II's rule, a reform movement, led by E. D. Morel, eventually forced the Belgian king to transfer the Congo (his personal possession) to the Belgian state in 1908. Chapter two addresses the foundational discourses on the Congo employed at the end of the nineteenth century. The Congo, like most other African states, was a European invention imagined through these colonial discourses. The discourses that defined and delineated the "Congo" and the "Congolese" were intimately involved in its conquest, colonization, and suppression. They produced a Congolese subject upon which Belgium and other international actors could act, often violently.

Chapter three explores the violent conflict over the Congo's identity as an independent, autonomous entity in the 1960s. The discourses that evolved during Belgium's colonial rule of the Congo were rooted in the paternalistic notion of *Notre Congo* (Our Congo). When the Congo became independent in 1960 and its government began acting in ways that challenged Belgium's authority and wishes, the Belgium government responded by dismissing the sovereignty and autonomy of the Congo, as well as the legitimacy of its democratically elected leader, Patrice Lumumba. Lumumba attempted to articulate a counterdiscourse on Congolese identity, drawing in part from the Belgian colonial discourse and the rhetoric of Third World nationalism. However, his ability to circulate this counterdiscourse was stymied by his inability to access international discursive space, largely due to the actions of the United States. There, the government and media drew upon colonial imagery, informed by discourses of cold war competition, to produce its vision of the Congo. The material consequence of these discourses was the direct intervention of the U.S. government to "stabilize" and "order" the Congolese political space. Within the parameters of the

1960 crisis, this meant a disregard for the Congo's political institutions and the forced removal of Patrice Lumumba.

Chapter four examines the reinvention of the Congo into "Zaïre" by President Mobutu Sese Seko. More than mere linguistic change, the policies embarked upon by Mobutu's regime constituted an important reimagining of the Congo's identity. Mobutu's construction of a "Zaïrian" national identity represented the development of a counterhegemonic discourse for imagining the Congo. Through the appropriation of Third World discourses on nationalism, Western philosophical rhetoric, colonial imagery, and the discourses of cold war competition, Mobutu was successful, to a limited extent, in altering the dominant image and introducing new images of the Congo/Zaïre. Much of his success came from his ability to access international discursive space—space that had been unavailable or unattainable for Lumumba. Yet, his alternative discourses were consumed by external actors in different ways. Numerous Third World leaders eventually regarded Mobutu as a pariah because his pro-Western support was unacceptable within the established discursive parameters of nationalism. However, within the logic of cold war discourses, Mobutu and Zaïre were defined by the West as valuable and essential allies. Yet, as Mobutu's power gradually shrank to areas around the capital, many Western observers—clinging to the myth of linear state development with the Western state at its apex—portrayed Zaïre as "proof" of the failure of modernity (i.e., Western "civilization") in Africa.

Chapter five examines recent productions of the Congo's identity as a culmination of these past constructions. A multiplicity of competing voices has emerged for the authorship of the Congo's identity, from neighboring regional states to armed rebel groups, from Congolese officials to Western governments and organizations. In the closing years of the twentieth century, the country underwent two rebellions, invasions from several of its neighbors (some welcome, others not), a change in leaders, and a change in its name (back to the Congo), and reemerged yet again as a symbol of contemporary Africa—the embodiment of all the continent's woes. With the end of the cold war and the overthrow of the Mobutu regime, the sociopolitical structures in Central Africa have been dramatically reenvisioned, with ongoing conflicts over identity, authority, resources, and sociopolitical structures. These events illustrate the complexities in the relationship between political actors and the images they adopt, create, and reinforce, especially as new images compete with old in changing historical contexts. As such, approaches based on cold war frameworks or state-centric perspectives have been incapable of adequately reflecting or analyzing the region's complexities. These events also illustrate how persistent imaginings of the Congo as a "chaotic" space inhabited by "backward" and "uncivilizable" people not only shape how external actors interpret the events in the region but also how they have fundamentally shaped those events

The recent events in the Congo bring several of this book's key points into relief. First, discourses on the Congo/Zaïre's identity are linked to a political dynamic; they frame the cognitive map of actors, shaping the possibility of action. The ways in which the Congo/Zaïre was reimagined during the closing years of the twentieth century allowed certain actions and not others. During these years, a further multiplicity of discursive voices emerged in the construction of the Congo/Zaïre. In addition to the Mobutu regimes and the governments of the United States, France, and Belgium, neighboring regimes such as Uganda, Rwanda, Burundi, Angola, and Zimbabwe, as well as numerous nonstate entities have actively scripted alternative and competing truth claims. At the same time, Western powers' perceptions of the region have re-employed persistent images of the Congo as a chaotic, backward space. These discursive shifts create both opportunities and limitations for alternative voices from the region. The concluding chapter brings together the analyses of the four empirical chapters to reveal the continuities and discontinuities in the discursive production of the Congo over the last century. As such, I examine in particular the cumulative effect these discursive constructions have had on the inhabitants of the Congo.

Chapter Two

Inventing the Congo: Henry Morton Stanley, Leopold II, and the "Red Rubber" Scandal

> *To open up to civilization the only part of our globe which it has not yet penetrated, to pierce the darkness in which entire populations are enveloped, is, I venture to say, a crusade worthy of this age of progress, and I am happy to perceive how much the public feeling is in favor of its accomplishments; the tide is with us . . . Need I say that, in bringing you to Brussels, I have not been influenced by selfish views. No, gentlemen, if Belgium is small, she is happy and contented with her lot. I have no other ambition than to serve her well.*
>
> —Leopold II (quoted in Banning 1877, 152–3)

In 1876, King Leopold II of Belgium organized the International Geographic Conference to position himself within Europe's colonization of the African continent. As the above quote from his opening speech illustrates, Leopold II sought to portray himself as a benevolent, selfless leader interested in opening up Africa for civilization, trade, salvation, and exploration. From an early age, the king had shown an interest in the general European trend of colonization. In an attempt to include Belgium in this field of activity, he hosted the International Geographical Conference in Brussels. The outcome of this conference was the founding of the International African Association (IAA), with Leopold II as its chairman. Unbeknownst to most of the attendees at the conference, Leopold II had also established the Commité d'Etudes du Haut-Congo (CEHC) and hired Henry Morton Stanley, a young American newspaper reporter turned explorer, to explore the Congo River basin. In 1879, Leopold II deftly collapsed the IAA into his new creation, the International Association of the Congo (IAC). Leopold II also directed Henry Morton Stanley to establish treaties with local leaders that effectively ceded their land to the Belgian crown (not the Belgian state) and to build a railroad and establish the groundwork for a colonial state, controlled by Leopold II. The result was the creation of the Congo.

Leopold II was the last European leader to engage in the imperial partitioning of Africa. By the time he emerged on the scene, most of the African continent had already been claimed by Britain, France, Portugal, or Spain. Fear that imperial rivalries would get out of hand led these European powers to meet in Berlin from 1884–85. The Berlin Conference had two principal objectives: to establish formal rules and procedures for the realizing of territorial claims and to resolve competing claims to, and interests in, the newly "discovered" Congo River basin. The first objective was resolved by requiring imperial powers to quickly establish recognizable military presence throughout their territories to prove "effective occupation." The second issue, concerning collective exploitation of the Congo River basin, was resolved by awarding Leopold II "international" recognition for his private estate, called the État Indépendant du Congo (Congo Free State).

Leopold II and his colonial representatives then embarked on the dual campaigns of military pacification and economic exploitation of the region. This exploitation primarily revolved around the harvesting of wild rubber for export to Belgium. In their attempt to realize heightened profits, the whites—working for the colonial state and various commercial enterprises (a number of which were parastatals controlled by Leopold II)—used forced labor, coercion, and extreme violence. Reports of these abuses were greeted with shock and outrage in the rest of Europe and the United States. Eventually, Leopold II's rule became tarnished by the image of "Red Rubber"—rubber stained by the blood of the Africans forced to gather it. An international reform movement, led by E. D. Morel, gathered strength and ultimately forced Leopold II to transfer the Congo to the Belgian state in 1908.

Despite its attempts to appear otherwise, the colonial project did not follow a natural, predetermined, uncontested path based on its own internal dynamic. Through repetition, the colonizing discourses of identity became a stabilizing power, producing a script that "naturalized" the domination and domestication of the Congo. The colonial project was a contested affair, and the discourses that emerged on Congolese social and spatial identities reflected the negotiations and struggles over meanings between colonized and colonizers and among the colonizers themselves. What emerged was a series of historically constructed and specific encounters that influenced understandings and actions on both sides of colonial/colonizer divide. As such, it should be noted that no single force exerted complete agency in the authoring of the colonial project. This chapter will focus on several of the significant actors and forces: Henry Morton Stanley, King Leopold II, his colonial agents, the Africans living in the space that became defined as the "Congo," and the various Western actors who resisted Leopold II's representation of his colonial project.

Perhaps more than any other single figure, Stanley was regarded in Western circles as *the* authoritative voice on the Congo at the end of the nineteenth century. Stanley had already gained international fame during the first of his four expeditions to Africa. In 1871, Stanley went to Africa to find the "lost" Scottish missionary/explorer David Livingstone for the *New York Herald*. His second expedition took him to Lake Victoria and Lake Tanganyika and down the Congo River. Lasting from 1874 to 1877, this trip resulted in Stanley's "discovery" of Lake Edward, Stanley Falls, and Stanley Pool. On this trip, Stanley became the first white man to traverse Africa from the east coast to the west, and to chart the course of the Congo River. Leopold II saw in this region a potential colony, something for which he had long craved. Under the guise of various international associations, Leopold II hired Stanley to acquire the land for himself. During his 1879–84 expedition for Leopold II, Stanley was responsible for establishing the physical space of the "Congo," assimilating that space into the larger colonial structures, and scripting the colonial subjects' identity and history to necessitate their conquest. Stanley established control (or at least juridical authority) over this colony-to-be, as well as the foundation of the nascent colonial state. Stanley would return to Africa a final time, leading the disastrous 1887–89 "rescue" of Emin Pasha (Hugon 1993; Forbath 1977).[1]

Stanley emerged as the principal author and authority of Congolese identity during the age of conquest. Stanley produced numerous newspaper reports, travelogues, exploration narratives, and works of fiction that publicized his accomplishments and views. His writings, particularly the newspaper reports for the *New York Herald* and his travelogues—*How I Found Livingstone* (1872), *Through the Dark Continent* (1878, 2 vols.), and *The Congo and the Founding of Its Free State* (1885, 2 vols.)—were incredibly popular both during and after his lifetime. Stanley's representations of the Africans became an accepted "truth" in the West, repeatedly re-employed over the next one hundred years, as subsequent chapters will show. One of the reasons Stanley was able to achieve this authoritative position was because he required all of his white companions to sign contracts promising they would not write or publicly speak about their travels until well after he had published his journals. Thus, Stanley reduced any direct challenge to his position as *the* expert and guaranteed his narratives' place as *the* standard interpretation.

Importantly, the Africans Stanley wrote about did not have a written tradition from which to offer alternative interpretations. Moreover, these Africans did not have access to the European or American printed media or speaker circuits that Stanley utilized to articulate and circulate his discourses. While it is important to note that they did not have access to European-sanctioned discursive space, Africans did play an important role in articulating and contesting the social and spatial identities produced within the colonial project. They engaged in a number of resistance strategies against colonial conquest. Cultural theorist Anne McClintock has noted, "In the colonial encounter, Africans adopted a variety of strategies for countering colonial attempts to undervalue their economies. Amongst these strategies, mimicry, appropriation, revaluation and violence figure the most frequently" (1995, 229). As this chapter notes, all four strategies were employed against European incursion into Africa.

Once the Congo became defined, dominated, and "internationally" recognized as King Leopold II's personal estate, the monarch actively had to sell his colonial vision to the Belgian populace.[2] Much to Leopold II's dismay, the general Belgian populace had little to no interest in imperial or colonial conquests, largely due to a high degree of provincialism (Gann and Duigan 1979, 26). Unlike Britain and France, where the colonial projects were shaped by the narratives produced by missionaries, explorers, writers, academics, and other colonial agents, in Belgium the initial colonial discourse was orchestrated more exclusively by Leopold II and his propagandists. Thus, in addition to Stanley, the main Western authors of the colonial discourse were Leopold II (through his speeches and writings), his colonial agents in Belgium and the Congo, and various procolonial publications, controlled to varying degrees by the king. Of these, the most popular were *La Belgique Coloniale, Le Congo Illustré,* and *Le Mouvement Géographique*.[3] Building upon Stanley's authorship of the Congo, Leopold II and his colonial agents also drew from the preexisting Africanist discourses generated by other European colonial powers. Thus, it is important to establish that, as latecomers to the "scramble for Africa," Leopold II and his agents employed and reinvented much of the colonial rhetoric already in circulation for their own project.

Ultimately, Leopold II's colonial project in the Congo became the target of international scorn. Images of colonial brutality, immortalized by the "Red Rubber" campaign of the Congo Reform movement, brought tremendous pressure on Leopold II and the Belgian state. As such, this chapter will conclude with a discussion of the international context within which the colonial project was pursued. Particular attention will be paid to the works of the international reform movement, led by E. D. Morel.

The Congo, like most other African states, was a European invention, defined and delineated through colonial discourses. This chapter examines the invention of the Congo by focusing on four central elements of the colonial project. First, the construction of Congolese social identity needs to be interrogated. Colonial agents produced images of Africans in which specific attributes, characteristics, and meanings were defined and assigned. The act of constructing the identity of the region's inhabitants was the act of inventing a knowable Congolese subject. Second, simultaneous to the construction of Congolese social identity was the invention of the Congo's spatial identity. The physical space of the Congo was defined and delineated, with specific meanings and characteristics attached to that territory. In both cases, indigenous systems of knowledge regarding social and spatial representations and practices were denigrated and Western representations, meanings, and practices forcefully imposed. Third, the discourses on Congolese social and spatial identity were combined within a colonial script to produce specific material practices. By constructing knowable subjects, the colonizing agents could act upon what they knew. Within the parameters of the colonial script, certain courses of action became possible, and often times preferred, while others became unthinkable. For example, the "crusade" of which Leopold II speaks in the opening quote is made possible and plausible because he has defined the region and its inhabitants as lacking in civilization, progress, and light. Finally, an understanding of the context in which the colonial project was enacted and realized needs to be understood. The ultimate failure of Leopold II's Congo venture and his abdication of that territory to the Belgian state can only be understood within a framework that highlights the international context within which he was operating.

Defining Congolese Social Identity

> On the 14th August, 1879, I arrived before the mouth of this river to ascend it, with the novel mission of sowing along its banks civilised settlements, to peacefully conquer and subdue it, to remould it in harmony with modern ideas into National States, within whose limits the European merchant shall go hand in hand with the dark African trader, and justice and law and order shall prevail, and murder and lawlessness and the cruel barter of slaves shall for ever cease.
>
> —Henry Morton Stanley (1885: I, 59–60)

In this passage from his *The Congo and the Founding of Its Free State*, Stanley articulated the central themes of the colonial discourse on the Congo that he helped to author—themes such as civilization and salvation, commerce and conquest, exploration and incorporation. At the root of this discourse, and the colonial project in general, was the representation of Congolese social identity. As the anthropologists Jean and John Comaroff note, "The essence of colonization inheres less in political overrule than in seizing and transforming 'others' by the very act of conceptualizing, inscribing, and interacting with them on terms not of their own choosing; in making them into the pliant objects and silenced subjects of our scripts and scenarios; in assuming the capacity to 'represent' them" (Comaroff and Comaroff 1991, 15). For Europeans to claim authority over the Congo, they first had to define a Congolese social body and attach characteristics to that social body that allowed their colonial conquest. These discursive acts represented the invention of a Congolese social identity.

On one level, the process of representing Congolese social identity involved delineating the dimensions of a recognizable social body; establishing the parameters of "Congolese" citizenry. Prior to the colonial project, the region contained numerous and disparate ethnic, cultural, and linguistic communities, including the Kingdom of Kongo at the mouth of the river and the Bolia states in the tropical forest, as well as the Lunda, Luba, and Imbangala, to name but a few.[4] There was no "imagined community" of Congolese—at least not from the perspective of the soon-to-be-called "Congolese" (Anderson 1991). Within the minds of the Western colonial audience, however, the colonial discourse ethnographically homogenized the Congolese subject. A collective *they* was invented, whose identity was discursively linked to the territorial construction now known as the Congo. The disciplinary power of the colonial state was able to further reify these constructed categories of identification and classification to produce social identities for political regulation. The colonial powers' production of colonial subjects subdivided the Congolese social body through the socially regulated categories of tribes, ethnicity, race, age, gender, and so forth. By producing identity through these categories, the colonizing powers produced identities as these categories (see Brown 1995, 58).

Colonial authorship of a Congolese social identity was concerned, first and foremost, with fixing and policing boundaries of difference. This was further achieved by attaching characteristics and meanings to the delineated social body. Historically, identity is a relational term that is defined through perceived or invented alterity (Said 1978; Todorov 1984; Taussig 1993). As political theorist William E. Connolly has noted, "Identity requires difference in order to be, and it converts difference into otherness in order to secure its own self-certainty" (Connolly 1991, 64). During the European colonial projects of the eighteenth and nineteenth centuries, the construction of the non-European as *Other* was instrumental in the conception and realization of colonial conquest. Imagining the Other relied on constructing the European *Self,* usually through the employment of binary oppositions and the demarcating and policing of boundaries of difference. As such, alterity was the basis of the definition of Congolese social identity within the colonial project. Whites were portrayed as physical embodiments of culture and civilization, while Africans were presented as the lack, or negation, of these characteristics.

Within the colonizing discourse, simply to speak of the "Congolese" constituted the invention and authorship of the Congo's citizenry, fixing a referent upon which the colonizers could act. Knowing, naming, and ordering the Congolese subject was a precondition for colonial domination and domestication of the region. It should be noted at the outset that the colonial invention and conquest of the Congo was built upon the foundation of a longer history of constructing the African Other within European knowledge. As such, the colonial authors of Congolese identity operating at the end of the nineteenth century were drawing upon discursive trends and rhetoric already in circulation.[5] At the time of Portugal's "discovery" of the Congo River in 1482, the Christian/European view of nonbelievers was that they were savage idolaters, sinners untouched by God's redeeming love. The dominant belief was that salvation could only come about through increased, and controlled, contact with Europeans. Thus, slavery was defended as being not only justifiable but desirable, since it would be the means of salvation for the Africans, introducing them to Christianity and (Western) civilization. However, by the eighteenth century, discourses on the African Other became less entwined with religious beliefs and were more the product of the Enlightenment. Though the overriding referent had changed—from God to Reason— the disposition to non-Europeans remained the same. Now, the Enlightenment enabled European domination of other cultures based on the notions of cultural supremacy and a perceived racial superiority. Non-European societies were seen as lacking in basic elements of "civilization," such as a civil society, sociopolitical structures, and rational thought. The Enlightenment performed the function of establishing the European individual and polity as the sole embodiment (and thus bearer) of "culture."[6] The salvation mission increasingly gave way to the civilizing mission.[7]

These elements of the Enlightenment discourse were carried over into the nineteenth century, which also saw the introduction of Darwinism and its emphasis on social evolution. Social Darwinism was increasingly used to support the racist theories of colonialism (Grovogui 1996; Lindqvist 1992; Fabian 1983; Said 1978). Consistent with the need to define and distinguish between Europeans and non-Europeans, explorers and missionaries to Africa would rhetorically dismiss commonalities and focus on exoticized differences, such as hairstyles, facial markings, and other physical traits. African social practices, religious beliefs, and forms of sociopolitical organization were either ignored or portrayed in terms that heightened their perceived exoticism and/or barbarism. As before, Africa and Africans were portrayed as existing in a different temporal and spatial moment than the Europeans: one before salvation, reason, or culture (Fabian 1983). Thus, at the end of the century, when Congolese identity was being forged by Leopold II's colonial agents, the signs, symbols, and rhetoric of that identity were already in circulation. Texts produced by Stanley and other colonial agents became part of a long-established tale that post-Enlightenment Europeans told each other about the advance of "civilization" into the darkest recesses of the globe.

One of the central features of the colonization of the Congo entailed the representation and fixing of a Congolese subject through alterity. As such, the invention of the Congolese Other was intimately tied to the imagining of the colonizing Self. For Belgian colonial agents, the construction of the Congolese was intimately tied to the creation of the emerging Belgian national identity. Establishing the Congolese as the Other helped construct an imagined Belgian national culture. Moreover, Belgium's international self-image was largely shaped by its possession of the Congo. As a colonial power, it had moved beyond its physical and economic limitations to take its place amongst the larger, stronger nations of Europe, such as France, Britain, and Germany. For Leopold II, acquiring colonies would, as he put it, "prove to the world that [Belgium] is also an imperial people capable of dominating and of enlightening others" (quoted in Gann and Duigan 1979, 30). In the case of Henry Morton Stanley, it is significant that he employed the African Other in his ongoing invention of his own identity. While he passed himself off as a middle-class American with an elaborate background, he was really born a poor, illegitimate Welsh orphan named John Rowlands. Because he spent most of his life (re)inventing his own identity, his writings on the Congo should be seen as, to some degree, part of his project to align himself with a certain Euro-American, civilized, white "self."[8]

Imagined racial differences were a defining element in the construction of Congolese social identity.[9] In keeping with existing rhetorical trends, Africans were portrayed in terms of the racialized exotic Other. The Belgian colonial press was rife with articles, drawings, and photographs of the facial markings, tattoos, and hairstyles of various Congolese "tribes." In addition to focusing on the supposedly "fixed" markers of race such as physical, mental, and social traits, Stanley also invoked racialized images of African savagery, barbarism, cannibalism,[10] indolence, greed, and so forth. For example, in one typical journal entry, Stanley speaks of the Africans' "wild effrontery & nosy curiosity," "unreasonable hostility," and "lying tongues & black hearts" (Bennett 1970, 126). In his writings, Stanley repeatedly employed animal metaphors, which served to situate the African between the whites (i.e., humans) and the beasts on a racialized evolutionary ladder. Stanley often referred to Africans as "beasts" and "apes" and compared them to dogs, often as the canine's inferiors. For example, Stanley writes that during a skirmish, "'Bull,' the British bulldog, had seized one of the Watura by the leg and had given him a taste of the power of the English canines of his breed before the poor savage was mercifully despatched by a Snider bullet" (Bennett 1970, 201).[11]

The Belgian popular press also repeatedly employed animal metaphors when describing Africans, or, even more popular, presented photographs of Africans with apes or chimpanzees (see figure 2.1). Such images provided "evidence" for various evolutionary and anthropological paradigms of the time and identified African subjects—by proximity—as more animal than man, emphasizing their inhumanity. The use of photography was emblematic, verifying the existence of an objective, "scientific" attitude.

Africans were frequently portrayed as children, unable to check their "natural" yearnings. In a typical passage defining Congolese social identity, Stanley wrote "A barbarous man is pure materialist. He is full of cravings for possessing something that he cannot describe. He is like a child which has not yet acquired the faculty of articulation" (1878: I, 80). Here, Stanley denied the "childlike" African the agency to articulate his/her own identity, allowing Stanley to speak for/of the subject. Furthermore, characterizing Africans as "like a child" authorized the imposition of a paternalistic relationship.

Simultaneous to this construction of "African as child" was another rhetorical maneuver: the projection of Africans as feminized, helpless victims. After the banning of the European slave trade, many white writers, including Stanley, focused on the smaller but continuing slave trade in eastern Africa. The trade was dominated by Muslim East Africans—dubbed "Arabs" by the Europeans—and had stretched into Central Africa by the nineteenth century. Stanley and Leopold II gave considerable attention to the effects of this slave trade on the region (for example, see Stanley 1885: II, 134–67), thereby imagining the Africans as being victims of both nature (i.e., Africa's hostile environment) and the Arab slave trade. Such representations amounted to an explicit call for Western intervention under the flag of the protection of Africans.

In addition to the existing image of the savage barbarian living in the wilderness of the African jungle, Stanley wove together the rhetoric of Africans as victimized and "childlike" to produce the image of the docile native. Taken together, the savage and docile images constructed an important "before/after" dichotomy for the European civilizing process. The "natural" African was characterized as a savage, merciless brute. Once the African came into repeated contact with the white man, he (and Africans were almost always portrayed as male) became "colonized" in the sense of being docile and malleable—in other words, domesticated.

The savage/docile imagery was an important rhetorical maneuver in the logic of the civilizing mission. Existing European discourses on racial difference were rooted in binary oppositions: black/white, savage/civilized, primitive/cultured, traditional/modern, dirty/clean, greedy/temperate, lazy/industrious, emotional/rational, agricultural/industrial, pagan/Christian, and so forth. These binary oppositions were fundamental to constructing boundaries of difference between whites and nonwhites. Anthropologist Michael Taussig refers to this as the

Figure 2.1: Chimpansé du bas Ubangi
Source: *Le Congo Illustré*, February 11, 1894, 3(3), 24.

space between, "in which civilization takes measure of its difference through its reflection in primitives" (Taussig 1993, 79). Yet, if these paradigmatic oppositions were held to be overly rigid, the civilizing mission—built on the logics of conversion and domestication—would be undermined. The promise of evolution needed to be held out. An inhabitable intermediate space between the supposed inferior African tradition and the projected/promised modernity of colonialism had to be defined. This docile native embodied that space, not quite embraced by modernity but always in danger of sliding backward to African traditions. In Stanley's narratives, it was only through the intervention of the civilized West that the African would advance along this diachronic line of progress—"evolving" from savagery to civilization.

The markers of clothing and labor were often employed in the construction of the Congolese subject. Clothing became a literal mark of culture and civilization. For example, Stanley, like other colonial writers/agents of this time, spent great amounts of time discussing the nakedness or near nakedness of the African natives. Their lack of clothing was presented as evidence that they were less evolved than whites. Furthermore, the farther Stanley traveled into the interior, the more he focused on the inhabitants' lack of clothing. Within the colonial discourse, the journey into the interior of Africa was presented as a journey back in time, where spatial advancement was equated with temporal reversal. The interior was portrayed as existing in "anachronistic space"—"prehistoric, atavistic and irrational, inherently out of place in the historical time of modernity" (McClintock 1995, 40). Clothing served as a marker for that journey: the fewer clothes, the more primitive.

Clothes served another function in the colonial narrative. When Africans were presented in "Western" clothing, they were symbolically reflecting their own inferiority through the supposed irony of this spectacle. Thus, African claims to such adornment were undermined through ridicule. When Stanley portrayed such Africans, he drew attention to their masquerade of "civilization" and, thus, their lack of it. In Belgian magazines, the recurring portrayal of Africans in "European" clothes provided humorous "evidence" of their own inferiority and suggested black/white differences could not be overcome by superficial trappings of "civilization" (see figure 2.2). Comically portraying Africans in Western clothes gained wide employment among imperialist cartoonists, who sought to ridicule Africans by drawing them as monkey-like caricatures prancing about in battered top-hats and tails. For whites, clothes served as a naturalized marker of their Western culture (and humanity), while on Africans these same clothes could only constitute a hollow imitation of Western culture, making the superiority of Western culture and inferiority of the Africans self-evident.

Finally, Africans were repeatedly portrayed as lazy and unmotivated, incapable or unwilling to engage in work. Within the colonial

Figure 2.2: A mocking portrayal of "civilized" Congolese
Source: *Le Congo Illustré*, 1892, 1(13), 104; originally published in *Scraps*, May 25, 1889, 301.

project, the embrace of physical labor, aimed at correcting and exploiting nature, helped define Western civilization. Since labor was not in the Africans' "nature," the white men had to force this civilizing activity upon Africans for their own good. Stanley and his white companions did this through their roles as supervisors. For example, Stanley's bags, equipment, and provisions were all carried by Africans. The great roads and railway he claimed to have built were physically built by Africans under white "supervision."

It is important to note here that Africans often responded to European intrusions and representations of their social identities by engaging in a number of resistance strategies, namely mimicry, appropriation, revaluation, and violence (McClintock 1995, 229). Stanley's expedition faced repeated armed resistance as it journeyed through the region he was claiming for Leopold II. His travelogues are rife with examples of villages and towns putting up armed resistance to his forceful incursions. After the Congo Free State was established, it endured repeated armed rebellions and Belgians had to forcefully squelch unrest throughout their occupation of the Congo (see Vellut 1987; Isaacman and Vansina 1985; Jewsiewicki 1980; Ranger 1977). Armed resistance by the inhabitants of the Congo can be seen as an attempt to articulate their identities and resist colonial representations, given that other means of expression were forcefully denied to them by the colonial power.

The practice of mimicry can be seen in African attempts to mirror the colonially imposed identity in order to resist the colonial project. For example, the Queen of Musyé was able to stall Stanley's drive into the interior by holding him against his will while claiming to protect him from the cannibals and savages who lived further upriver. By exploiting white stereotypes of cannibalism and the barbaric interior, the queen was able to temporarily thwart Stanley's encroachment on the trade she controlled (Stanley 1885: I, 424–432).

Furthermore, there were acts of revaluation by Africans that can and should be regarded as part of strategies of resistance. The most obvious was the refusal of Africans to accept European notions of property ownership and exchange value. In his work on "commodity culture," cultural theorist Thomas Richards observes that Stanley's porters did not accept the value Stanley attached to the goods they carried; therefore, they were forever dropping, discarding, misplacing, or walking away with them (cited in McClintock 1995, 230). This reflects efforts to capture, redeploy, and resist the colonizers' ability to reproduce value. Rather than examining their political and social implications, Stanley attributed these actions to the natives' "natural" indolence and thievery. He would often execute the porters for such infringements (which may in fact indicate that on some level he did understand their political ramifications). Throughout the texts of Stanley and other colonial agents, the voices of the silenced subjects are audible in the numerous accounts of "irrational" behavior, mockery, and the varying degrees of active resistance.

Africans living in what became known as the "Congo" did not have a written tradition or access to the European or American printed media or speaker circuits that the colonizing agents utilized to articulate and circulate their constructions of Congolese social identities. As a result, they were unable to speak for themselves directly to Western audiences. The failure of Africans to access discursive space can be contrasted to Leopold II's ability to articulate and circulate colonial discourses on Congolese social identity, which was graphically displayed in 1897 at a small Belgian village a few kilometers outside of Brussels. The village of Tervuren was the site of the Colonial Exhibition for the 1897 World's Fair, which hosted over a million visitors. There, a Palais des Colonies was made up of numerous rooms trumpeting the glories and benefits of Leopold II's possession of the Congo: a Salon d'Honneur featuring statues and artifacts praising Leopold II and his colonial agents; a Salle d'Ethnographie crowded with various pieces of "Congolese" life: ivory tusks, shields, spears, masks, fabric, utensils, and tools, as well as paintings and sculptures by European artists and miniature models of "authentic" huts and villages; a Salle des Importations featuring Western products introduced to the Congo (many of which remained the exclusive possession of whites); and a Salle des Exportations and a Salon des grandes cultures, both of which featured the raw materials extracted from the Congo, such as cocoa, coffee, cotton, and rubber (Luwel 1967; Lüsebrink 1993). Through this exhibition, the Africans were positioned as depoliticized objects of knowledge disassociated from their cultural "artifacts" and "natural resources" (Ferguson 1996, 183).

At the height of Leopold II's colonial project, there occurred across Europe an important shift from the scientific racism of anthropological, ethnographic, scientific, and travel writings to the more public display of commodity racism. Photographs, advertisements, and, in particular, museums and imperial exhibitions "converted the narrative of imperial Progress into mass-produced *consumer spectacles*" (McClintock 1995, 33). These exhibitions also reflected the commodification of resources now "owned" and controlled by the European colonial powers. Leopold II was at the forefront of this movement, organizing World and Universal Exhibitions across Belgium (Lüsebrink 1993). Through these spectacles, Belgian national identity, the Belgian colonial project, and the constructions of the Congolese social identity became products for international consumption (see Vints 1984). In fact, these exhibitions were part of the dissemination of these identities through the public definition, performance, and display of difference. The making and existence of such portrayals gave Leopold II and his agents significant power over that which was portrayed: the Congo's identity. Undoubtedly, the greatest and most important of these spectacles was the World's Fair of 1897.[12]

A telling spectacle was played out on the grounds in Tervuren, where 267 Congolese men, women, and children were on display. The Africans were housed in three villages: a river village (in which the natives paddled around a small pond in a dugout canoe), a forest village, and a "civilized" village. The inhabitants of the first two villages were presented as examples of "authentic" life before Belgian intervention, with their "primitive" accouterments and practices. A do-not-feed-the-natives sign completed the zoo-like atmosphere of the display. The "civilized" village was made up largely of African soldiers, who thrilled the crowds with proof of their "evolution" by marching in step and performing in a military band. This scene provided an illuminating example of how the colonial project was gendered, for the male soldiers were the symbols of "civilized Africans" while the females in the village were portrayed as the physical and symbolic site of "tradition." In the colonial narrative of "advancement," the former must triumph over the latter.

The Colonial Exhibition was intended to promote awareness of and support for Leopold II's colonial venture. Perhaps the message of the exhibition was best represented by the sculpture that dominated the Salle d'Ethnographie. The piece, by Charles Samuel (1862–1939), depicted an African "native" clad in a loincloth (fabric was used to clothe the male's nakedness), spear in hand, falling away from a towering Arab slave trader. At their feet was a naked African woman on the ground, arm outreached for assistance. The African woman was portrayed as helpless, and the African male, shown cowering, as inadequate in providing her "protection." Such images as these implied that masculinity and power resided in the Belgian white who was needed to provide protection, salvation, and civilization to the feminized and helpless Congolese already oppressed by "Arabs." The sculpture can be regarded as a symbolic justification of the overall Belgian colonial project, a point illustrated by its continued privileged place in the Royal Museum for Central Africa in Tervuren today.

Delineating and Defining the Congo's Spatial Identity

> *The fearful scourges of which, in the eyes of our humanity, these races seemed the victims, are already lessening, little by little, through our intervention . . . In those vast tracts, mostly uncultivated and many unproductive, where the natives hardly knew how to get their daily food, European experience, knowledge, resource and enterprise, have brought to light unthought-of wealth.*
>
> —Leopold II (1903, 5)

In the passage above, Leopold II defines his colonial project in the Congo as one rooted in compassion and duty. What is significant in this passage is the construction of the Congo's spatial identity. On one hand, he portrays the physical space of the Congo as "mostly uncultivated" and "unproductive," with the implicit portrayal of the region as untouched by human enterprise and the explicit call for European intervention. On the other hand, Leopold II speaks of the Congo as a recognizable physical space, a uniform and autonomous entity. Defining the spatial identity of the Congo was an important aspect of the colonial project. It entailed dismissing preexisting spatial representations, meanings, and practices Africans attached to that space and imposing colonial representations, meanings, and practice. At the most basic level, defining spatial identity entails delineating physical space, drawing symbolic boundaries and borders. To that end, Stanley was responsible for inventing the physical space of the "Congo" were one did not exist before. During his 1879–84 expedition for Leopold II, Stanley traveled on foot throughout the region, physically demarcating the geographical limits of Leopold II's possession. In effect, Stanley colonized by traversing. The physical space that he delineated was roughly eighty times the size of Belgium. The areas contained numerous and disparate ethnic, cultural, and linguistic communities. From this diverse mix, Stanley created a single entity. Moreover, Stanley was responsible for assimilating that space into the larger colonial structures.

But constructing a spatial identity entails more than simple territorial delineation. It involves producing and attaching meaning to that physical space. It involves scripting spatial representations and spatial practices. To a certain degree, the colonially scripted spatial identity of the Congo was tied to the production of Belgian national identity. It provided a physical "mirror" in which Belgian national culture, manhood, and identity were performed and reflected. As the colonial project gained momentum (especially after the transfer of Congolese sovereignty to the Belgian state in 1908), the Belgian national identity became even more closely tied to the Congolese referent.[13] As anthropologist Renée Fox has observed, the "vast African territory that stretched far beyond the restricting boundaries of Belgium, and yet 'belonged' to it, provided Belgians with an horizon, and with an existential as well as a geographical frontier" (1984, 225). The colonial space helped produce a racialized sense of superiority among many white Belgians that helped bridge the numerous divisions in Belgian society.[14]

There were significant temporal assumptions attached to the representation of Congolese physical space. At the time of Portugal's "discovery" of the Congo River in 1482, the Christian/European view of nonbelievers was that they were sinners who occupied a different temporal as well as physical space than Europeans, one before salvation. As such, non-Europeans were characterized as savage idolaters, sinners untouched by God's redeeming love. Such a characterization allowed Europeans to dispossess the Africans of their land. Emerich de Vattel summarized the predominant view of European jurists when he stated that nonwhites had no "physical, legal, or emotional attachment to land or territory worthy of European respect" (quoted in Grovogui 1996, 51). Such discursive moves were employed by Stanley, Leopold II, and other colonial agents as well. The physical space of the Congo was portrayed as an unclaimed and timeless space, as yet unorganized by societies and economies. It was defined as anachronistic space, a space existing before history and antithetical to Western modernity.

Yet, the colonial representation of Congolese space was more complex than a simple portrayal of it as a land before time. In his writings, Stanley imagined the interior of Africa as an empty space, unpeopled (except for the savages, incapable of articulation) and waiting for the white man to develop it. Stanley was instrumental in portraying the Congo as a resource-rich space *waiting* for European cultivation and exploitation. It was presented as being "unimproved" and thus at the disposal of the European. As cultural theorist Mary Louise Pratt observes, "The European improving eye produces subsistence habitats as 'empty' landscapes, meaningful only in terms of a capitalist future and of their potential for producing a marketable surplus" (Pratt 1992, 61).[15] Stanley's narratives were saturated with this "improvement" imagery. A representative example is one enlightening passage from the *New York Herald* (August 10, 1872):

> Ah, me! What wild and ambitious projects fill a man's brain as he looks over the *forgotten and unpeopled country,* containing in its bosom such store of wealth, and with such an expanse of fertile soil, capable of sustaining millions! What a settlement one could have in this valley! See, it is broad enough to support a large population! Fancy a church spire rising where that tamarind rears its dark crown of foliage, and think how well a score or so of pretty cottages would look instead of those thorn clumps and gum trees! Fancy this lovely valley teeming with herds of cattle and fields of corn, spreading to the right and left of this stream! *How much better would such a state become this valley, rather than its present deserted and wild aspect!* But be hopeful. The day will come and a future year will see it, when happier lands have become crowded and nations have become so overgrown that they have no room to turn about. It only needs an Abraham or a Lot, an Alaric or an Attila to lead their hosts to this land, which, perhaps, has been *wisely reserved* for such a time (Bennett 1970, 75–6; emphasis added).

In another passage, he stated that, "I came to the conviction . . . that industry well directed, and plans vigorously pursued, *might vastly improve what Nature had so carelessly left in disorder*" (1885: I, 134; emphasis added).

However, from the point of view of the African inhabitants, these spaces that Stanley saw as blank slates were saturated with history, meaning, and social practices. Yet, Stanley and other colonial agents dismissed these systems of knowledge. On one occasion, when the inhabitants were explaining the surroundings to Stanley, he wrote: "They also gave us a vast number of names of places; but their ideas of locality were so very vague, and as each channel and islet of the main river bears its distinctive titles, their information had no practical value" (1885: II, 109). Stanley and other colonial agents were engaged in a struggle of spatial semantics, appropriating the physical context in which the colonizer/colonized literally occurred. Within this struggle, the colonizers tried to place the African inhabitants within a map of their own making. The colonial project attempted to erase traditional sociopolitical and economic systems and practices that were tied to indigenous spatial representations and replace them with Western representations, practices, and meanings.[16] This is most clearly seen in the representation of Congolese political and economic space.

Precolonial Africans tended to conceive of political space within the region as a multilayered structure of concentric circles of diminishing control, radiating from the various cores (Kopytoff 1987, 29). This perception reflected trends in African political organization. Before colonization, political structures in the region, as elsewhere in most of Africa, were multiethnic in nature, with most ethnic groups divided between different political jurisdictions. African political and social boundaries were rather fluid and shifting. Authority and power were dispersed into diverse and fluctuating forms of sociopolitical organization: from states to noncentralized societies (Bohannan and Curtin 1995, 89). For example, before Stanley's arrival, the Kingdom of Kongo—at one time one of the most centralized precolonial African states—had disintegrated into a fragmented, multilayered society devoid of any real chiefs (Callaghy 1984, 340).

Stanley's explorations in Africa coincided with the global expansion of Europe's Westphalian state system, which entailed markedly different conceptions of political space. The Westphalian state system, canonized in 1648 at the end of the Thirty Years War, rested on the concepts of political sovereignty, spatial demarcation, and territorial integrity. At the center of these concepts was the notion of the "state" in which an autonomous and sovereign power ruled within a specifically defined territorial space. At the end of the nineteenth century, this model of sociopolitical organization was exported from Europe, through coercive force, to the newly created colonies around the globe, replacing older, often more complex forms of sociopolitical organization.[17] Stanley was an important transmitter of this new order to central Africa. As he stated, he "remould[ed] it in harmony with modern ideas into National States" (Stanley 1885: I, 59–60).

The colonial agents' discursive dismissal of existing spatial systems and practices enabled the imposition of the "state" concept as it was defined by the dominant Western discourses. The Congo became part of the "universalization" of the European state system that privileged the "state" as the single legitimate entity within the international realm. Traditional, indigenous sociopolitical structures and practices, as well as their autonomy and "sovereignty," were viewed as illegitimate and erased. Integration into the Westphalian state system required (and continues to require) a construction of sovereignty (with the simultaneous delegitimization of existing systems and practices) and the construction of a physically, spatially, and temporally defined entity in line with the state idea of modernity (Walker 1991 and 1993; Strang 1996). This was achieved by a double move executed by the colonial project. The "Congo" was invented as an *autonomous* spatial entity (a "state") within the Western Westphalian discourse. Yet, through the imagining and authoring of its citizenry—"Congolese"—as savage, uncivilized, and childlike, its "sovereignty" was denied and transferred to Leopold II and his colonial structures.

With regards to existing economic space, Stanley and other colonial agents forcefully replaced existing systems and symbols of value exchange with a capitalist system grounded in the exploitation of native (often unpaid) labor. As Pratt has noted, "subsistence lifeways, nonmonetary exchange systems, and self-sustaining regional economies are anathema to expansive capitalism. It seeks to destroy them wherever it finds them" (Pratt 1992, 154–155). Thus, traditional economic exchanges were represented as "irrational" and "fetishistic," resulting in the disavowal of them as legitimate systems. This move was symptomatic of the struggle to dictate the terms of colonial contact by controlling its dominant material and symbolic values. Central to this strategy was the rhetorical invention by Stanley and other colonial agents of the *idle* and *lazy* native. This was perhaps the most tirelessly invoked trope of Congolese and Africans in general. Yet, once employed, this trope made it possible to achieve control over natives, their bodies, and their labor. As McClintock has keenly observed, "The discourse on idleness is, more properly speaking, a discourse on work— used to distinguish between desirable and undesirable labor. Pressure to work was, more accurately, pressure to alter traditional habits of work" (McClintock 1995, 252–3).

Central to this project was the introduction of wage labor into the economies of Central Africa. Stanley prided himself with the belief that he introduced capitalism to Central Africa: "[T]o have a white man in their midst offering to buy what strength lay in their arms and willingness in their spirits for labor! It is an event which neither they, and certainly not their fathers, had ever heard or dreamed of" (1885: I, 143). A central and recurring feature in Stanley's narratives was the introduction of commerce to Africa. In fact, his writing is rife with references to the Congo's untapped wealth, the civilizing effect of labor, and the African's "natural" desire for trade and commerce with the West. In part, this provided the script for violently "opening up" the African interior for Western exploitation. Because he claimed to "introduce" commerce and trade, Stanley could shape and define it as he saw fit. The Congolese, as well as other Africans, were forcefully incorporated into an economic system that exploited them in multiple ways: through the payment of low wages, forceful removal from fertile lands, introduction of taxation systems that ensured their employment to Westerners, introduction of cash crops controlled by the Western–dominated markets, and, in numerous cases, forced labor. Thus, within the colonial project, indigenous spatial representations and practices (especially political and economic) were forcibly replaced by spatial representation and practices rooted in the European Westphalian and capitalist systems

Leopold II was able to claim hegemony of this newly invented physical space (via the International Association of the Congo) due to Stanley's use of over 400 "treaties" signed by himself (as Leopold II's representative) and local African leaders. These treaties gave the IAC "legitimate" claim to the territory in the eyes of the European community. These forms of documentation were important elements of international law, providing the juridical justification for European colonization. In part, these treaties were highly important because, as written discourses, they were preservable. Recognition of the "Congo" and Leopold II's control over the Congo basin was first granted by the United States (see Bontinck 1966). Formal "international" recognition was granted by the 1884–85 Berlin Conference. There were no Congolese or other African representatives at the Berlin Conference. The "international" (read "European") legal code that authenticated such actions only provided the Africans with the "right to dispose of themselves"—that is, "to transfer their 'hereditary' right to their 'soil' and self-rule to foreign powers. African rights were not absolute rights but privileges bestowed by colonial powers upon pacified native populations" (Grovogui 1996, 80; see Grotius 1623; Banning 1877; Vitoria

1917; Oppenheim 1920). Within the "international" juridical discourse and the "international" state system that it helped construct, the Africans were simultaneously authored and erased, an important practice of exclusion/inclusion. African presence was notably absent from the proceedings, thus allowing Europeans to achieve sole authorship of "Africa," from the make-up of its map to the anthropology of its "tribes."

In the case of the Congo basin, the signatories of the Berlin Conference recognized that the IAC (created and controlled by Leopold II) was a sovereign institutional structure and, as such, entrusted it with ensuring cooperation and equal access to the region. In Leopold II's name, Stanley had "legally" dispossessed the inhabitants of their own land and established "effective occupation" of the territory. Though the IAC was not a government but a private company, it was recognized by the states within the international community, and Leopold II was granted juridical sovereignty over the region (Keith 1919, 63). Thus, the "Congo" was formally assimilated into the expanding European state system.

The "international" facade of the IAC was not long in collapsing as Leopold II took increasing control over the Congo. By a royal decree on May 29, 1885, Leopold II replaced the IAC with the État Indépendant du Congo (Congo Free State), which established the region as his own personal possession. At first this move was greeted with some resistance by other European colonial powers. However, Leopold II was able to weather the storm by maintaining a promise of "free trade" and neutrality, as well as by drawing on his established image as a benevolent philanthropist dedicated to civilizing Africa and combating the Arab "scourge."

Scripting the Colonial Project: Violence and Conquest

[The Congolese is one who is] entirely hostile to all idea of work; which only respects the law of force, and knows no other argument than terror.

—1903 judgment by the President of the Congo's Supreme Court of Justice (quoted in *West African Mail*, February 3, 1905, 1068)

By defining the Congo's social and spatial identities, the colonizing powers were able to engage in specific courses of action. They had made the Congo "known" and could act upon what they "knew." As the above quote illustrates, the colonizing script on identity had dramatic material effects, mostly clearly the use of violence. The colonial project did not follow a natural, predetermined, uncontested path based on its own internal dynamic. The discourses of colonial conquest had to be explicitly articulated and circulated. Through repetition, they became a stabilizing power, producing a script that "naturalized" the domination and domestication of the Congo.

The continual production of a "knowable" Congolese subject resulted in the image of Africans as emasculated, dehumanized, passive, and the antithesis of the colonizing whites. Once this image had been articulated and accepted as "truth," colonial agents like Stanley were able to act in ways that may have been otherwise unthinkable. In fact, Stanley became infamous for his cruelty and violence. During his expeditions, floggings, beatings, and executions were administered regularly for "crimes" varying from desertion to the dropping of a pack. Stanley was proud of this reputation and actively sought to promote it in his writings, as the drawing from *How I Found Livingstone* illustrates (figure 2.3). Stanley considered Africans to be inferior creatures who only understood violence: "Whatever deficiencies, weakness, and foibles that [Africans] may develop must be so manipulated that, while they are learning the novel lesson of obedience, they may only just suspect that behind all this there lies the strong unbending force *which will eventually make men of them,* wild things though they now are" (1878: I, 71; emphasis added). In this passage, Stanley considers the Africans "things" that may "eventually" be made men.

The representation of Africans as "things" that only understood force allowed Stanley (and the colonial administrators who followed) to engage in devastating brutality. Such a maneuver is representative of what anthropologist Michael Taussig calls the "colonial mirror of production," where the colonizer mimics the savagery imputed to the savage (Taussig 1993, 66). In a sense, it is the simulation of an imagined savagery in order to dominate or destroy it. In a fairly typical dispatch to the *Herald,* Stanley casually observed that his expedition attacked a village and "burned three of [the African chief's] villages, captured, killed or drove away the inhabitants" (Bennett 1970, 25). Murder and enslavement became acceptable, even necessary, given his construction of the African's identity. In another dispatch, Stanley wrote: "without hesitation I had [several unruly porters] tied up and flogged, and then adorned their stubborn necks with the chain kindly lent by [Arab slave trader] Sheikh bin Nasib" (Bennett 1970, 62). Here he treats Africans as slaves, even putting them in slave irons—a blatantly hypocritical act

"LOOK OUT, YOU DROP THAT BOX, I'LL SHOOT YOU."

Figure 2.3: "Drop that box, I'll shoot you"
Source: Henry M. Stanley. 1872. *How I Found Livingstone*. New York: Harper and Brothers.

considering his outspoken criticism of the Arab slave trade. Stanley's excessive and violent treatment of the inhabitants was rooted in his need to construct and maintain boundaries of difference between himself and the Africans.[18]

Violence and the threat of force were legitimized—even required—by the dominant colonial discourses. In a June 16, 1897 letter to one of his colonial agents, Leopold II wrote: "In barbarous countries I know that a strong authority is needed to bring the natives, who have never been accustomed to it, under the practice of civilisation. To this end it is necessary to be at the same time firm and paternal" (quoted in Boulger 1898, 254). Just as Stanley's authorship of Congolese identity allowed him to engage in violent courses of action, so too did Leopold II's colonial discourse justify and necessitate the use of force. Leopold II reportedly asserted that forced labor was "the only way to civilize and uplift these indolent and corrupt peoples" (quoted in Stengers 1989, 19). These "fantastical rites of imperial violence," to borrow a phrase from Anne McClintock (1995, 27), were scripted by the colonizing discourses of Congolese social and spatial identity. The imaginative range essential to the execution of colonial violence was an imagining drawn from that which the whites imputed to the Africans, and then mimicked (Taussig 1993, 65–66). That is to say, asserting that Congolese are savages that only understand force requires that the colonizing power engage in savage acts of violence to achieve their goals.

An official Belgian government inquiry reported in 1919 that the population of the Congo had been reduced by half during the years of Leopold II's rule (quoted in Hochschild 1998, 233). Demographer Léon de St. Moulin supports this finding, stating that the Congo's population declined by at least a third, possibly by half (1990, 303). If the official 1924 population figures of 10 million are accepted, that means roughly 10 million died under Leopold II's reign. However, as demographer Sabakinu Kivilu has pointed out, the 1924 figures are highly suspect (1990, 329). While debate continues over the exact figures, it is quite reasonable to state that *several million* Africans died during Leopold II's control of the Congo. The causes of death—beyond "natural causes"—included murder, starvation, exposure, and disease, all of which had their immediate roots in the colonial project.

Besides the astronomical numbers, what makes the loss of life in the Congo more startling was the degree of state-sanctioned violence that accompanied it. Evidence abounds of colonial officials such as Léon Rom lining their gardens with human skulls, indiscriminate torture and beatings, forced starvation, institutionalized maiming and disfigurement, forced relocation, kidnapping and blackmail as forms of "taxation," and outright murder. The semiofficial handbook given to each agent and state post, *Manuel du Voyageur et du Résident au Congo*, contained specific instructions on hostage taking (Donny 1897: I, 137–140). These activities and the official policies authorizing them have been detailed, and often sensationalized, by such writers as Adam Hochschild (1998), Jules Marchal (1996) and Daniel Vangroenweghe (1986). While most analysts accept the occurrence of these atrocities, there is some debate over the *degree* to which they took place.

What was the reason for the brutality of the campaign? Most scholars focus on Leopold II's insatiable greed, fueled by the presence of raw rubber at a time when demand was rapidly increasing.[19] Desperate to make a profit off of his colonial enterprise, Leopold II and his commercial compatriots encouraged agents to use whatever methods possible to attain the highest levels of rubber accumulation.[20] To that ends, forced labor, blackmail, hostage taking, violent repression, taxation, and straightforward coercion became standard practices for ensuring the gathering of rubber. While this violence was doubtlessly motivated by economic pressures and the need to create labor discipline, it was also very much a passionate, and gratuitous, end in itself.

With its rhetoric of development, civilization and salvation, the colonial discourse not only sanctioned but required brutality. At the most basic level, the inhabitants of the Congo were denied their humanity by the colonial project: They were largely seen as animals or subhumans, inhabiting a physical space that was rich in resources and the legal possession of Leopold II. In 1885, on the very day the Congo Free State was proclaimed, Leopold II declared by royal decree that all "vacant" land in the Congo was the property of the state. Since Leopold II possessed the Congo, the rubber and other "natural" resources were the colonizers' by right. Under the logic of the "civilizing" discourse, forcing the Africans to gather those resources was not only allowable, but it was for the betterment of the Africans. Brutality against Africans, like slavery before it, was enabled and encouraged by scripted discourses. The murdering and mutilation of the Congolese was always tied to these discourses. To treat the inhabitants of the Congo in different ways would have required a different discourse of Congolese identity, a different conception of "reality."

Embedded in the colonizing discourses were other specific "plans of action" for the conversion and domestication of the Congolese subject. Since the Congolese identity was largely constructed through binary oppositions between blacks and whites, it was understood that the mere presence of whites would promote civilization and development. Thus, Belgian domination and conquest of the Congo was required for "evolution by example," a view expressed in the following passage from Henry Ward's *Five Years with the Congo Cannibals*[21]:

> Time and the influence of white men of upright character, as missionaries, traders and government officials, dwelling among them, and identifying their sympathies with the lives and welfare of the natives, will effect great changes in the people of the Upper Congo. As civilisation spreads, and the ways of the white men become known to the dwellers in the far interior, a desire to imitate the more agreeable modes of living then presented to their gaze will spring up in the breasts of these poor African savages liberated by that time, let us hope, from the devastating scourge of Arab slave-raiding in their midst (Ward 1891, 163).

The colonial project was partially realized through commercial engagement and trade in ways that necessitated the erasure and replacement of traditional noncapitalist practices. Traditional economic exchanges were often cast as "irrational" and "fetishistic" in an attempt to destroy them. Likewise, the discourse on African "laziness" was an attempt to establish control of Africans and their labor. Furthermore, the natives had to be dispossessed of their land. Discursively, this process was effectively accomplished through the portrayal of the Congo as a space existing before history; that is to say, an unclaimed and timeless space, as yet unorganized by societies and economies. As Pratt notes, Africa's "very primalness [was] a sign of the failure of human enterprise. Neglect became the touchstone of a negative esthetic that legitimated European interventionism" (Pratt 1992, 149). For example, Belgian Prime Minister M. de Smet de Naeyer, during a 1903 debate on the Congo in the Belgian House, declared "The native is not entitled to anything; what is given to him is a pure gratuity" (quoted in *West African Mail*, 3 February 1905, 1068).

Leopold II argued that having a colony would provide profit for Belgium (Stengers 1972, 264–5; Hochschild 1998, 57–74). It would do so not only by providing valuable resources but also by providing, as the king himself put it, "an outlet for her surplus production of men, things and ideas" (quoted in Gann and Duigan 1979, 30).[22] The colonial discourse stressed the material benefits the country would receive from its control over the Congo (see Slade 1962, esp. ch. 3). For example, when *Le Congo Illustré* ran an article asking "*Pourquoi il nous faut une vaste colonie*" the answer was spelled out in purely economic terms, stressing the trade generated between Belgium and the Congo and the profit the Belgians received (7 April 1895, 49–51).

The colonial discourse also employed the rhetoric that commerce was a vehicle for spreading European culture—civilization via trade. For example, *Le Mouvement Géographique* ran an article on June 27, 1897, entitled "*Historique du commerce européen au Congo*" that, while stressing the material benefits that Congolese trade had brought to Belgium, placed greater emphasis on the role of commerce and trade in bringing civilization to the Congo. Yet, rhetorical moves such as these were initially largely unsuccessful given that Africa was historically of little importance to the Belgian businessman (Gann and Duigan 1979, 24). Belgian economic interests would eventually embrace the Congo, but only after the colonial project was firmly underway.

Leopold II was more successful in garnering external support for his venture by employing the rhetoric of free trade, wisely realizing that capitalizing on Belgium's neutral status would be to his advantage. Thus, while other European powers were engaged in the "scramble for Africa" (better characterized by Joseph Conrad as a "scramble for loot"), Leopold II's colonial project was perceived as nonthreatening by other imperial powers because he ensured free access to the territory. By promising not to impose customs or import duties in the "untapped" and "resource-rich" Congo, Leopold II produced the image of a free trade paradise. As Stengers has noted, "It was this wonderful promise which alone won him recognition for his state" among his European colonial competitors (1972, 273).

The colonizing script also employed the rhetoric of salvation. Like the European conquest of the Americas, Leopold II's colonial project in Africa was partly scripted through the ideology of religious salvation (see Todorov 1984; Pratt 1992). However, a more dominant theme in the Belgian conquest was the "salvation" of the natives from the so-called Arabs. Within Leopold II's colonial project, the Africans were rhetorically presented as needing rescuing not only from damnation and backwardness but also from the evil of the Arab slave trader. For example, in a November 6, 1876, speech to drum up support for his nascent colonial vision in Africa, Leopold II capitalized on the "dark" specter of slavery:

> Gentlemen, The slavery which is still continued over a considerable portion of the African Continent is a plague-spot which all friends of civilisation must desire to see obliterated ... The horrors of this state of things, the thousands of victims which the slave trade causes to be massacred every year, the still greater number of perfectly innocent beings who are brutally dragged into captivity and condemned wholesale to hard labour for life ... [We must act to end this] odious traffic, which is a disgrace to the age in which we live, and to tear away the veil of darkness which still hangs over Central Africa (quoted in Banning 1877, 162–3).

As the colonial project gathered momentum, much of the rhetoric focused on the Arab slave trade, including extensive coverage in *Le Congo Illustré*.[23] Rhetorically casting himself as a white warrior driving out the Arab scourge helped authorize the Belgian "protection" of the Congolese "victims." It also gained Leopold II and his colonial aspirations a high degree of moral support early on throughout Europe and the United States. In a very material sense, this script enabled colonial agents to engage in extremely violent wars of conquest and repression in eastern Congo to "liberate" it from the Arabs.

Leopold II was also successful in garnering domestic and international support by employing the rhetoric of the "civilizing mission," a.k.a., the "white man's burden" (see Gong 1984). Through the colonial discourse, the Congolese were portrayed as uncivilized people, evidenced by their "backward" beliefs and practices. Great emphasis was placed on discussions of the supposed propensity of the Congolese for savagery and violence, as well as the practice of polygamy, human sacrifice, and cannibalism. Simultaneously, the colonial discourse constructed an image of whites as civilizing agents. Europeans, because of their "natural" superiority and rationality, had a *duty* to spread their culture to the "backward" corners of the world. These discursive maneuvers necessitated the conquest and colonization of the Congolese in order to violently expunge their "backward" beliefs and practices and move them further along the path of evolution.

Discourses of the European civilizing mission also employed the language of expanding scientific knowledge. As Mary Louis Pratt has observed, the Enlightenment-inspired intellectual quest to "fill in the blank spaces of the map" was one of the driving elements in the colonial discourse, producing "the rest of the world" for European consumption (Pratt 1992, 5; also 15–37). The need to define, name, catalogue, and "know"—central elements of the project of modernity—became key pillars of the Belgian colonial discourse, enabling the conquest of the Congo. There was a need to "fill in" the map of Central Africa, to "penetrate" the interior beyond the cataracts, to discover the source of the Nile, and to observe, document, and (hierarchically) categorize the peoples, animals, and fauna of the region. Defining and ascribing meaning to the Congo through scientific exploration and scholarship was an effective act of power and control.[24] Leopold II's organizing and hosting the 1876 International Geographic Conference was but one example of the employment of scientific exploration for the advancement of the colonial project.

A central aspect of the colonial project involved the silencing of African identity discourses, or the closing off of discursive spaces for indigenous voices. For example, within the Congo the village was the traditional reservoir of memory and identity. The colonial project represented the village as a site and symbol of "savagery" and "degeneracy" that needed to be erased and replaced in the name of civilization (see Mudimbe 1994, 141–142). Equally, the Belgian colonial agents continued Stanley's practice of dismissing indigenous systems of signs and symbols. To take but one example, the colonial agents made little attempt to learn indigenous languages, holding that they were "incomprehensible" (see Picard 1896, 160; *La Belgique Coloniale* 1896, 292). European systems of knowledge were privileged and forcefully imposed to prove their "universalism." The diverse—and often antagonistic—memories/histories, local economies, discursive systems, and indigenous identity constructs of the Africans in the Congo region were confronted with a seemingly monolithic colonial system supported by a vision of progressive enrichment and, of course, a high degree of coercive force.

Taken together, these elements of the colonial project performed a number of functions. The Congo was defined in such a way as to deny the sovereignty of its people. Portraying the inhabitants of the Congo as incapable of handling power and authority allowed them to be dominated by force. The only "right" extended to these newly named Congolese was their right to dispossess themselves of their land. Traditional sociopolitical structures, discourses, and forms of authority were violently besieged, and in their stead, the Western state structures were forcefully installed. The colonial construction of the Congo entailed an invasion and repression not only of African political and economic space but of its epistemological space as well.

The International Context: "Red Rubber" and the Congo Reform Movement

> [A] system has been introduced by King Leopold II in the Congo Basin, imitated in some respects by others, which is turning its servants into brute beasts, disgracing European prestige, befouling civilisation, and jeopardising the whole future of European effort in the Dark Continent.
>
> —E. D. Morel in *West African Mail*, 24 February 1905

As the above quote notes, the colonial project in the Congo did not unfold within a vacuum. In fact, Leopold II's colonizing endeavors were profoundly influenced and shaped by their larger context. Western criticism of colonial rule in the Congo did not garner significant international attention until E. D. Morel, a young British shipping agent, realized that Leopold II's "free trade" state was a façade, based on the use of forced labor in the gathering of rubber. Morel began an international campaign against Leopold II, founding the Congo Reform Association (CRA) in 1904. In this concluding section, I focus on how Leopold II's colonial project was interpreted and (re)presented within the international (that is, Western) community at the time. Specific attention will be paid to how various actors, particularly Morel and his reformist colleagues, portrayed Congolese identity, Belgian identity, and Leopold II's colonial project.

Although early reports of atrocities against the Congo's inhabitants had been produced from foreign missionaries,[25] Morel is generally credited with focusing Western attention on the violence of Leopold II's rule (see Marchal 1996; Vangroenweghe 1986; Louis and Stengers 1968; Hochschild 1998). As a shipping agent during the late 1890s,

Morel noticed that Belgian ships arriving from the Congo were loaded down with rubber, ivory, and other resources but returned containing only arms and ammunition. Morel suspected the use of forced labor and the abrogation of the free trade promises made at the Berlin Conference. Bolstered by reports he received from (non-Belgian) missionaries and from Roger Casement, the British consul in Boma, Morel became a virulent opponent of Leopold II's rule, touring the European speaker circuits, producing hundreds of pamphlets, and publishing the *West African Mail*, a weekly newspaper covering African news in general. Morel and his supporters coined the phrase "Red Rubber" to connect the wild rubber from the Congo with the blood spilled by the Congo's inhabitants, who were forced to gather it. Eventually, the CRA established branches and affiliates across Europe and the United States, drawing support from thousands, including politicians, clergy, celebrities, and nobility. Through their publications, speeches, and public gatherings, Morel, the CRA, and its supporters successfully produced an alternative discourse that challenged not only Leopold II's discourse on the Congo but also norms of "international" behavior.

Just as Belgian national identity had become tied to Leopold II's colonial project, nationalist discourses were also intimately linked with other European colonial projects. By the nineteenth century, the colonial discourses of imperial powers such as Britain, France, Germany, and the United States were grounded in the rhetoric of their own cultural superiority (see Hammond and Jablow 1970; Miller 1985; McClintock 1995; Kaplan and Pease 1993). For instance, the British colonial discourse established the English individual as the sole embodiment of "civilization," while the French discourse privileged the superiority of French "culture," and so forth. This meant that it was not enough for Africans to be colonized by Europeans but that they must be integrated into a specific European society. These discursive trends informed the campaign against Leopold II's "Red Rubber" rule in the Congo. Specifically, Morel and the Congo Reform movement's tactics involved painting Belgians as uncivilized or, more specifically, as illegitimate bearers of civilization. This move was an attempt to excise Leopold II and Belgium from the ranks of the more "civilized" European colonial powers. Thus, the civilization of the "international community" was itself reinscribed through the exclusion of Belgium. Importantly, the Congo's need to be dominated and domesticated was never questioned. Rather, it was Leopold II's/Belgium's role as author of that civilizing mission that was called into question.

Belgian barbarity was therefore a major theme in the alternative discourse constructed by Morel and the Congo Reform movement. In *A*

Campaign Among Cannibals, Edgar Canisius, an American who worked for the rubber concession company Société Anversoise du Commerce au Congo, wrote "I have heard and seen much of the callousness of the Chinese, but certainly their indifference to human suffering does not exceed that of the average Congolese Belgian" (1903, 70). Morel filled his pamphlets and the *West African Mail* with horrific reports smuggled out of the Congo, primarily by missionaries working there. Roger Casement returned to England in 1903 to write his report on the atrocities for the foreign office. In this report, he provides detailed documentation and graphic examples of abuses, mainly the use of the *chicotte* (a type of whip) and the chopping off of hands and other body parts as punishment for failing to procure the required amount of rubber. These reports recast the Congolese as victims of Belgian barbarity. Such specific evidence fueled Morel's campaign and strengthened the ranks of the Congo Reform movement.

Leopold II and his colonial state were at risk of losing their sovereign claim to the Congo by losing their ability to author the Congolese social identity. As international relations theorist Cynthia Weber has observed: "states are 'written' effects of attempts to exert effective control over representation, both political and symbolic. If a state is unable politically or symbolically to represent its people, then it risks losing its source of sovereign authority" (Weber 1995, 28). Leopold II's critics held that there *was* a need for civilization, just not Belgian civilization, since Belgians were apparently as uncivilized as the natives. In effect, Belgian practices in the Congo endangered European and the U.S. colonial narratives: They threatened to bring to light the violence underpinning all colonial and imperial projects. Excising Belgium helped Europeans to erase their own violence from their colonial narratives and myths.

Perhaps the best representative of the excising of Belgium can be found in Morel's pamphlet *The Scandal of the Congo: Britain's Duty*, in which he writes: "Civilisation has been outraged [by Belgian rule in the Congo] . . . The personal rule responsible for this wrong has ceased morally to belong to the category of civilised states" (1904c, 9). This rhetorical move placed Leopold II and Belgium outside of "civilisation." Much of this literature demonized Leopold II, painting him as greed or evil incarnate. The line between Leopold II and Belgium collapsed, so that the atrocities in the Congo were not just a result of Leopold II's greed but of Belgium's lack of civilization.

The view that the Congo needed civilizing, but not by Belgians, was immortalized in Joseph Conrad's popular *Heart of Darkness*, published in the spring of 1899. The novel was written after Conrad traveled up the Congo River, witnessed Belgian rule first hand, and established a personal friendship with the British consul Roger Casement. The plot centers on the British character Marlow's journey into the interior of the Congo to remove Kurtz, a company official who has "gone native." Conrad employed familiar stereotypes of the Congo and the natives, most centrally, the spatial trope that travel into the interior represented backward movement across time and space: "Going up that river was like traveling back to the earliest beginnings of the world, when vegetation rioted on the earth and the big trees were kings . . . We penetrated deeper and deeper into the heart of darkness . . . We were wanderers on a prehistoric earth . . . The prehistoric man was cursing us, praying to us, welcoming us—who could tell?" (Conrad 1988, 35, 37). The Africans are presented as beasts, cannibals, savages, and childlike primates. These primitives and the African environment they inhabit are what drag Kurtz off the pedestal of civilization. As Conrad writes, "The wilderness had patted him on the head, and behold, it was like a ball—an ivory ball; it had caressed him and—lo!—he had withered; it had taken him, loved him, embraced him, gotten into his veins, consumed his flesh, and sealed his soul to its own by the inconceivable ceremonies of some devilish initiation . . . He had taken a high seat amongst the devils of the land" (Conrad 1988, 49).

Kurtz functions as a symbol of the Belgian colonial project. Because he is not as high up the "civilization" ladder as the British Marlow, Kurtz is unable to combat his "forgotten and brutal instincts" (Conrad 1988, 65). Marlow's hold on "culture," though tenuous, proves to be stronger, and he is able to conquer Africa and his own demons (69).[26] It should be stressed that Conrad believed strongly in the civilizing mission for Africa and the Congo. In fact, he was an avid supporter of British imperialism and a propagandist for the empire during the Boer Wars. His criticism was reserved for Belgian imperialism, which he felt was inadequate for promoting Western civilization and economic development. This was also the theme of his 1896 short story, sarcastically entitled "An Outpost of Progress" (Conrad 1975).

Linked with the presentation of the illegitimacy of Belgium's civilizing/colonizing project was its characterization by the Congo Reform movement as a *contagion*: Belgian rule was portrayed as a disease that threatened the "legitimate" colonial projects of the other European powers. H. R. Fox Bourne, secretary of the Aborigines Protection Society, stated: "Let it be remembered that in the heart of Africa, vitally affecting the welfare of all the surrounding portions of the continent which are in present or prospective occupation by the European Powers is a *poisonous growth of spurious 'civilisation'* which *contaminates* and more than threatens overwhelming injury to all its neighbours" (1903, 302–303; emphasis added). As Morel wrote, Leopold II's actions were "befouling civilisation, and jeopardising the whole future of European effort in the Dark Continent" (*West African Mail,* 24 February 1905: 1103). One of Morel's more provocative pamphlets was unsubtly titled *The Belgian Curse in Africa* (n.d.)

This image of the Belgian as a bad/illegitimate colonizer became a popular trope in larger European colonial discourses, being re-employed in literature and even cinema.[27] By decrying Belgian colonial practices, other imperial powers were drawing attention away from their own colonial atrocities. By painting Leopold II as a "bad" colonizer, other European powers were casting themselves as "good" colonizers. Thus, Leopold II became, to a certain extent, the *Other* within the "international community" that Morel and the Congo Reform movement appealed to as its audience.[28] What was at stake was less the fate of the Congo than the authoring of a set of international norms for a projected international (civil) community.

In the "Congo Question" pamphlet, Morel's rhetoric is representative. At one point, he writes: "England, France and Germany cannot allow the disease introduced into the West and Central Africa by King Leopold of Belgium to be further extended. Nor do their responsibilities end there. The source of the disease must be dealt with. The canker must be rooted out and destroyed. The Congo State must be called to account for its crimes against civilisation" (n.d., 377). This passage constructs an image of Belgian colonialism as a contagion, an implied international community as its interpretive community, and an explicit call for intervention based on supposed international norms.

Leopold II's critics challenged most aspects of Leopold II's colonial policy yet did not rescript his imagined Congo, re-employing the very same rhetoric against itself. For example, they argued that Leopold II and his colonial agents were exploiting the African's "inherent" barbarity. An example of this was the image of the Congo's "cannibal army." Leopold II's colonial state, understaffed and extremely cost conscious, had established as its coercive arm an army known as the Force Publique, manned by Africans and officered by whites (largely non-Belgian Europeans). Re-employing the pervasive image of Congolese as cannibals, Leopold II's critics simply asserted that these soldiers had not been "cured" of their "natural" habits (see Bourne 1903, 76, 299–300; Burrows 1903, 212; Morel n.d., 364–376). While other European colonial powers employed (or impressed) "their" Africans into military service, they were able to escape similar accusations because the cannibal trope was no longer an active part of their colonial discourse (they often claimed to have "corrected" this African habit through their own colonizing presence).

While criticism was leveled at Leopold II and his colonial rule for failing to provide the promise of the European "civilizing mission," more pervasive themes among his critics concerned commerce and free trade. On the one hand, Leopold II created the image of the Congo as a resource-rich free trade paradise, but on the other hand, the king had established monopolistic holdings and imposed tariffs in order to realize profits from his colonial venture. Morel produced a tract entitled *The Economic Aspect of the Congo Problem: The Kernel of the Question* (1908) that charged Leopold II with violating the mission entrusted to him by the European powers at the Berlin Conference. Morel argued Leopold II was thwarting African development and civilization by maintaining an exploitative monopoly. In *The "Commercial" Aspect of the Congo Question* (1904d), Morel praised other European powers for using commerce as a vehicle for development and civilization in Africa. But, he asserted, such a "commercial" relationship did not exist in Congo, where forced labor, taxation, and exploitation in the gathering of "Red Rubber" were the modus operandi. In the *West African Mail* (7 October 1904), he accused Leopold II of establishing a monopoly and cutting other Europeans out of the picture.[29] As these examples illustrate, Leopold II's critics were often more concerned with Leopold II's squashing of free trade than the native's "human rights." In this, they were reproducing Leopold II and Stanley's mythology that capitalism was intrinsic to the Congo's "development."

Morel and the Congo Reform movement imagined Congolese social identity in much the same way as the dominant Belgian colonial representations. The images of the inhabitants authored by Stanley, Leopold II, and other colonial agents were taken as "true" and generally not challenged by the Reform movement. Both the colonial and "Red Rubber" discourses employed the tropes of the Congolese as cannibals, savages, barbarians, or children. However, the representation of the Congolese as helpless victims was heightened in this more paternalistic alternative discourse. Whereas Leopold II portrayed the Africans as helpless victims of Arab slaver traders, this new alternative discourse imagined the Africans as helpless victims of Leopold II's cruelty and greed, as evidenced by the numerous cartoons reprinted in English and American popular press (see figures 2.4 and 2.5). Mark Twain was recruited by Morel and, in 1904, entered the debate with his famous *King Leopold's Soliloquy*, a scathing attack on the monarch's barbarity against "those twenty-five millions of gentle and harmless blacks" (Twain 1961, 32).

If the basic elements of Congolese social identity remained unchallenged, this reform discourse radically challenged the self-image of Leopold II and the Belgians. Leopold II fought back, bribing editors and reporters to suppress negative coverage and publish pro-Belgian pieces (see Willequet 1962). He hired spies and double agents, from the well-connected General Henry Shelton Sanford to the entrepreneur/explorer May French-Sheldon, to infiltrate both the CRA and foreign governments (Boisseau 1996). He attempted to flood the public realm with supportive coverage. For example, Demetrius C. Boulger, a pro-Leopold II agent in the United States, published the sympathetic tome *The Congo State, or The Growth of Civilisation in Central Africa* (1898). As the "Red Rubber" scandal grew, Boulger also weighed in with "The Congo State and Central-African Problems" for *Harper's* (February 1900, 373–388) and "The Attack on the Congo Free State" in *The North American Review* (15 December 1903, 825–836). Another agent on Leopold II's payroll, Frederick Starr, produced a series of articles for the *Chicago Tribune* and the book *The Truth About the Congo* (1907). In these writings, the natives were portrayed as savage or childlike cannibals who only understood force: Starr even asserted that "it is doubtful whether the Congo native has as keen a sense of physical suffering as ourselves" (1907, 23). In this work, Starr also criticizes missionaries for their "complaining spirit" (1907, 61) while excusing any abuses of power on the part of colonial officials on the ground that the sun in Africa makes all whites "a little crazy," an interesting, though unoriginal, trope in the representation of African space (1907, 43). The Belgians, and Leopold II in particular, were characterized as being saintly providers of civilization, culture, and economic development. Boulger, for example, proclaimed that "If there is any quarter of the globe where international rivalry, jealousies, and criticism should cease, it is in Central Africa, where the Congo State has sprung into existence before our eyes, and where, for twenty years and more, King Leopold of the Belgians has been engaged on a work of noble beneficence" (1900, 373).

Despite Leopold II's attempts, the alternative discourse of Morel and the Congo Reform movement gained greater sway in the West than his own scripting of the colonial project. This shift occurred for several reasons. The CRA successfully appealed to a "humanitarian" community of Americans and Europeans outraged by the abuses in the Congo. Moreover, rival powers were increasingly frustrated by their inability to access the Congo's wealth, a point Morel exploited in his anti-

Figure 2.4: "In the Rubber Coils"
Source: *Punch*, November 28, 1906.

Leopold II writings and speeches. Finally, the beginning of the twentieth century saw a growing sense of nationalism in Europe that was fed by the "Othering" of Leopold II and Belgium. However, any attempt by

Figure 2.5: "King of the Rubbernecks"
Source: *Daily Pioneer Press*; reprinted in *West African Mail*, March 16, 1906, 1214.

one European power to intervene directly in the Congo would clearly have challenged the norms of sovereignty and disrupted the precarious balance of power. Under pressure, Leopold II provided a solution to the situation by selling his personal estate to the Belgian government in March 1908—thus, instituting a change in its name to the "Belgian Congo." Brussels agreed to assume over 100 million francs' worth of debt, pay 45.5 million francs to complete several of the king's building projects (including renovations to his palace in Laeken), and pay

Leopold II an extra 50 million francs as "a mark of gratitude for his great sacrifices made for the Congo" (Marchal 1996, 349).[30]

Leopold II's successors continued the process of constructing and imposing a colonial state in the Congo, violently extending Belgian occupation of the Congo's physical space and forcefully suppressing indigenous resistance. Violent repression and forced labor remained the rule of the day for quite some time (see Marchal 1999). Yet it should be stressed that Belgian attempts to create a monolithic colonial state repeatedly failed, largely because it was financially and physically unable to extend its coercive force throughout the region. Since its inception, the colonial state had to rely on aligning itself with other groups—such as the Church, businesses, and co-opted indigenous agents and structures—in its attempts to achieve dominance within Congolese society. Even then, this dominance—and the underpinning Belgian discourses of political space—was never completely successful.

Despite the "Red Rubber" scandal, the representations established by Stanley, Leopold II, and his colonial agents remained the primary authoritative statements on Congolese identity. The alternative discourse produced by Morel and other reformers did not offer a fundamental reimagining of the Congo; the ways the colonial project first defined and inscribed the Congo's social and spatial identity were largely accepted and re-employed by the Congo Reform movement. Thus, the Congolese identity that emerged in the works of Stanley, Leopold II, and his colonial agents remained the dominant version for the next half century and served to underpin Belgian colonial domination of the Congo until its independence in 1960.

Chapter Three

Congo as Chaos, Lumumba as Diable: Independence and the 1960 Crisis

> The objective of the Brussels Universal Exhibition is to present an impressive, overall picture of man's achievements to make life on earth more civilized and agreeable . . . For the Belgians, this Exhibition takes place at a very important moment in the nation's history. It is exactly fifty years ago, that Belgium became responsible for the administration of vast territories in Central Africa. The Belgians . . . have no imperialistic history, tradition or ambition. Unlike the British, the Dutch, the Portuguese and the Spanish, they had no part in the great periods of colonial conquest and expansion . . . However . . . they have shown how much a small, but technically very advanced country can do for the development of backwards areas.
>
> It cannot be denied that somebody had to do this job in Central Africa.
>
> —L. Bruneel, President of the Congo and Ruanda-Urundi section of the 1958 Exhibition (quoted in *The Belgian Congo To-Day*, April 1958, 3)

Most visitors to Brussels are probably familiar with the Atomium, one of the city's most recognizable icons. The towering structure of nine spheres linked by tubes is 102 meters tall and was built to represent the atomic lattice of iron crystals, magnified 165 billion times. The Atomium was created to serve as the centerpiece, celebrating scientific progress, for the 1958 Brussels Universal Exhibition. Situated at the northern foot of the Atomium, the Belgian Congo and Ruanda-Urundi[1] section of the Expo stretched out for 20 acres (Wyvekens 1989, 158). An estimated 350 million people visited the seven pavilions that made up the Congo section of the 1958 Expo (Cockx and Lemmens 1958, 166).[2] The pavilions (dedicated to themes such as agriculture, Catholic missionaries, mines, energy, and transportation), a grand hall, and a seven-acre tropical garden were intended to provide visitors with "the whole Congo story" (*Congo belge et Ruanda-Urundi* 1958). The theme of the display was the material and spiritual uplifting of the natives achieved by fifty years of Belgian rule. As the section's president, L. Bruneel, proclaimed, "[The Congo Section] simply aims at showing men of good faith, what the Congo has become since Belgium has taken its administration in hand, and what are its future prospects, if peace and racial harmony continue to prevail in Central Africa" (quoted in *The Belgian Congo To-Day,* April 1958, 12). The 1958 Expo sought to illustrate to the world the Belgian mastery of modernity, most explicitly symbolized by the towering Atomium, as well as its colonial project. Through multilayered displays, the Congo and Belgium were defined and the colonial project narrated, praised, and justified. Throughout the Expo, visitors could watch military routines performed by the Force Publique while meeting African tourists flown in from the Congo. Like the 1898 Tervuren Expo, displays such as this one worked to construct an image of a subject as though it were a realistic representation, or a picture of the "truth" (Mitchell 1988, 60).

The Congo section of the 1958 Expo sought to present an image of Belgium and its colonial project to the world, an image where Belgian colonialism was making life "more civilized and agreeable." But this image was undermined by subsequent events. In January 1959, riots broke out in Leopoldville, the capital of the Belgian Congo. These riots shocked a sleepy Belgian populace who had assumed that the nationalist movements sweeping across Africa would somehow bypass their colony. Just a few years earlier, Belgian Minister of Colonies André Dequae asserted that "the natives have neither political consciousness nor interest" (quoted in *Belgian Congo To-Day,* January 1954, 8). In the wake of the 1959 riots, the Belgian government moved quickly to decolonize. In his annual New Year's address, King Baudouin (the grandson of Leopold II's nephew and successor, Albert I), announced that Belgium would give its colony the "gift" of independence "without undue haste." The Belgians organized a series of roundtable meetings with prominent Congolese leaders and eventually established a timetable for independence. The political structures put in place were similar to the Belgian parliamentary system, and in national elections Patrice Lumumba was elected prime minister. In a gesture of national unity, Lumumba appointed his chief rival, Joseph Kasavubu, as president.

On June 30, 1960, King Baudouin presided over the independence ceremony that transformed the Belgian Congo into the Republic of the Congo. However, on July 5, 1960, several units in the Congolese army, the Force Publique, mutinied, demanding promotions, pay raises, and the removal of white officers. At the time of independence, the Force Publique remained a colonial structure, with its black soldiers suffering harsh treatment at the hands of exclusively white officers. Many Belgian officers flatly told their troops that independence was "for civilians" and that they should "ignore it" (quoted in Kitchen 1967, 19–20). As rioting and unrest spread, Lumumba attempted to control the revolt by promoting all African soldiers one step, removing some Belgian officers, and appointing a Congolese, Joseph Mobutu, as a quasipolitical overseer of the military structure. However, a number of Belgian officers refused to step down. Belgian troops stationed in the Congo intervened and actively engaged the Congolese army and civilians. In what amounted to an invasion, on July 9, 1960, the Belgian Council of Ministers dispatched additional paracommandos to the Congo, against the wishes of the Congo government. As a result, more Congolese troops mutinied against their white officers and violence intensified.

On July 11, Belgian naval forces attacked the Congolese ports of Matadi and Boma. The same day, Moise Tshombe, the regional leader of the southern province of Katanga, announced his region's secession and asked for Belgian support. The Belgians responded positively. On the following day, Lumumba and Kasavubu (after being denied assistance from the U.S. ambassador), cabled the Secretary-General of the United Nations and asked for UN military assistance. The UN responded by sending a multinational force to the Congo in order to "restore law and order." Despite Lumumba's wishes, the UN did not move to dislodge Belgian troops from the Congo. Frustrated, Lumumba turned to the Soviet Union for assistance, which sent several planes and material. Fearing a superpower showdown over the Congo, UN Secretary-General Dag Hammarskjöld began the intensive diplomatic activity of trying to return Belgian troops to their barracks, keep Russian troops out of the Congo, and have the multinational UN force maintain domestic peace. Hammarskjöld made no substantial move to confront Tshombe over secession, despite Lumumba's urging.

Sensing Western discontentment with Lumumba and with strong encouragement from his European advisers, President Kasavubu fired Prime Minister Lumumba on September 5, 1960. Lumumba responded the same day by firing Kasavubu, creating a standoff with both leaders claiming legitimacy. The internal political situation was further muddled on September 14, when Mobutu, encouraged by the Central Intelligence Agency (CIA), announced a military coup and created yet another national government. By this time, the U.S. government had already decided Lumumba must be removed, and the CIA was plotting to assassinate the Congolese leader. Despite being under UN protection/house-arrest, Lumumba managed to escape from Leopoldville and flee toward Stanleyville. However, he was captured en route. Lumumba was then flown to Katanga, where he was handed over to the secessionist forces. Lumumba was beaten, tortured, and eventually murdered.

In this chapter, I examine how the 1960 Congo crisis was rooted in the conflicts over Congolese identity and who had the authority to author that identity. Identities of states, like other social identities (however multiple and changing), are formed by being located or locating themselves within social narratives. As Margaret Somers notes, "it is through narrativity that we come to know, understand, and make sense of the social world, and it is through narratives and narrativity that we constitute our social identities" (Somers 1994, 606). Narratives of national identities are generally formed by a gradual layering on and connecting of events and meanings, usually through three steps: the selection of events themselves, the linking of these events to each other in causal and associational ways (plotting), and interpreting what the events and plot signify (Cornell 2000). These three acts of narrativization (selecting, plotting, interpreting) lay at the heart of identity construction within international relations.

However, these identity-constructing narratives are rarely of our own making. External forces are constantly at play, seeking to select, plot, and interpret the events and meanings by which identities are narrated. Actors do not create their own narratives at will. They are limited by the availability of accepted representations and narratives. As Somers and Gibson note, "Which kind of narratives will socially predominate is contested politically and will depend in large part on the distribution of power" (Somers and Gibson 1994, 73). Within the 1960 crisis, the Congo's sovereignty and the identity of its citizenry were rewritten and reinscribed by multiple discourses claiming authorship. At stake was how the Congo was to be "imagined."

Identities are formed by the gradual layering on and connecting of events and meanings, and this opens up numerous points of contestation. For example, which events will be selected, and by whom? How will these events be linked to other events to form a causal relationship? Who will perform that act of emplotment? Who will interpret what the events and plot signify? That is to say, whose interpretation of the narrative—and the identities that narrative helps construct—will become dominant?

It should be stressed that these different narratives had direct material consequences. For example, the Belgian government operated within a framework informed by its colonial narrative of paternalism and ownership. As such, these discourses authorized the government's dismissal of Lumumba's claims to sovereignty and autonomy. Likewise, the U.S. government, operating within its own scripted narrative of cold war competition and Congolese barbarity and chaos, pursued interventionist policies that included the forceful removal of Patrice Lumumba. For his own part, Lumumba engaged in authoring alternative discourses on Congolese history and identity but was ultimately unable to access the international discursive spaces from which to circulate these alternative narratives. Agency can only be understood by recognizing the various narratives in which actors find themselves.[3] This approach resituates power in history away from a focus on subject *positioning* (as reflected in the traditional international relations theories of (neo)Realism, (neo)Liberalism, and Marxism) to one of subject *construction*.

This chapter examines the 1960 Congo Crisis from the perspective of clashing narrativization by exploring how competing forces selected, plotted, and interpreted their narratives of Congolese identity. The chapter illustrates not only the political dynamics of discourses surrounding independence, but also the lingering effects of established rhetoric, the rise of new (non-Congolese) "voices" on the Congo's identity, and the continuing difficulty that indigenous Congolese voices faced in being heard within the larger international community. The primary actors involved in this conflict over selecting, plotting, and interpreting narratives were Patrice Lumumba, the Belgian government, and the American government, against a backdrop of numerous "lesser" actors. Particular attention will be paid to the differences in causal emplotment, which refers to the meaning-making process in which actions and events are situated within larger, accepted narratives. More specifically, it is the act of creating meaning, of making sense of the social world. As we shall see, the events of the 1960 crisis were emplotted by different actors into differing larger narratives: for Lumumba it was the narrative of Belgian exploitation, for the Belgian government it was the narrative of Belgian Paternalism and *"Notre Congo"* (Our Congo), while the U.S. government emplotted the events within the larger narrative of cold war conflict. The chapter will conclude with a discussion of accessing and controlling international discursive space.

Competing Narratives of *Notre Congo*: Paternalism versus "Atrocious Suffering"

> The independence of Congo constitutes the culmination of the work conceived by the genius of King Leopold II, undertaken by Him with a tenacious courage and continued with perseverance by Belgium. It marks a decisive hour in the destiny not only of Congo itself, but, I don't hesitate to state, of the whole of Africa.
>
> For 80 years, Belgium sent to your soil her best sons, first in order to rescue the Congo basin from the odious slave trade that decimated its populations; afterwards in order to bring together the different tribes who, previously hostile, together will constitute the greatest of the independent States of Africa; finally, in order to call forth a happier life for the various regions of the Congo that are represented here, united in one Parliament.
>
> —King Baudouin's Independence Day speech (quoted in Gerard-Libois and Verhaegen 1961, 318)

> Our lot was eighty years of colonial rule; our wounds are still too fresh and painful to be driven from our memory.
>
> We have known tiring labor exacted in exchange for salary which did not allow us to satisfy our hunger, to clothe and lodge ourselves decently or to raise our children like loved beings.
>
> We have known ironies, insults, blows which we had to endure morning, noon, and night because we were "Negroes."
>
> —Patrice Lumumba's Independence Day speech (quoted in Merriam 1961, 353)

On June 30, 1960, the Belgian government officially granted the Congo its independence as a sovereign state. But the ceremony that took place in Leopoldville encapsulated two extremely different visions of the Belgian colonial project in the Congo. As the above quote from King Baudouin's speech illustrates, the Belgian colonial policies continued to be informed by the rhetoric of salvation and civilization established by Stanley, Leopold II, and the earlier colonial agents, well after these figures passed from the scene. Newly elected Prime Minister Patrice Lumumba, however, articulated a very different interpretation of the previous eighty years; one which focused on the collective suffering and abuse of the Congolese by a harshly repressive regime. These two speeches were delivered from the same stage and the differences are extremely important, for the divergent interpretations of colonial history were central elements in the narrativization of Congolese identity. These narratives not only were in direct conflict on that June afternoon, but each provided the larger narrative by which the subsequent events were interpreted by each side. As such, it is important to explore how these conflicting narratives were structured and interpreted, and how they produced meaning for the events that followed the Congo's independence.

The Paternal Narrative of Notre Congo

The Congo section of the 1958 Expo presented the dominant colonial narrative of the Congo and Congolese for an international audience. At a time when other European colonial powers were engaging in a policy of decolonization, the Expo authenticated the Belgian colonial project and explained why the government had not moved faster in its own decolonization policy. A major feature of the Congo section was a thirty-minute interactive show entitled *Congorama*. The display—a combination of film, mobiles, sound recordings, animated maps, and automated miniature villages—illustrated "the different states of the Congo's progress from the night of prehistory to the light of civilization." A silent film provided a visual narrative of the colonial project, moving from images of Africans in the jungle to their employment as porters, from the building of the railroad and white settlements to the growth of larger cities. Throughout the film, the railroad was used as a pervasive symbol of evolution, liberating the Africans from their portership and providing the imagery of forward progress. Most of the scenes involved panoramic displays of an unpopulated landscape. The few Africans in the film were portrayed either in traditional clothes in rural settings or in European clothes walking around town, constructing a distinct dichotomy between "backwardness" and "modernity."[4]

These elements of the colonial history were selected and linked together in causal and associational ways that produced the dominant narrative of Belgian colonial domination in the Congo. At its core were the salvation and civilizing discourses articulated by Henry Morton Stanley, Leopold II, and his colonial agents decades beforehand. On the threshold of Congolese independence, the young King Baudouin proclaimed that the "purpose of our presence on the African continent was defined by Leopold II; to open up these backwards countries to European civilization; summon their populations to emancipation, to freedom and to progress after having freed them from slavery, disease and misery" (*Belgian Congo To-Day*, January 1959, 3). In the wake of Belgium's inheritance of the Congo from Leopold II, the colonial state had instituted a colonial practice they themselves termed "Paternalism" that was informed by the dominant discourses on Congolese and Belgian identity (Hodgkin 1956, 51–59; Young 1965, 59–72). Paternalism, with its overt emphasis on the white man as *father* and African as *child*, became the philosophical framework (and justification) of the Belgian occupation of the Congo.[5] This policy was articulated in Governor-General Pierre Ryckman's treatise *Dominer Pour Servir* (Dominate to Serve/Domination for Service) (1948).[6] Even as late as 1959, this paternal metaphor continued to inform Belgian colonial policy. When speaking of the Congo's rural population seven months before independence, Belgian Minister of Colonies Auguste de Schrijver stated, "I see these simple populations outside the large urban centers, and I feel myself more than ever the father of a family" (quoted in Young 1965, 59).

Familial rhetoric was a central aspect of most European colonial projects, but rarely as overtly and explicitly as in the Belgian case. As cultural theorist Anne McClintock has noted, the family trope was important for at least two reasons. First, "the family offered an indispensable figure for sanctioning social hierarchy within a putative organic unity of interests" (McClintock 1995, 45). Subjugation of women and children to the male adult was an accepted and natural fact within Western thought. Thus, imperial and colonial practices were naturalized by reference to this established social hierarchy. What is more, colonial violence against the Congolese was effectively relegated to the "domestic" sphere of the family and, thus, apoliticized. Second, "the family offered an invaluable trope for figuring *historical time*" (McClintock 1995, 45). Both the social hierarchy (white over black; male over female) and historical change ("evolution" and "development") were presented as natural and inevitable. As McClintock argues: "Projecting the family image onto national and imperial progress enabled what was often murderously violent change to be legitimized as the progressive unfolding of natural decree... The trope of the organic family became invaluable in its capacity to give state and imperial intervention the alibi of nature" (1995, 45).

As the superior half of this familial relationship, Belgian national identity during the twentieth century had become increasingly tied to its overseas venture. Belgian daily life was saturated with images, rhetoric, and representations that narrated its national identity through the referent of the Congo (see Vints 1984; Jacquemin 1985; Jacquemin 1991; Blanchard et al. 1995; Tousignant 1995). The Congo was envisioned as *Notre Congo*. Through circulation and repetition, this image became embedded in Belgian daily life. Take, for example, chocolate. During the twentieth century, chocolate became one of the defining commodities of Belgium and Belgian identity (along with beer, diamonds, and lace). The cocoa for the chocolate was not indigenous to Belgium but had to be imported. Interestingly, the Belgian chocolate industry was able to acquire cheaper cocoa from other European colonies in Africa than from its own. In the 1930s, the government in Brussels launched a campaign to encourage the buying of Congolese cocoa, to keep the profits within the family, so to speak (Vellut 1996; Vantieghem 1996). Regardless of its source, Belgian chocolatiers employed the Belgian Congo as part of their marketing strategy. Images of Congolese and Leopold II frequently adorned wrappers and advertisements. Côte d'Or, for example, sold a "Congobar," and Delhaize featured Leopold II in their chocolate campaigns. In the case of Jacques Chocolates, the company included collectable stickers in their product, depicting various images from the Congo: "representative" images from various "tribes;" scenes from the Congo's colonial history; examples of Congolese wildlife and fauna; and numerous images of Congolese "evolution" since colonization, such as the railroad, medicine, and technology. These stickers could be affixed, like stamps, in a book glorifying the colonial project and its history. The book was suitably entitled *Notre Congo*.

Images of colonial successes and future payoffs abounded in Belgian society: in literature (see Halen 1995; Halen and Riesz 1993), cartoons (most famously, *Tintin au Congo*), art (see Quaghebeur et al. 1992), popular culture (see Jacquemin 1991 and 1985), cinema, urban space (Vincke 1993; see sculpture of "La race noire accuillie par la Belgique" in Parc du Cinquantenaire and Rue du Colonies in Brussels), and in travelogues and historical accounts (such as Poulaine 1931; Gendarme 1942; Rhodius 1959). Children's literature and textbooks featured tales of Belgian victories in and responsibilities to Africa (François 1943; see also De Baets 1991, 91–95; Halen and Riesz 1993; Verhaegen 1992). As political scientist Crawford Young has noted, "the Belgian public drew substantial vicarious satisfaction from the successful image of the Congo and basked in the complacent glow of its own myths about imposing achievements in Africa" (Young 1965, 20).

As the colonial project selected and plotted these elements to construct Belgian and Congolese identities, meaning was assigned to the events and symbols. Perhaps the most pervasive theme in the narrativization of the Belgian colonial mission was the view of the Congolese as *still evolving*. The predominant discourse held that some progress had been made in civilizing them, and these successes were typically represented by symbols of Western technology and industry:

hydroelectric dams, railroads and highways, mining facilities, plantations, urban sprawl, primary schools, and health care facilities. These were the physical markings of "civilization" the Belgian colonial project had etched on the surface of its Congo, material and physical markers of "development." However, it was felt that, by and large, the Congolese still remained precariously close to their savage roots. They were still to be regarded as "children" in need of Paternalism. For example, Professor Guy Malengreau of the University of Louvain wrote in 1955:

> In reality . . . the great mass of the Congo's inhabitants are incapable of governing themselves. This will be so for a long time to come . . . To enlarge the political rights of the colony's inhabitants would be in reality to abandon the fate of millions of natives to a handful of men whose interests are often in opposition to those of the bulk of the population for whom Belgium's guardianship is today the only protection (1955, 356).

At the time of independence, many Belgians often expressed the view that the Congolese were savages who "were up in the trees just fifty years ago" (Merriam 1961, 57–8).

The Belgian colonial narrative also relied on a specific spatial interpretation that regarded Congolese space as an extension of Belgian domestic space, and such representation engendered important material practices. Economic interests remained the central focus of the Belgian colonial vision, as they had been at the outset under Leopold II (see Jewsiewicki 1979; Willame 1972, 17). To that end, the images most Belgians had of the Congo were cast largely in economic terms, regarding the colony as a "sound business venture" (Hoskyns 1965, 33). Significantly, most of Belgium's economic investment in the Congo was centered in the southern region of Katanga, where copper, cobalt, tin, zinc, and uranium (from 1944 to 1960) were mined. In that region, Belgians had over $3.5 billion invested and an expatriate population of roughly 40,000 Belgian citizens. The region provided 60 percent of Congo's foreign currency earnings, most of which was held by one corporation, Union Miniére du Haut-Katanga (UMHK).

Stanley's colonizing rhetoric continued to influence the colonial project, as evidenced by the Belgian colonial state's adoption of his former moniker, Bula Matari (breaker of rocks) for itself. As Crawford Young observed: "The metaphor captured well the crushing, relentless force of the emerging colonial state in Africa . . . European administrators found this semiotic imagery congenial, as it suggested the irresistible hegemony deemed necessary to performance of their guardian role" (Young 1994, 1). Through the simultaneous use of Bula Matari and Paternalism, the colonial state tried to rhetorically construct itself as a "tough father." Its African "children" would be "raised" by discipline and control. The Belgian colonial state sought to establish itself as the pervasive, omnipresent (and omnipotent) father figure in the Congolese spatial domain.

But it wasn't—not by a long shot. The colonial state failed to establish complete hegemony over other competing social forces within the Congo, from armed insurgents to traditional sociopolitical structures, such as chieftancies and kinship alliances. Due to its financial and physical limitations, the colonial state had to unite with the Church and Belgian corporations to establish a semblance of hegemonic control.[7] Together, this triumvirate of state/Church/business formed the foundation for Belgian colonial rule. It is important to note that the state was often eclipsed by the other two. For instance, the physical and educational needs of the Congolese were usually administered to by the Church, not the state. Missionary orders ran the majority of the colony's health clinics and schools. To a large degree, the Church "filled in" for the state by performing functions commonly associated with the state under the Western understanding of state practices. In many places, the Church even issued its own currency (vouchers) and organized its own military protection (Mudimbe 1994, 136). Interestingly, the Church divided up the Congolese space into regions, each controlled by a different order. These zones became the domain of the ruling order, with education and salvation administered accordingly. This practice was also followed by Protestant missions in their different denominations. In the words of anthropologist V. Y. Mudimbe, the Congo became a "spiritual checker-board on which each unit or square was occupied by a definite religious style" (Mudimbe 1994, 110). Moreover, the major economic corporations also compartmentalized Congolese space and performed functions frequently assumed by Western political theories as the state's domain. For example, business firms such as Union Miniére initiated extensive welfarist policies as part of their "manpower stabilization" policies: providing their laborers with housing, health care, education, and so forth. Or as one businessman in Katanga put it: "See how well we look after our cattle" (quoted in Slade 1960, 4). It was, to a large degree, an extensive welfare system under the rubric of Paternalism.

Another product of the colonial narrative and its policy of Paternalism was the emergence of an elite social class. Called *évolués,* these were Congolese who had relatively advanced education[8] and/or civil service jobs (see Willame 1972, 24–27; Slade 1960, 12–14). The *évolués* were regarded as symbols of the "civilizing" mission. They were defined by the colonial government as those blacks in the midst of the transition from "traditional" tribal customs to Western "developed" culture. The colonial state engaged in the act of measuring and documenting the level of "civilization" individual Congolese had reached. In fact, the colonial government established a strategy for hierarchically ordering Congolese society through the introduction of the Carte du Mérite Civique.

Established by Governor-General Jungers in a July 12, 1948, decree, the Carte was awarded to Africans who could prove that they were "living in a state of civilization." An African had to go through an application process to show that he or she was free of "uncivilized" practices, such as polygamy, witchcraft, and theft. The regulations for the Carte specified that "it must be shown by his acts that he is *penetrated* with European civilization and conforms to it" (quoted in Young 1965, 85; emphasis added). The process was an attempt to quantitatively define "civilization" and judge Africans adherence to it; perhaps no other colonial policy better captures the Belgian's attempt to fix and control Congolese identity within its own scripted narrative of development and culture. It should be noted that many in the African clergy declined to apply for the Carte or its "*immatriculation*" successor because they felt it would have distanced them from their followers. By 1958, the colonial state recognized only 1,557 Africans as "civilized" (Young 1965, 78; see also Brausch 1961, 24).

At the turn of the twentieth century, Belgian rule had maintained rigid control over discursive space and its system of signs and symbols, including access to the French language (Samarin 1989). But by midcentury, the *évolués* had mastered this system and were pressing for a greater voice in the colony's future. Begrudgingly, Brussels increased the "legitimate" domestic space for Congolese. Overall, the changes were relatively small and slow in coming. Still suffering from socioeconomic constraints and the hegemonic selection system, Congolese achieved limited access to higher education in the 1950s and promotion within a tightly regulated civil service. Restrictions in the form of de facto segregation and access to alcohol were gradually lifted. Furthermore, *La Voix du Congolais,* a nationwide publication that became a forum for indigenous ideas and art, was established (Mudimbe 1994, 123). To a certain degree, *La Voix du Congolais* helped construct, in Benedict Anderson's terminology, an "imagined community" among Congolese elites. Through these growing discursive spaces, Congolese writers were able to publish and distribute their work.[9] Yet, most of these changes were largely reserved for the *évolués,* and not the masses.

Moreover, because the colonial state only permitted "cultural" or "mutual self-help" indigenous associations, most of the political movements that emerged, such as Alliance des Bakongo (ABAKO), were firmly rooted in ethnic or regional identities (MacGaffey 1997, 53–57).

The white settler population in the Congo—as elsewhere in Africa—was predictably resistant to policies from the metropole that weakened their hold on power and increased that of the Africans. Furthermore, the changes that the Belgian colonial state allowed were frustratingly meager to the Africans when compared to the decolonization practices of England and France. The situation came to a head in January 1959, when anticolonial riots broke out in Leopoldville. In their wake, the official Belgian position was that the Congolese were rapidly approaching a stage in their development that justified independence.[10] On January 13, 1959, King Baudouin proclaimed that "our firm resolution, today, is to lead the Congolese populations, without harmful procrastination, but also without thoughtless haste, toward independence, in prosperity and in peace" (*Belgian Congo To-Day* January 1959, 3). But the question remained: *When?* The colonial narrative established that the Congolese "children" were still in the process of civilizing. In a speech to a joint session of the U.S. Congress on May 12, 1959, King Baudouin stated that: "all my countrymen join me in the desire to raise the population of the Congo to a level that will enable them freely to choose their future destiny. *As soon as they are mature, as soon as they have received the loving care in education that we can give them*, we shall launch them forth on their own enterprise and independent existence" (*Congressional Record*, June 1959, 7969–7970; emphasis added). Thus, it became clear that the Belgian government considered the Africans still too undeveloped to handle self-rule.

The riots and growing unrest of the late 1950s threw into question the images that the Paternal colonial project had attempted to construct. The image of Africans as children graciously accepting the white's strong, guiding hand toward higher development—so prominently articulated at the 1958 Expo—was challenged by their violent resistance. Within the logic of the colonial narrative, however, this violence confirmed the pervasive and underlying image of the Congolese as inherent savages. If the colonial project was now regarded as flawed, it was not due to deficiencies in Paternalism but because of the seeming impossibility of uplifting an inherently savage and barbaric race.[11]

The first tentative steps toward decolonization had occurred under the 1954–58 coalition government of Socialists and Liberals, who had succeeded in temporarily breaking the Social Christian's hold on power (see Slade 1960, 39–42; Hoskyns 1965). Once the decision to decolonize was made, the will to prolong the transition vanished. Foot-dragging on the part of the colonial government was regarded as increasing anti-Belgian sentiment among the Congolese and damaging Belgium's long-term interests and investments. In keeping with the Paternal discourse, independence and freedom were presented as being "gifts" bestowed upon the Congolese "children" by the benevolent parent. Yet, many Belgian politicians feared that Paternalism had not yet adequately raised these "children" to "adulthood" and that the Congolese "children" would be easy prey to Communism.[12] Such perceptions played an important role in framing Belgium's response to Patrice Lumumba and the events of the 1960s.

The Challenge of Lumumba's Narratives

In the wake of the January 1959 riots, a more pronounced nationalist/pro-independence discourse emerged in the Congo (Fierlafyn 1990; Nyunda ya Rubango 1980). The most popular articulator of these discourses was Patrice Emery Lumumba, a young politician from Stanleyville who attempted to make his Mouvement National Congolais (MNC) a nationally based party. Lumumba's popularity was tied to the fact that he authored important counternarratives that challenged dominant Belgian views of the colonial project. He offered an interpretation of the previous eighty years that focused on colonial exploitation, repression, and resource extraction. However, there simply was not the space within the colonial narratives for Congolese to articulate a counterinterpretation. To continue the familial analogy of Paternalism, the "children" were not allowed to talk back to the "parents." By disrupting and even opposing the accepted narratives, Lumumba was seen by most white Belgians (both in the Congo and Belgium) as radical, unstable, and dangerous.

Patrice Lumumba's self-identity had undergone substantial shifts in the years leading up to his election. As an *évolué*, Lumumba had received his Carte d'Immatriculation (the successor of the Carte du Mérite Civique) in 1954 and became president of the local club of *évolués* after moving to Stanleyville. He was multilingual, speaking French, Lingala, and KiSwahili fluently. In 1956, Lumumba was sentenced to a year in prison for reportedly embezzling funds as a postal clerk. After his release, he worked for a local brewery, rising to the rank of commercial director. He helped form the MNC, becoming its leader and serving another prison sentence in 1959 for reputedly fomenting riots in Stanleyville. He was begrudgingly released by colonial authorities in January 1960 to attend the Roundtable Conference on decolonization in Brussels. The MNC won the most votes in the May 1960 elections and Lumumba formed a coalition government, with himself as prime minister and defense minister.

Throughout the 1950s, Lumumba's political thinking was firmly in keeping with the framework established by the colonial narrative, as is evident in his book *Congo, My Country* (written in 1956, but published posthumously). Reproducing basic tropes in the colonial discourse, he wrote: "Belgium's mission to the Congo is essentially a civilising one . . . [it aims at] giving the natives an understanding and appreciation of civilization" (Lumumba 1962, 11). Echoing the rhetoric of Paternalism and historic evolution, he noted: "To introduce the ferment of political life prematurely among the ignorant and irresponsible masses in response to a craving for modernization would be to introduce the ferments of discord and dissension . . . The Congo cannot, of course, escape the same laws of nature; it will follow the same course of development as Belgium and finally its inhabitants will have to enjoy political rights" (1962, 31). Thus, to a large extent Lumumba's own thinking was informed by the Belgian colonial discourse.

Lumumba's position changed, however, after his visit to Ghana in December 1958 for the All-African People's Conference. This meeting of African nationalist parties was organized by Ghana's President Kwame Nkrumah to support the anticolonial struggle and to strengthen the ideas of Pan-African unity. It proved a valuable meeting place for African national leaders to share ideas and develop anticolonial strategies. This trip proved formative for Lumumba, who afterward drew heavily from the pronationalist, anticolonial rhetoric espoused there. Returning to Leopoldville, he proclaimed that independence from Belgium should be considered a "right" not a "gift." However, Lumumba never completely embraced the more revolutionary strands of anticolonialism. His feelings toward Belgium remained ambivalent, and he seemed to maintain a notable degree of faith in Belgian goodwill until the end of his life (Musabachime 1987; see also Simons, Boghossian, and Verhaegen 1995; Mutamba Makombo 1993; and Fierlafyn 1990).

In articulating a narrative of Congolese identity, Lumumba was the sole Congolese politician stressing a "national" identity rather than one based on region or ethnicity, as did most other political leaders, such as Joseph Kasavubu and Moise Tshombe. Much of this had to do with Lumumba's conception of Congolese space, which bound a specific population ("Congolese"). Subscribing to the dominant Western view that territorial space was the sole spatial form in which to secure a political community, Lumumba accepted the colonially constructed space of the Congo as entailing a single, unified political entity (see Niemann 2001). For him, Congolese sovereignty was posited within the population that dwelt within that space. That is to say, Lumumba viewed sovereignty as a right of the Congolese population. While other politicians privileged smaller, fragmented spaces bound by ethnicity, language, or regional memories, Lumumba tied Congolese identity to the larger colonially demarcated space of the Congo. Employing the rhetoric of nationalism, Lumumba sought to create a unified identity for the people inhabiting that territory.

Lumumba narrated a national identity through selecting, plotting, and interpreting events from colonial history. By grounding Congolese identity in the collective social memories of suffering at the hands of Belgian colonizers, Lumumba articulated what it meant to be "Congolese." This conception was clearly articulated in his Independence Day speech, which followed Baudouin's recitation of the Belgian colonial narrative. As such, Lumumba was offering an alternative narrative of the colonial project and Congolese identity. Since this speech is representative of the nationalist discourse Lumumba authored, and because it became used by the Belgian and American governments and media as "evidence" of Lumumba's irrationality and immaturity, it bears quoting at length. In the opening passages, he stated:

> Our lot was eighty years of colonial rule; our wounds are still too fresh and painful to be driven from our memory.
>
> We have known tiring labor exacted in exchange for salary which did not allow us to satisfy our hunger, to clothe and lodge ourselves decently or to raise our children like loved beings.
>
> We have known ironies, insults, blows which we had to endure morning, noon, and night because we were "Negroes." Who will forget that to a Negro the familiar verb forms were used, not indeed as with a friend, but because the honorable formal verb forms were reserved for the whites?
>
> We have known that our lands were despoiled in the name of supposedly legal texts which recognized only the law of the stronger.
>
> We have known that the law was never the same depending on whether it concerned a white or a Negro: accommodating for one group, it was cruel and inhuman for the other.
>
> We have known the atrocious sufferings of those banished for political opinions or religious beliefs; exiled in their own countries, their end was truly worse than death itself.

> We have known that there were magnificent houses for the whites in the cities and tumble-down straw huts for the Negroes, that a Negro was not admitted in movie houses or restaurants or stores labeled "Europeans," that a Negro traveled in the hulls of river boats at the feet of the white in his first class cabin.
>
> Who will forget, finally, the fusillades where so many of our brothers perished or the prisons where all those brutally flung who no longer wished to submit to the regime of a law of oppression and exploitation which the colonists had made a tool of their domination?
>
> All that, my brothers, we have profoundly suffered (quoted in Merriam 1961, 352–53).

In contrast to Baudouin's speech, Lumumba's provided an important alternative narrative of the colonial project that exposed the repression, exploitation, and violence that the Belgian narrative sought to erase. Lumumba's speech politicized the tensions and resistance between whites and blacks that Baudouin's narrative romanticized or dismissed within the depoliticized framework of Paternalism. Moreover, Lumumba's speech created a counterimage of the Congolese population. The Congolese, in Lumumba's narrative, were not children or savages, immature or irrational. Rather, they were presented as part of a "we"—as victimized men and women who had survived with dignity, humanity, strength, and unity. Paternalism was replaced with a different but still familial metaphor—"brotherhood."

Lumumba's narrative on the Congo's identity contained a fundamental tension because of his intertwining elements from the preexisting colonial and the emergent African nationalist discourses. This tension has been explored by Partha Chatterjee in her work on Third World nationalism (1986, 1996). Chatterjee argues that anticolonial nationalism separated the domain of culture into two spheres—the material and the spiritual. She argues that the spiritual sphere is an "inner" domain bearing the "essential" marks of cultural identity (1996, 217). It is within this realm that Third World leaders have expunged the colonial presence in order to articulate an "authentic" national identity. In Lumumba's case, the "essential" markers of this identity had to be created and articulated. Lumumba chooses not to use preexisting ethnic, linguistic, or regional markers to delineate this identity but rather to offer a narrative of the colonial project based on shared memories of exploitation and brutalization.

It was within the "material sphere" that claims of Western civilization were mostly strongly asserted—bolstered by science, technology, economic organization, and Western methods of statecraft. Chatterjee observes that the anticolonial nationalists studied, replicated, and incorporated these accomplishments into their own cultures. Lumumba fits this description, accepting not only the colonially created embodiment of the Congo but also the Western-scripted concepts and practices that constituted the Congo. On the one hand, Lumumba employed the logic, language, and practices of Western stateness articulated within the colonial discourse. On the other hand, operating within the discourses of African nationalism, Lumumba sought to Africanize the colonial state institutions: replacing white state officials with Congolese and reaping the benefits that such a transition would entail (in terms of both power and wealth). Lumumba, like most other postcolonial leaders, viewed the state as the primary vehicle for forging national cohesion. In fact, one of the direct causes of the 1960 crisis was the fact that the coercive institution underpinning state power, the army, was *not* Africanized. White Belgian officers remained firmly in control. As Belgian army commander Gen. Janssens infamously wrote on a blackboard for his Force Publique troops prior to independence: "before Independence = after Independence." This event is frequently cited as being part of the catalyst for the initial uprising (See Gérard-Libois and Verhaegen 1961, 1076–1079; Weissman 1974, 56; Kitchen 1967, 19–20).

The Force Publique served as an important element in calming many whites' anxieties over black self-rule, largely because they were disciplined, ordered, and, most importantly, firmly under the control of their white officers. In the 1958 Brussels Expo, just as in the 1898 Tervuren Exhibition, the Force Publique were presented to the audience as the living symbol of colonial success. They continued to be heralded as the symbol of colonial progress in "civilizing" the natives. When the Belgian colonial project put a face on its success, it was that of the Force Publique soldier. For example, in the propaganda film *Main dans la Main* (Hand in Hand), made by the Belgian Colonial Office (InforCongo) about the 1958 Expo, Force Publique soldiers were clearly the "stars," guiding whites through the Congo section. As *La Libre Belgique* infamously stated on July 5:

> The whole future of the Congo is at stake. There is only one thing: the *Force Publique,* which remains the miracle of this Congo that used to be Belgian. The *Force Publique* today is the only solid institution in this country. Its soldiers have an *esprit de corps,* they all have the same martial attitude, the same smile up to the ears, the same efficiency, too. The *Force Publique* has delivered a prodigious demonstration: well officered, well

trained, the Congolese are capable of achieving great things (*La Libre Belgique*, July 5, 1960).

Ironically, this was published on the very day of the Force Publique mutiny.

The nightmare that many whites—especially those in the Congo—anticipated seemed to be realized with the popular election of Lumumba, who was viewed by many Belgians as a trouble-making nationalist. When the Force Publique openly rebelled against their white officers, the Belgian government saw that the "only solid institution" had reverted to savagery. Within the Belgian-produced discourse, these events became proof that the Congolese were immature and incapable of self-rule. The parents *had* to intervene.

Punishing the Children: Interpreting Congolese Independence

Independence has been a tragic error and all measures must be taken to save Belgian lives.

—La Libre Belgique, July 8, 1960, 91

The Belgian government's intervention in the Congo was based on how the events immediately following independence were emplotted and interpreted within their larger narrative of Congolese identity. There are two important elements of this narrative worth highlighting at the outset. First, the Congo was often conceived as an extension of Belgian domestic space. Thus, the 1960 crisis and the Belgian government's response were regarded, to a certain degree, as a domestic affair—or more precisely, within the language of Paternalism, a family affair. Thus, the Belgian government operated from a self-perceived right and responsibility to intervene. Second, sovereignty and independence had been defined as *gifts* rather than *rights*. Tied to this understanding was the belief that sovereignty and independence were intimately linked to a developmental stage within a modernist paradigm. Within the Belgian government's narrative, the Congolese proved within the first few days of independence that they were not "developed" enough for the "gifts" of sovereignty and self-rule, so the gifts could and should be taken back. Moreover, the Congolese (mis)use of those gifts was seen as threatening to white lives, interests, and investments. Therefore, independence *had* to be taken away.

Reclaiming the Gift of Sovereignty

Despite the transfer of power in 1960, the mentality of *Notre Congo* remained. Belgian interests and investments within the Congo were still defined by the Belgian media and government as extensions of Belgian domestic space. For example, Belgian Minister of Justice Merchiers justified the invasion during a press conference on July 28:

> The tragic turn taken by events in the Congo has obliged the Belgian Government to act with all speed in order to give the white inhabitants the measure of protection dictated by the supreme laws of humanity and the imperative duty of saving men, women and children in immediate and terrible danger. The Government in all conscience was forced into this course of action by the mutiny of those same Congolese troops whose task it was to maintain order (Ministry of Justice 1960, 5).

Notably, this official announcement on the intervention was delivered not by the *foreign* minister, but a minister of *domestic* affairs. Concern for the "white inhabitants" was presented as the motivating factor. Ignoring Congolese law and authority, these whites supposedly had recourse to the so-called "supreme laws of humanity" that the Belgians themselves sought to define. The government and press stressed the protection of "Belgian lives" from the beginning, as the passage from *La Libre Belgique* quoted on the previous page illustrated. At the time of the intervention, no Belgian citizens had been killed. Furthermore, in the minister's statement, the entire Congolese space was envisioned as one of *disorder,* despite the fact that the Force Publique mutinies that precipitated the intervention were isolated incidents. Within the Belgian government's narrative of events, the Force Publique had abdicated its role of "maintain[ing] order" by rebelling against their white Belgian officers. This emphasis was important, because the Force Publique had long served as the symbol of Belgian colonial success in "civilizing" the Congolese. The mutiny had a tremendous effect on Belgian popular opinion because it meant that, in the familial rhetoric of Paternalism, even the "good children" had turned against the "parents." By continuing to see the Congo as an extension of its domestic space, and focusing on the failure of its trained Congolese troops to provide "order" in that space, the Belgian government attempted to directly reinstate its coercive control rather than appeal to the newly elected Congolese authorities.

It should be noted, however, that Belgian discourses on the Congo's unity were ambiguous at best. The colonial project was originally built on the image of a unified Congolese physical space. Yet, the territory's size had created problems for the colonial government. From the outset, the Congo was too large for the colonial government to establish effective and complete control. For that reason, there was a high degree of deconcentration and decentralization of Congolese space under Belgian rule. In practice, *Notre Congo* was a fragmented and compartmentalized space made up of administrative regions, church zones, substate spaces, business domains, and monopolistic concessions. Thus, the twentieth-century Belgian colonial discourse constructed the Congo as a *collection of spaces*, rather than as one unified/uniform space. Moreover, all these compartmentalized spaces were not regarded as equal. The most important region—before and after independence—was Katanga. As *La Libre Belgique* editorialized, "For us the elements of the problem are simple. In the state of almost total anarchy into which the Congo has fallen, the most important consideration is to save what can be saved. If it is possible in Katanga to restore law and order with the collaboration of a local government composed of sober and sensible Africans, then we should not hesitate for a moment" (July 13, 1960). Katanga was more closely linked to Belgian "domestic space" than other parts of the Congo, because the majority of Belgian citizens and investments were in this region.[13] The move to define the Congo as an extension of Belgian domestic space was seriously challenged by the Congolese government and international powers, and Belgian troops were forced to allow United Nations troops to perform the functions of coercive control that they had tried to monopolize. However, Belgian troops resisted handing over control of the breakaway region of Katanga, which they still regarded as a privileged space. The Belgian soldiers initially provided direct support for Tshombe's breakaway government. Later, Belgian as well as French, Rhodesian, and South African mercenaries constituted the backbone of Katanga's armed forces. Moreover, the Belgian government and economic community provided important political and economic support, including the shipment of arms.

Prior to independence, Belgian rhetoric repeatedly regarded self-rule as a developmental stage within the modernist paradigm. Take, for example, these passages from the Belgian government's January 13, 1959, declaration of decolonization of the Congo:

> In exercising her sovereignty, Belgium has assumed responsibilities toward all the inhabitants of the Congo. In the course of the political evolution defined in this declaration, it is her duty to maintain a sound administration and to keep it under her control. She will hand over these responsibilities as the new Congolese institutions gradually prove they

are capable of maintaining order and respect for public and private obligations, and the protection of persons and property . . . [T]he Congolese people will show their wisdom and maturity by undertaking with us the shaping of the new structures, and by assuming conscientiously the serious responsibilities its future involves (Belgian Government Information Center 1959, 25–27).

This point was further articulated by King Baudouin, who explicitly connected "freedom" with specific material trappings such as "institutions," "staffs," and "technicians":

In a civilized world, independence is a status which combines and guaranties [sic] freedom, order, progress. The concept of freedom is impossible without sound and well-balanced institutions, experienced administrative staffs, a well-established social, economic and financial organization directed by experienced technicians, an intellectual and moral edification of the people, without which a democratic regime is merely mockery, deception and tyranny . . . We, of the Mother Country, and the white men in the Congo, have a task as counsellors and guides that must be continued, while it undergoes a transformation and loses its importance as progress is gradually achieved (quoted in Belgian Government Information Center 1959, 5–7).

Thus, within the discourses it created, the Belgian government established that the Congolese had to prove themselves civilized and developed in order to have the gifts of sovereignty and self-rule bestowed upon them. Baudouin's rhetoric and Belgium's actions bring to mind Nietzsche's insightful commentary on gift gifting in *Thus Spoke Zarathustra*: "You force all things to and into yourself that they may flow back out of your well as the gifts of love. Verily, such a gift-giving love must approach all values as a robber: but whole and holy I call this selfishness" (Nietzsche 1982 [1954], 187).

The Belgian government interpreted the events following Congolese independence as evidence that the "children" had not become developed enough to be independent. Their intervention was underpinned by the continuing belief in African inferiority. Indeed, among many whites, "*A bas les macaques!* (Down with the apes!)" was a common refrain. The rhetoric that the "children" had proved themselves unworthy was predominant within the Belgian government and media throughout the 1960 crisis. The "inherent" savagery and barbarism of the Congolese had returned to the surface now that Belgium's civilizing hand had been removed. For example, the Belgian Ministry of Justice released a pamphlet entitled "Evidence" that placed the blame of the violence on the inability of Congo officials to control the "brutal savagery" of the Congolese (Ministry of Justice 1960, 6).[14] Since the events of July "proved" Congolese savagery within their narrative, the Belgian government felt justified in their intervention. Though the Belgian press and government read Congolese actions within a framework that reinforced "savage" imagery, those actions can also be regarded as symbolic expressions of resistance. As Crawford Young has argued, Congolese anti-European violence in the post-independence era "was a kind of ritual humiliation of the colonial structure" by the politically and socially dispossessed (Young 1967b, 13).

"Sale Nègre" versus "Sensible African"

Just as Lumumba offered an alternative narrative of the colonial project, so to did he challenge Belgium's interpretations of the 1960 crisis. While the Belgian government and media denied the historicity of the crisis by explaining it in terms of the Congolese's "natural" barbarity, Lumumba articulated a narrative based on specific historical and political events—namely, Belgian intervention. In Lumumba's interpretation of events, the initial uprising by numerous Force Publique soldiers was due to their continued mistreatment at the hands of their white officers. In the wake of these mutinies, Lumumba and Kasavubu traveled across the country in an effort to quell the rebellion. Lumumba raised all soldiers a grade and promised future reforms. However, Lumumba and Kasavubu met with limited success, largely because of the actions of Belgian military forces on the ground, who continued to move against Congolese soldiers and civilians. Lumumba also regarded the secession of Katanga as resulting from Belgian intervention and complicity. He interpreted the events following independence within a narrative framework dominated by the portrayal of an interventionist and exploitative Belgium. As Lumumba often pointed out, the engagement of Belgian troops was in direct violation of the treaty of friendship that explicitly stated that Belgian forces stationed in the Congo could not intervene except on demand of the Congolese minister of national defense. The minister of defense was Patrice Lumumba himself.

Lumumba's ability to promote his interpretation of events was limited in part because he lacked credibility in the West, particularly in Belgium. Within the Belgian media, Lumumba became the personification of Congolese impertinence, immaturity, and savagery. They portrayed him as an unstable, nationalistic radical (Morue 1980). In her study of the Belgian newspaper *La Libre Belgique,* Christine Masuy notes that media representations of Lumumba became increasingly demoniacal over time. Much of the coverage focused on Lumumba's physical attributes—his "choppy" French, white and broad teeth, and goatee—to present the Prime Minister in purely negative terms (Masuy 1997). Similar rhetorical and representational moves were enacted across Belgian media in general (see Halen and Riesz 1997; Piniau 1992).

This image of Lumumba as *diable* (devil) was prevalent in the press coverage of his Independence Day speech. Lumumba's actions were read within the framework of Paternalism as proof of his immaturity and irrationality. *La Libre Belgique* referred to the speech as "*un affront au Roi et à la Belgique*" and sharply chastised "*l'insolence*" of this upstart African (1 July 1960, 1). Almost without exception, the Belgian media attacked what they regarded as Lumumba's audacity to criticize Belgian colonial practices, instead of accepting the "gift" of independence with "grace" and "dignity" (*Le Soir,* 1 July 1960, 1, 3, and 7; 2 July 1960, 7; see also Morue 1980, 23–28). As historian Catherine Hoskyns points out, "In Belgium the speech was taken as proving right those who had always maintained that Lumumba was fanatical and unreliable and likely to sabotage Belgian interests. During the mutiny, when Belgians had to decide whether or not to trust Lumumba, they remembered this speech" (Hoskyns 1965, 86), which many Belgians viewed as "strident, contemptuous, and ill-tempered" (Lefever 1965, 4).

Increasingly, Lumumba became presented as a devil by the larger European media. The European press occasionally referred to him as "*le sale nègre*" (Kalb 1982, 49; Michel 1962, 110–111). When Lumumba stayed at Blair House during his visit to Washington, D.C., the Belgian and French press expressed outrage that he slept in the same bed that King Baudouin and Charles De Gaulle had each slept in a few months earlier (*La Libre Belgique,* 14 February 1961). Lumumba effectively became the scapegoat for Belgian fears and disappointments (Willame 1997, 189–195). Moreover, because Lumumba was regarded as threatening to Belgian interests, he was portrayed as being bad for *Congolese* interests—for Brussels, the two still being one and the same. For it was the Belgian government alone, like the wise father it imagined itself to be, who was the better judge of what was in the Congo's "best" interest.

These representations of Lumumba provide an interesting contrast to the Belgian media and government's representations of Moise Tshombe, leader of the Katanga secession. Discussing the government's intervention on behalf of Tshombe, King Baudouin stated: "Whole tribes led by *sober and honest men* have asked us to stay and help them build a *real independence* in the midst of the chaos which now reigns in what was once the Belgian Congo. Our duty is to give a favourable reply to all those who *loyally* request our cooperation" (*La Libre Belgique,*

22 July 1960; emphasis added). As opposed to Lumumba, Tshombe and his followers were characterized as being sensible, sober, honest, and loyal. In fact, it was their loyalty that determined their portrayal as being sensible, sober, and honest.[15]

As the Congo Crisis became a concern to other international actors, Brussels was not able to pursue its interventionist policies unfettered, and this constituted a severe blow to Belgium's self-image and reputation. *Le Soir* bemoaned: "Never in Belgium's memory has our prestige been so low" (quoted in *Time*, 22 August 1960, 22). In Parliament, the Foreign Affairs Minister Pierre Wigny complained of the country's emasculation by international law: "Do we really have to prove with legal phrasing and quoting of legal text books the rightness of our intervention?" (quoted in *Time*, 25 July 1960, 23).

On July 5, 1960, the very day of the Force Publique mutiny, *Le Soir* printed a cartoon depicting a drowning drunk whose bottle is rescued by a lifeguard, letting the drunk go down. This image seems to be an apt analogy for Belgium's response to the 1960 Congo Crisis: Lumumba was portrayed as the drunkard (or at least an idiot) who gets in over his head, the lifeguard (Belgium) dives in to rescue only what it considers to be of value, the alcohol (Katangan wealth), while the victim (Lumumba/Congo) is left to drown. Yet, in the end, the Belgian government's narrative and its claim as the primary author of Congolese identity were challenged from many sides, including Lumumba, the UN, the Soviet Union, and numerous independent Third World governments. The greatest challenge to Belgium's discursive authority, however, came from the U.S. government, whose hegemonic position in global affairs would eventually lead to the dominance of its authorship of the Congo's identity.

From Father Belgium to Uncle Sam

> Should the Congo crumble into chaos and become a successful object of Communist penetration, the Soviet bloc will have acquired an asset without price—a base of operations in the heart of Africa from which to spread its tentacles over this newest of continents. The avoidance of this very real danger is the immediate objective of our policy in the Congo.
>
> —Under Secretary of State George Ball (1961, 2)

While the Belgian government emplotted the events of the 1960 crisis within their larger narrative of Paternalism and Lumumba emplotted the events within the larger narrative of colonial repression and exploitation, the government of the United States operated within a framework supplied by the narrative of cold war competition. As George Ball's statement above notes, the Eisenhower administration's interpretation of the 1960 Congo Crisis shifted discussions of the Congo's identity away from varying interpretations of colonial history to assumptions about cold war competition, which focused on the fear of Congo as chaos and the threat of communism.

In the post–World War II era, the United States constructed a national image of itself as definer and protector of "Western" values, namely freedom, democracy, and the free market. In his insightful work on U.S. foreign policy and the politics of identity, IR theorist David Campbell argues that U.S. identity was strongly tied to constructions of otherness, particularly given the imagining of "America" as an idealized, ahistoric nation, reaching beyond its geographical boundaries (Campbell 1992, 144).[16] As political scientist Kennan Ferguson notes, during the cold war the "dominant political discourse of the United States positioned it as the custodian of identity, policing and locating allies and enemies, threats to, and infections of the American body politics" (Ferguson 1996, 167; see also, Weber 1998). Defining itself as the protector of "Western" values and global hegemon authorized the U.S. government to resolve international "problems." One such problem was what the American government officials and media called the "Congo Question." Rhetorically framing the situation as the "Congo Question" placed authorship of both the question and the answer in the hands of the questioner, in this case the Eisenhower administration, the State Department, and the CIA. In responding to this "Question," three elements of the U.S. government's "answer" stand out. First was the continued reliance of rhetoric from the earlier discourse of Stanley and other colonial agents. While the Belgian government's discourse had evolved beyond the colonizing discourses of Leopold II to the colonial discourses of *Notre Congo* and Paternalism, the American discourse was firmly rooted in earlier images of the Congo as a chaotic, savage, and primitive jungle.

Second, this imagery was emplotted within the framing narrative of cold war competition. In the cold war context, the American government interpreted "chaos" as a fertile soil from which "red weeds" grow, to use a metaphor employed by *Time* magazine (12 September 1960, 29). American views of Soviet aims in the Third World had been established by U.S. Chargé d'Affaires George Kennan's infamous "Long Telegram" from Moscow that asserted: "Toward colonial areas and backwards or dependent peoples, Soviet policy, even on official plane, will be directed toward weakening of power and influence and contacts of advanced Western nations, on theory that insofar as this policy is successful, there will be created a vacuum which will favor Communist-Soviet penetration" (Kennan 1946 [1993], 24). Thus, the cold war rhetorical maneuver meant constructing the Congo as easy prey for Communist conquest. These two existing discursive trends—Congo's inherent backwardness and cold war anxiety—converged to narrate the Congolese as irrational, immature, and easy targets for Soviet influence.

Finally, the narrative authored by the Eisenhower administration and circulated by the U.S. media portrayed Patrice Lumumba as the embodiment of this image. This portrayal was achieved in three combined maneuvers. First, Lumumba was presented as an irrational and immature leader. Second, Lumumba was portrayed as either a Communist or under the sway of the Communists. Finally, Lumumba was constructed as being the *cause* of the Congo's problems. Within this narrative, the logic of the U.S. government dictated that to overcome the troubles, the troublemaker had to be removed.

Congo as Chaos

A defining element of the U.S. government's narrativization of the 1960 Congo Crisis was the re-employment of the rhetorical devices scripted by Stanley, Leopold II, his colonial agents, and the Congo Reform movement. These images shaped not only public policy but the larger American cultural understanding of the Congo, having been repeated, circulated, and reproduced in American culture throughout the twentieth century. From Stanley's earliest reports to novels like Joseph Conrad's *Heart of Darkness* to repeated Hollywood cinematic constructions, the Congo became synonymous with savagery, primitivism, chaos, barbarianism, cannibalism, and unchecked nature. Graham Greene's popular novel, *A Burnt-Out Case,* was published at the time of the 1960 crisis and is representative of this tradition. The novel reinforced established tropes of Africa as "a continent of misery and heat" (Greene 1960, 17), beyond Western rationality and understanding. The story revolves around the protagonist's trip to a Congolese leproserie to escape the modern world. For Greene, the Congo is a blank slate, "nowhere," "the end of the end," and "the furthermost place from Europe." Such images were also reproduced in contemporary movies. In American theaters, the image of the African continent as a dangerous land-that-time-forgot in need of conquering/civilizing permeated such popular films as *King Solomon's Mines* (1950), its sequel *Watusi* (1959), the Mau-Mau/civil rights/decolonization warning *Something of Value* (1957), and, perhaps most explicitly, in *Congo Crossing*

(1956). These images, drawn from the colonizing discourse of Stanley and others, formed the basis of the cognitive map most Americans, including policy makers, had of Africa, of which the Congo was seen as the quintessence.

The events of 1960 were interpreted within this cognitive framework. For instance, *Time* magazine's coverage of the Congo's independence was enunciated in the language of supposed Congolese primitivism. Its headline proclaimed "Belgian Congo: Freedom Yes, Civilization Maybe" (*Time*, 11 January 1960, 24). A photograph of Congolese citizens dancing at an independence rally was accompanied by the caption: "Congolese Celebrating Independence: Striding out of the Stone Age to Especially Composed Cha-chas" (*Time*, 11 July 1960, 33). The rhetoric continued to stress the otherness of the Congolese, often in derogatory ways. One reporter covering the May election asserted "most of the half-naked illiterate black voters had no idea what the candidates were talking about" (*Time*, 30 May 1960, 23; note the continuing use of clothing as a marker of modernity). This rhetoric was informed by, and simultaneously reinforced, the view that most Congolese were still uncivilized and ignorant of political practices. In his memoirs, President Eisenhower referred to the Congolese as "a restless and militant population in a state of gross ignorance—even by African standards" (Eisenhower 1965, 573).

The Force Publique's mutiny was perceived through such discursive lens. In the initial coverage of the mutiny, *Time* ran a photograph of rioters with the caption: "Congo Tribalists Fighting In Leopoldville: With a Primeval Howl, a Reversion to Savagery" (*Time*, 18 July 1960, 17). The text of the report was even more telling: "With a primeval howl, a nation of 14 million people reverted to near savagery, plunged backward into the long night of chaos" (*Time*, 18 July 1960, 17). Such reporting relied on established constructions of Congolese as primitive savages and failed to note that the civilian population was not generally involved in the uprising, and only a few sectors of the Force Publique were in mutiny (Kitchen 1967, 22). The political dynamics behind the mutiny were disregarded or delegitimized in American narratives. As *Time* reported: "There seemed *no logical explanation* for the madness that swept the Congo. The Congolese involved gave *no coherent answers* except to ask bitterly where were the pay raises and easy jobs and plentiful food that had been promised by the politicians?" (*Time*, 18 July 1960, 17; emphasis added). These rhetorical moves worked to separate the political motives from the event in the eyes of the reader, casting it instead as "madness."

In their narrative of Congolese identity, American government officials portrayed the Congolese as not civilized or mature enough to "handle" complex notions of Western democracy or other "modern" political concepts. In a State Department policy paper on the Congo, Ambassador Timberlake stated: "the fact is that the Congo is years from more than a facade of democracy . . . [Not one Congolese understood] even the most elementary principles of democracy" (U.S. State Dept. "Policy Paper," 25 January 1961, 50; quoted in Orwa 1985, 136). The dominant American view was that the Congolese were incapable of ruling themselves. Once such a notion was disseminated and internalized, Congolese sovereignty and independence became meaningless. Just as King Baudouin and the Belgian government chose to ignore the "façade" of Congolese sovereignty, so too did the U.S. government, but for a different set of reasons.

Under-Secretary of State George Ball asserted the Congo "was not yet able to maintain its independence without outside help" (Ball 1961, 4). Informed by the discourse of cold war competition, it became of paramount importance that such "outside help" did not come from the Soviet Union. For example, Kennedy used the fear of Congo going Communist as an issue in his campaign against Nixon. This anti-Soviet drive was the basis for U.S. policy in the Congo and is aptly illustrated by Ball's summary of American policy:

> But what in the long run do we seek to achieve in the Congo? . . . [A] stable society under a stable and progressive government. That government may be "non-aligned" in its international policies. That is for it to decide. But it should be strong enough and determined enough to safeguard its *real independence*. And it is important that it maintain *with us*, and with European states that are contributing to its successful development, the kind of friendly and constructive relations that will serve our mutual purposes . . . We wish to insulate the African Continent from the kind of military intervention by the Sino-Soviet bloc that has created such problems in other parts of the world (Ball 1961, 2–3; emphasis added).

This rhetorical maneuver drew a distinction between "real" and "false" independence, with the United States as definer and enforcer of that boundary. "Real" independence meant having friendly relations with the United States and its allies. Conversely, any non-pro-Western foreign policy implied a false independence and, as such, sovereignty was not an acceptable legal norm to protect against intervention. Importantly, this passage states that to be acceptable, the Congo's foreign relations should serve "our mutual purposes." Ball further elaborates U.S. policy:

> *First,* our objective in the Congo, as elsewhere in Africa, is a free, stable non-Communist government for the Congo as a whole, dedicated to the maintenance of genuine independence, and willing and able to cooperate with us and with other free nations in meeting the tremendous internal challenges it must face... *Second,* ... to ward off the dangers of civil war and great-power intervention (Ball 1961, 19–21).

Again, the U.S. government defined "genuine" independence exclusively in terms of a pro-Western position. Sovereignty and independence were defined within a context that implied a continued submissive relationship to external Western powers.[17] What is also curious about Ball's policy position is its stance against "great-power intervention." Clearly, Ball and the U.S. government only had the "Sino-Soviet bloc" in mind and not themselves.

Since the end of World War II, American policy toward the Belgian Congo reflected the tension between Washington's avowed anticolonial stance and its fear of Communist ascendancy. This contradiction was partly resolved by reinterpreting Belgium's colonial relationship with Congo. In a 1959 speech, U.S. Consul General Green stated that the U.S. government did not consider Belgian policy to the Congo as one of colonialism per se: "[The United States is] condemning the kind of colonialism which existed in the 18th and 19th centuries and whose existence is neither possible nor desirable in a free world . . . I am convinced that the Belgian Government and the Belgian people are just as opposed to such outdated forms of colonialism as we are ourselves" (*Belgian Congo 59,* January 1959, 7). Because the Belgians were assumed to be "like" Americans, the United States supported Belgian policy toward the Congo. At the beginning of the crisis, the United States deferred to what it saw as Belgium's sphere of influence so as not to emasculate the Belgian government, undermine Belgium's self-image, or threaten the North Atlantic Treaty Organization's (NATO) solidarity (Weissman 1974, 43; Schraeder 1994; Orwa 1985, 68). Thus, reported atrocities committed by Belgian troops were downplayed by the U.S. government,[18] and the United States initially supported and followed its NATO partner's actions in the Congo (see Weissman 1974, 57, 63, and 103).

However, as the crisis progressed and the Eisenhower administration became increasingly convinced that Patrice Lumumba was a Communist troublemaker, Washington became more critical of the

Belgian government's policy. In particular, the U.S. government refused to accept the Belgian representation that Katanga and Tshombe were legitimate options. To do so would have left the rest of the Congo in "chaos." While that was less of a concern for the Belgian government, who viewed the Congo as compartmentalized space, the U.S. government viewed Congolese social space as a uniform whole, and resisted attempts to "Balkanize" that space lest some parts fall under Communist control. The Eisenhower administration and the CIA interpreted secession as chaos, and chaos as synonymous with communism. Assistant Secretary of State for African Affairs G. Mennen Williams stated that "if Katanga seceded, then up to 20 other areas might want to do the same. This would have led to chaos, and opened the door for Communist and extremist penetration" (Williams 1967, 148). Under-Secretary of State Ball argued that the "armed secession in the Katanga plays into the hands of the Communists. This is a fact that all Americans should ponder" (Ball 1961, 21). Such sentiment was echoed in numerous cartoons, such as the one in figure 3.1.

Painting Lumumba Red

The bulk of the U.S. discourse on the Congo involved a construction of Lumumba that overdetermined his eventual removal. In representing Lumumba as "irrational," American media and government officials took their cue from the Belgians. Proof of Lumumba's irrationality was found in his nationalist beliefs and criticism of Belgian colonialism, both of which were expressed in his Independence Day speech. In their coverage, *Time* magazine and other American publications portrayed Lumumba's speech as evidence of his emotionalism, irrationality, and immaturity.

The rhetoric of irrationality can be found throughout the Western media's portrayal of Lumumba. Taking *Time* magazine as a representative example, here is a collection of some of the adjectives used by it to describe Lumumba during the last half of 1960: "The Embezzler," "goateed," "convicted embezzler," "choleric," "Wiry," "the Batetela tribesman," "desperate," "Sly," "lean," "bearded," "vainglorious," "reckless," "erratic," "unpredictable," "paranoid," "touchy," "demagogic Premier," "the chief troublemaker," "the troublemaking Premier," "erratic Premier," "erratically irresponsible," and "mischief-making."[19] Terms like "demagogic" and "desperate" rendered him politically illegitimate in the eyes of the American government and media, despite his position as the democratically elected leader of an independent Congo. The descriptions of mental qualities "erratic" and "irresponsible" focused on Lumumba's unfitness to rule; the use of

Figure 3.1: "Is there a doctor in the house?"
Source: *Minneapolis Tribune*, August 1960. Reprinted with permission, the *Star Tribune*.

physical qualities were embedded with other meanings. Interestingly, much of the rhetoric revolving around Lumumba focused on his goatee. For the U.S. media audience at this time, the goatee had become a loaded symbol for subculture and Communism. The goatee was a symbol of the beat subculture, which mainstream America considered subversive and Communist (the addition of "-nik" to the term "beat" after the 1957 Russian Sput*nik* satellite sealed this association). Thus, the U.S. media's focus on Lumumba's goatee translated its meaning into a U.S. cultural context where "goatee" was equated with subversive, communist, troublemaker.[20]

These media representations are important for, in the case of the 1960 Congo Crisis, they not only *reflected* the dominant discourse on the Congo but clearly *shaped* American policy toward the Congo. American politicians, largely unfamiliar with Congolese history and politics, formed their opinions of the situation from the popular press, as is evident by the high number of popular press articles quoted in the *Congressional Record* (see Lemelin 1997, 219–238). For example, Senator Styles Bridges used a report from the *Washington Evening Star* as evidence that Lumumba was an "ex-convict . . . who has fallen into the Red trap" (*Congressional Record,* 12 August 1960, 16281). Likewise, Sen. Olin Johnston spoke authoritatively on the Senate floor from a report in the *National Review:* "[Lumumba] is a cheap embezzler, a schizoid agitator (half witch doctor, half Marxist), an opportunist ready to sell out to the highest bidder, ex officio big chief No. 1 of a gang of jungle primitives strutting about in the masks of cabinet ministers" (*Congressional Record,* 17 August 1960, 16641).

After Lumumba demanded that the Belgian troops leave, James K. Penfield of the U.S. Bureau of African Affairs sent a memo to the State Department (June 20, 1960): "This is indicative of the lack of maturity and ability on the part of the Congolese and probably implies as well some degree of Communist influence on Prime Minister Lumumba and his immediate entourage" (quoted in Kalb 1982, 29). Thus, criticism of Belgium was interpreted as evidence of his immaturity and communist leaning. Further evidence of communist influence was "found" in Lumumba's articulate press reports. As *Time* reported, "For an ex-post office clerk with a limited education, Lumumba was sending off some fairly polished and legalist notes. Their phraseology led foreign diplomats to wonder who was writing his stuff. The answer seemed to be that Lumumba is now surrounded by a growing coterie of Red-lining [*sic*] advisers" (*Time,* 29 August 1960, 20).[21] Thus, the eloquence of the multilingual Lumumba disrupted established images of him. Instead of altering their perception, Western observers merely assumed that someone else must be behind Lumumba.[22]

Such discursive representations of Lumumba worked to undermine his claims to political legitimacy. Working within that framework, the U.S. government, primarily through CIA station chief Lawrence Devlin, helped mastermind President Kasavubu's "firing" of the prime minister on September 5. The U.S. government also played a deciding role in the September 14 military coup by Mobutu, who was receiving funds and directives from the CIA (Weissman 1974, 95–99; Tully 1962, 220–223). The self-declared purpose of Mobutu's (first) coup was to "neutralize" both Lumumba and, to a much lesser extent, Kasavubu, who had proven ineffective in curtailing Lumumba's power and popularity within the Congo.

Claims to autonomous sovereignty by Lumumba and his supporters were dismissed within American-produced narratives. Believing the Congolese were too immature and ignorant to understand and operate democratic institutions and practices, the U.S. government directly intervened to thwart and curtail those institutions and practices. For example, the United States resisted the reconvening of the democratically elected Parliament out of fear that it would lead to a strengthening of Lumumba's position (a subtle admission of his popularity and ability to "speak" for the Congolese) (Weissman 1974, 104–105). As the CIA and State Department actively intervened in Congolese politics to make sure that their agenda was realized, American media and government officials increasingly portrayed Lumumba as the cause of the problem. Lumumba was named as the "chief troublemaker," and the crisis was seen as the result of "Lumumba's troublemaking." For example, in figure 3.2 Lumumba is portrayed as a serpent, wrapping around the UN building in a death grip. This image is strikingly similar to figure 2.4, in which King Leopold II-as-snake is choking a Congolese male, suggesting that while the actors may change, much of the imagery on the Congo remains remarkably the same.

The narratives of Congolese primitivism and cold war competition converged to produce a reading of the 1960 crisis in which any and all solutions required the removal of Lumumba. By late August, *Time* had already concluded "Congo might yet prove able to govern itself. But after two hectic months in office, Lumumba hardly seems the man for the job" (*Time*, 29 August 1960, 21). For the Congo to become "civilized" and "genuinely" independent, Lumumba had to go.[23] Western media and policy makers began envisioning a post-Lumumba Congo (Weissman 1974, 86–87), employing what Hannah Arendt (1968) refers to as "infallible prediction." Their rhetoric became propaganda, scripting a future Congo already achieved through self-fulfilling prophecies of, in this case, the forceful removal of the Prime Minister.

This conclusion had already been reached in Washington. The CIA decided that the Congo crisis could only be resolved if Lumumba was permanently removed—something Kasavubu and Mobutu had failed to accomplish. CIA Director Dulles cabled Leopoldville: "In high quarters here it is the clear-cut conclusion that if [Lumumba] continues to hold high office, the inevitable result will at best be chaos and at worst pave the way to communist takeover of the Congo ... Consequently we conclude that his removal must be an urgent and prime

Figure 3.2: Lumumba, as snake, squeezes the UN
Source: Bob Palmer, *News-Leader*, Springfield, MO, 31 July 1960.

objective" (CIA Cable, Dulles to Station Officer, August 26, 1960; quoted in Schatzberg 1991, 22–23 and U.S. Senate Report 1976, 15).

The actual events surrounding Lumumba's murder remain highly contested to this day. Although the Belgian government officially apologized for Lumumba's assassination in February 2002, the specific roles and degrees the CIA and Belgian intelligence forces played in Lumumba's arrest, beating, transfer, and murder, and the subsequent cover-up, remain unclear (see DeWitte 2001). Much of the information about these events has become the stuff of legends—such as the rumor of a CIA operative driving around Elisabethville for a week with Lumumba's body in the trunk of his car. What is clear, and well-documented in a U.S. Senate Report (1976), is the fact that the CIA initiated several plans to assassinate Lumumba, from the hiring of hit men to the importation of a lethal dose of poison in a diplomatic-immunity pouch. The organizing force of these activities was Lawrence Devlin, the CIA's station chief in Leopoldville. As Dulles's cable, quoted above, illustrates, however, Devlin was operating on orders from higher authorities, and these "highest quarters" seemed to include the president. In testimony before a Senate hearing, CIA station officer Hedgman stated that it was his understanding that President Eisenhower had directly authorized the assassination of Lumumba (U.S. Senate Report 1976, 25).

The rhetorical demonization of Lumumba continued after his death. For example, Sen. Paul Dague addressed the Senate by reading from a *Washington Post* article: "His 7 weeks in office were catastrophic... While the country disintegrated, Lumumba smoked hashish, drank gin or danced with his fleet of concubines... but showed no interest in the problems of government... He was vicious. He was corrupt... He was incompetent. There is not much to mourn" (*Congressional Record*, 16 February 1961, A955).

Yet, it is worth stressing that U.S. policy toward the Congo should not be regarded as monolithic, as there were significant differences of opinion within the U.S. government, namely between pro-European and pro-African forces within the State Department and, more notably, between the State Department and the CIA (Schraeder 1994; Kalb 1982; Weissman 1974a). Furthermore, there were important shifts between the Eisenhower and Kennedy administrations. Kennedy's administration was less prone to read events in the Congo in such binary cold war terms as was Eisenhower's. Yet, in a broad sense, the shift from Eisenhower to Kennedy came too late. Lumumba was murdered three days before Kennedy's inauguration (perhaps not by coincidence), and the basic elements of the Congolese discourse had been firmly established. Though Kennedy's administration might have been willing to embrace nationalists elsewhere in Africa and the Third

World, its view of the Congo was still informed by images and rhetoric that articulated it as an ahistoric, premature, savage, and chaotic land. Though the shift in U.S. administrations did not alter the foundation of Western discourses, it did establish an element that would inform U.S. policy toward Congo (and Africa) for decades to come. While the Eisenhower administration was driven by a communist-centric vision, Kennedy's was shaped by "liberal Messianism," which entailed an obsessive focus and promotion of American Liberalism (see Weissman 1974a, 211). Perhaps the most important result of this move was the emergence of a discourse on development commonly known as Modernization theory. The most representative of these works was W. W. Rostow's *The Stages of Economic Growth*, published in the midst of the 1960 Congo Crisis.[24] This new development discourse was, at its heart, a reframing of the civilizing discourses of colonialism.[25] Quite simply, the United States considered that it had a moral obligation to redeem the mistakes committed in Africa by Europe.[26] The major difference was that this new civilizing mission was no longer grounded in claims of European cultural superiority but in "objective" economic theories. What remained consistent was American monopolization of "authorship" (defining progress) and "expertise" (achieving development) and the forceful dislocation of traditional African systems, practices, and knowledges. Africa, defined as a "traditional" space (Rostow 1960, 39,45), was set in opposition to Western "modernity." In terms of U.S. policy, this meant that "traditional" elements—economic, social, and/or political—had to be rooted out, if not by the Congolese themselves, then by a benevolent United States acting in the Congolese's "best interest." This move represented a return to the core elements within the previous discourses of colonialism, Paternalism and *Notre Congo*.

Competing Narratives and Control Over Discursive Space

> *Reiterating Ghana's position in the Congo situation . . . the legal Prime Minister, Patrice Lumumba, must be immediately and unconditionally released from prison, all Belgians who have infiltrated back into the Congo to sabotage the independence of that country must be sacked forthwith and all colonialists who are seeking to control and dominate the Congo must be eliminated. Unless these conditions are fulfilled and the normal process of parliamentary democracy thereby restored, the tragic mess which will*

> result in the Congo will be the inescapable responsibility of the
> United Nations Organization.
>
> —Ghanaian Pres. Kwame Nkrumah, December 15, 1960, radio address (1960, 2–3)

As Kwame Nkrumah's speech illustrates, the governments of Belgium, United States, and the Congo were not the only international actors involved in the 1960 Congo crisis. Other significant actors included the United Nations administration,[27] Premier Khrushchev and the Soviet Union, and the "Afro-Asian" bloc of the UN General Assembly, of which Nkrumah was a major voice. These actors articulated their own narratives of the 1960 crisis, adding their "voices" to the contestation over the Congo's identity. The crisis illustrates the rise in the number of voices claiming authorship and attempting to access international discursive space. This new multiplicity of discourses was due to several factors. The hegemony and coercive ability of the European imperial powers to support their truth claims had deteriorated over the first half of the twentieth century. After the two world wars, the United States claimed dominant authorship of the post-war international order. Guided in part by their liberal ideology, the United States created international organizations such as the United Nations, which greatly increased the discursive space available to Third World leaders. The UN provided a public platform from which numerous international actors—from Khrushchev to Ghanaian delegates—could articulate and circulate their own truth claims. Furthermore, the growth and increased availability of new technology, such as the radio and television, enlarged potential discursive space. There were, however, still substantial limits on an actor's ability to access this space. In this final section, I examine these alternative voices and the larger issue of accessing discursive space through which to articulate and circulate narratives and identity discourses.

Coming in the wake of the Korean War, the situation in the Congo offered the United Nations an opportunity to exercise its international authority and legitimacy. Indeed, the 1960 Congo Crisis is the first substantial attempt by the UN to engage in institutional peace-keeping practices. Yet, to a large extent, the UN Secretary-General's office operated within the cognitive framework authored by the U.S. government. There were clear reasons for this. As Stephen Weissman has noted:

> In mid-1960 it was appropriate to consider the UN a satisfactory vehicle for American policy. In the Security Council, the West held four out of five permanent seats and three out of six of the elected seats . . . In

the Secretariat a high percentage of the staff was at least basically Western in outlook. Americans, British and Frenchmen held 49 of 102 senior positions. [Dag] Hammarskjöld's closest advisers were all Americans who had survived a McCarthyite purge of the Secretariat in the 1950s (Weissman 1974a, 60ff.; see also Hoskyns 1965a, 112).

Though the UN Secretary-General's office pursued its own agenda, that agenda was clearly defined within the framework of American discourses, as evidenced in the rhetoric employed by the Secretary-General's office vis à vis Lumumba.[28] In a meeting with U.S. Ambassador Henry Cabot Lodge, Hammarskjöld referred to Lumumba as "stupid" and Antoine Gizenga, his representative, as "evil" and "unintelligent" (quoted in Kalb 1982, 58). Top UN officials viewed him as "a potential dictator bent on wrecking our operations" (Von Horn 1967, 195). By August, Hammarskjöld had concluded that the "UN effort could not continue with Lumumba in office. One or the other would have to go" (Kalb 1982, 50–51). The UN took an active role in removing Lumumba, from canvassing young Congolese expatriates (Gendebien 1967, 64–65) to directly participating in both Kasavubu's and Mobutu's coups (Weissman 1974a, 90, 95–99).

The UN administration also read the Congo Crisis within the narrative of Congolese immaturity. The UN's primary focus was to establish itself as the principal "authority" and source of law and order within the Congo. This claim contradicted Lumumba and Kasavubu's original invitation, which expressly stated the UN was *not* needed to "restore the internal situation in the Congo but rather to protect the national territory against acts of aggression committed by Belgian metropolitan troops" (UN Security Council Official Records 1960, 54). Hammarskjöld's actions were grounded in perceptions of Lumumba as the source of instability and the Congo as a "failed" state, despite ample evidence to the contrary. After circumventing the Congolese government and virtually ignoring Lumumba, Hammarskjöld announced in early August a plan in which UN advisors and technicians would be assigned to each government department. Hammarskjöld undermined the Congo's head of government and its established state institutions, suggesting a form of UN trusteeship.

Meanwhile, just as the Eisenhower administration interpreted the 1960 Congo Crisis through a narrative of cold war competition, so too did Soviet Premier Nikita Khrushchev. Khrushchev portrayed the Congo as a battleground, pitting African nationalism and self-determination against Western (neo)colonialist intervention (see Khrushchev 1974, 463–465). Khrushchev defined Congolese identity within a narrative of Third World nationalism, repeatedly emphasizing Congolese sovereignty in the sense of the inhabitants' "right" to self-determination. Rejecting the rhetoric of Congolese im/prematurity, the Soviet government portrayed the Congolese state as being endowed with rights of sovereignty, autonomy, and territoriality as defined by international law (i.e., the United Nations Charter). At the UN, Khrushchev declared that Lumumba's administration was the "only lawful" one in the Congo, as it was the only one that "enjoy[ed] the confidence of the Congolese people" (quoted in Lefever 1965, 100). Furthermore, Lumumba himself was portrayed in the Soviet media as a symbol of Third World resistance and nationalism (see, for example, Jankowiak 1997).

American fear of Soviet intervention was grossly exaggerated, and this was recognized by many key American policy makers at the time. In a July 25, 1960 State Department memorandum, it was observed: "The Communists do not have an efficient and well-established apparatus in the Congo that would permit them to manipulate existing forces" ("Memorandum From the Director of the Bureau of Intelligence and Research to Secretary of State Herter, 25 July 1960" 1992, 355). As Stephen Weissman has noted, there were several reasons for the "minimal Soviet input" in the Congo: Sub-Saharan African was a low priority in great-power competition; the Congo was simply too far away to guarantee safe passage of equipment, arms and men; and, finally, they recognized that Africa was a "particularly unfriendly terrain" (Weissman 1974a, 280–281). Thus, the Soviets used the Congo not as a possible "foothold" for global expansion, but as a site for propaganda. Their rhetoric stressed the victimization and martyrdom of the Congo, its people, and its leader.

The "Afro-Asian" bloc within the UN also based its construction of the Congo on elements of international law—namely the United Nations Charter—that emphasized national self-determination as a "right" rather than a "gift." To a certain degree, this bloc rejected the view that the Congolese independence was "premature" and its citizens "immature." The UN delegates within this bloc generally rejected the demonization of Lumumba, viewed the Belgian intervention as a direct violation of Congolese sovereignty, and advocated the unity of the Congo entity, as was evident in Nkrumah's radio address quoted at the beginning of this section. The Afro-Asian bloc repeatedly stressed to Hammarskjöld that it would support UN involvement only on certain conditions: ending the persecution of Lumumba, refusing recognition of Mobutu (who was seen as a Western creation), encouraging Congolese political reconciliation, and preventing Belgian military assistance from bolstering the Katanga regime (Hoskyns 1965, 234–236; see also Nkrumah 1960).

Viewing the Congo Crisis through the lens of national self-determination, the Afro-Asian bloc, especially key "leftist" states such as Ghana and Guinea, often rearticulated Lumumba's narratives. Though not a dominant force in the UN, the bloc was able to exert some degree of power, at times forcing key resolutions (and American acceptance of them) through the General Assembly. The bloc was particularly effective in countering Belgium's narrative of the crisis and hardening the UN's position against Tshombe. Its influence did not travel much beyond the floor of the UN, thus illustrating the limitations of this discursive space. The Belgian and American media largely ignored or dismissed the statements made by the Afro-Asian bloc. Moreover, the bloc did not represent a majority in the General Assembly. Finally, divided among the more militant leftist, moderate, and pro-Western states, the bloc lacked unanimity and complete cohesion, a point exploited by the Eisenhower administration (Weissman 1974a, 108–111, 149; see also O'Brien 1966, 3–27). The bloc was not able to challenge significantly the American government's discourse on the Congo's identity, nor was it able to stop the political machinations linked to that discourse.

The failure of the bloc to achieve its goals hints to the larger contestation over discursive space, mainly fought between the United States, Belgium, and Patrice Lumumba's government. Given the contestation over narratives and interpretations of events during the crisis, what was at stake was the ability to articulate and circulate those narratives and interpretations within the international community. With respect to the United States and Belgium, Washington had far greater discursive space within which to articulate and circulate its versions of Congolese "reality" than did Brussels. In large part, this was tied to the decline of Belgium's (always limited) power and the rise of the United States as a superpower during the twentieth century. In the previous chapter, I noted that Belgium, along with other European imperial powers, was regarded (within the international community it helped define) as the primary author of the identities of its colonized possessions. In the wake of the two world wars, European authoritative discourses, and European power to articulate, inscribe, and enforce those discourses, were greatly diminished. In their place, the United States had emerged as the dominant Western power that, instead of allowing a plurality of identity discourses, sought to privilege its own reading/writing while challenging and marginalizing other discourses. The United States enjoyed greater discursive space, not only because of its political hegemony, evidenced in its ability to shape policies in such organizations as the United Nations and NATO, but also because of its cultural hegemony. For instance, American publications such as *Time, Life, New York Times,* and *International Herald Tribune* had a far greater global readership than did *Le Soir* and *Le Libre Belgique*, the two major Belgian newspapers.

Furthermore, each government imagined different audiences. The Belgian government's discursive audience was primarily a domestic one. The international "community" to which it occasionally appealed to was conceived as the colonial one of hegemonic Western states. In contrast, the post–World War II U.S. government had developed more of an "international consciousness," largely because of its perceived superpower status. Its international audience explicitly (and successfully) included newly independent Third World states.

Finally, Patrice Lumumba was severely limited in his ability to articulate and circulate his alternative narratives and interpretations of events because he was unable to gain access to wider discursive space. Domestically, Lumumba's main vehicles for articulating and circulating his discourses were direct public speeches and the Congolese media. After Kasavubu fired him and Mobutu moved to "neutralize" him, Lumumba's mobility was severely limited and, more importantly, he was physically denied access to the radio station in Leopoldville, thus eliminating his ability to speak directly to the country's population. Moreover, Lumumba had limited access to international media sources. For example, the Belgian paper *Le Soir* reprinted Lumumba's Independence Day speech on page three of its special edition, after a front page editorial attacking Lumumba's "diatribe" and reproducing the full text of King Baudouin's speech. This one instance would prove to be the only time Lumumba would have his speeches directly reproduced in the international media. Most coverage of his Independence Day address derogatorily paraphrased it, as when *Time* wrote: "Patrice Lumumba, jealous of the limelight everyone else was enjoying, took the opportunity to launch a vicious attack on the departing Belgian rulers. 'Slavery was imposed on us by force!' he cried, as the King sat shocked and pale" (11 July 1960, 33). After Independence Day, no international publication printed an interview with Lumumba, which would have allowed him to articulate his interpretations to a wider audience. Lumumba's inability to access the international media meant that he was unable to circulate his discourses beyond a limited domestic stage.

Furthermore, Washington actively used its hegemonic control over discursive space against Patrice Lumumba. For example, the delegation he sent to the UN was denied seating, after intense maneuvering by the Eisenhower administration (Weissman 1974a, 106–108). When Lumumba traveled to the United States, he was not given audience with Eisenhower or other top-ranking government officials, limiting the scope of his discursive delivery. For example, while he did meet individually with the United Nations Secretary-General Dag Hammarskjöld, he was not given the opportunity to address the UN's General Assembly. In effect, Lumumba's ability to use international organizations as a platform for articulating and circulating his discourse was completely cut off.[29] Thus, Lumumba was denied a space from which to articulate and circulate his narrativization of Congolese identity. The implication of this silencing of Lumumba was that Western governments were able to claim to speak authoritatively of and for the Congo: direct intervention by the United States and Belgian governments meant that they would still control international authorship of the Congo's identity even after "independence."

Chapter Four

From Congo to Zaïre: Mobutu's Production of an "Authentic" National Identity

> Congolese! Show to the old world who claims to be more civilized than the black continent, that our ancestral African hospitality is not a vain word and that you are more human[e] than those in Europe who think they may submit people to the consequences of conflicts between African states and financial groups.
>
> —Joseph-Désiré Mobutu (quoted in Ba 1970, 87)

When Muhammad Ali climbed into the boxing ring on October 30, 1974, he was facing far stronger, bigger, and younger George Foreman. It would turn out to be the event that established Ali's reputation for brilliance as a fighter and a strategist.[1] Foreman appeared to be on his way to victory in the early rounds of the fight, pinning Ali to the ropes with his superior strength and size. But Ali's manager had loosened the ropes slightly, providing Ali with more space to maneuver. Foreman continually battered Ali with shots to the body. Yet, after every punching spree, Ali would shout "Is that the best you can do, George? Is that all you got?" He was openly mocking Foreman, calling into question his strength and manliness as a boxer. Ali even threw over a dozen "right leads," considered an insult to a boxer of Foreman's stature. Infuriated, Foreman fought back blindly: throwing jabs at imaginary targets, swinging at Ali where Ali was not, and draining himself of his energy. Preying on Foreman's weaknesses and fears, Ali was illustrating the first of his three gifts: knowing his opponents and using their weaknesses against them. By the eighth round, his second and third gifts kicked in: his amazing perseverance and his lightning-quick speed. By that time, Foreman was spent. Ali came off the ropes energized, landing several devastating punches on Foreman in quick succession and, within seconds, knocking Foreman out. As the bell ended the fight, Ali raised his fists in the air as the new champion, acknowledging the chant "*Ali! Boma ye!*" ("Ali! Kill him!") by thousands of screaming fans in Kinshasa, Zaïre, until recently know as Leopoldville, Congo.[2]

When Muhammad Ali entered the boxing ring for the fight billed as the "Rumble in the Jungle," it was also an event that showed the brilliance of Mobutu Sese Seko (né Joseph-Désiré Mobutu) as an international strategist and politician. After his second coup on November 24, 1965, Mobutu sought to change the Congo's image, renaming it, himself, and many of its cities under an "authenticity" campaign aimed at reclaiming the nation's African traditions. The Ali-Foreman fight, the brainchild of an up-and-coming promoter by the name of Don King, put the world's attention on the Congo, which had by then been renamed Zaïre. For the previous fifteen years, international media attention had focused on the rebellions and political unrest that plagued the Congo. Now Mobutu was presenting a new image. It was the image of a postcolonial Africa, boldly embracing the future while simultaneously grounding itself in an ancestral past.

The Ali-Foreman fight can be read as more than an international publicity stunt by a Third World leader. Two of the tactics utilized by Ali to reclaim his title—exploitation of opponents' weaknesses and perseverance—also became the tools utilized by Mobutu during his more than thirty years in power. He successfully exploited the internal divisions among the domestic opposition, as well as their desire for power and wealth. Mobutu was also able to capitalize on the fears of numerous external actors, whether it be the fear of Communism or the loss of economic privileges. Moreover, he outlasted most of his fellow cold war dictators, creating a new image for the Congo by manipulating past discourses, images, and symbols and by exploiting the weaknesses and fears of other international actors. Just as Ali's manager had loosened the ropes to give the fighter more room to maneuver, so too was Mobutu able to increase and manipulate discursive space for his constructions of "Zaïrian" identity.

Using the example of Mobutu's Zaïre, this chapter explores the complexities of identity production and consumption in international relations. Discourses on Zaïre/Congo's identity have been neither monolithic nor unchallenged. Discourses on identity are inherently open-ended and incomplete, and a plurality of discourses exists at any given time. Each discourse establishes a closure and dominance over other discourses but is always incapable of establishing a completely closed, stable, and fixed position (Doty 1996, 6). It is not enough to only examine the dominant or hegemonic discourses, for that gives only a partial picture and works to reify the imagery of domination. It is important to recognize that internal actors also have discursive agency and do not passively have their identity written for/upon them. Through his invention of Zaïre and his rhetoric of *authenticité*, Mobutu developed a counterhegemonic discourse on the Congo within international relations. Through the appropriation of Third World discourses on nationalism, Western philosophical rhetoric, colonial imagery, and the narratives of cold war competition, Mobutu was somewhat successful in articulating a counterdiscourse and altering the dominant image of the Congo. Much of his success stemmed from his ability to access international discursive space—space that had been unavailable or unattainable for Patrice Lumumba.

While it is important to examine the discursive *production* of identities, it is also imperative to examine how those discourses are interpreted or *consumed*. Quite simply, identity discourses are interpreted differently by different audiences. Cultural studies theorists have shown that audiences often resist discourse, or read/consume images in ways that might have been unintended by their producers. Stuart Hall conceives of any communication process as "produced and sustained through the articulation of linked but distinctive moments—production, circulation, distribution/consumption, reproduction" (Hall 1980, 128). The production of discourses (rhetoric, representations, and actions) is "encoded" with meanings based on specific frameworks of knowledge. When these discourses are consumed and reproduced, their meanings are "decoded" through the framework of knowledge held by the consumer. This point is significant to remember, because it suggests that meanings are not always decoded exactly as they were intended or consistently by all audiences. Much of the literature on identity in international relations either ignores or overlooks the second half of the production/consumption process. A more integrated approach to identity needs to address both aspects. This chapter examines the diverse ways in which Mobutu's discourses on Zaïrian identity were consumed by different groups within the international community.

Mobutu was limited in large part by the ways in which his alternative discourses were consumed by external actors. Over time, numerous Third World leaders came to regard Mobutu as a pariah because his pro-Western support was increasingly unacceptable within their discursive parameters of nationalism. The U.S. government read Mobutu and Zaïre within the discursive frameworks of cold war competition and accepted conceptualizations of sovereignty and notions of the state.

Within the logic of cold war discourses, Mobutu and Zaïre were defined as valuable and essential allies; however, as Mobutu's power gradually shrank to areas around the capital, many American observers clung to the myth of linear state development with the Western state at its apex. Thus, they argued that Zaïre "proved" the failure of modernity (i.e., Western "civilization") in Africa.

The first section of the chapter explores how the Mobutu regime invented a Zaïrian national identity, primarily through the use of narrative, delineation of national characteristics, and performance. The second section develops the argument that Mobutu's national identity discourses were produced for external as well as internal audiences. The third section contends that the discourses of a new Zaïre were, in fact, counterhegemonic. The fourth section explores how Mobutu's identity discourses were consumed by various audiences across the international community. This section illustrates not only disjunctures between the production and the consumption of national identities, but also the multiplicity of interpretations. The final section examines how the (re)presentation of Mobutu and Zaïre evolved within the Western community during the last two decades of his life. As such, this concluding sections offers a bridge to the next chapter.

Imagining "Zaïre"

> By the policy of Authenticity, the return to our sources, I hope to mentally decolonialize my people, that is to say, to modify the economic structures left by the colonizers, for they were not adapted to a young country in the process of development.
>
> —Mobutu Sese Seko (quoted in Du Bois 1973, 13)

After coming to power, Mobutu launched several campaigns aimed at garnering public support for the regime and constructing a national identity. Throughout this chapter, I will occasionally refer to Mobutu, members of his regime, his propagandists, and his supporters amongst the Zaïrian intellectual elites collectively as "Mobutu." While I clearly recognize the complexities of internal decision-making processes and discursive authorship under Mobutu's reign, I collectivize them for the sake of brevity. National identity discourses were not the sole production of Mobutu but involved numerous elites as well. Importantly, Mobutu and his elites were also fashioned by these discourses themselves. To a very large extent, these elites were reconstructed by what they created. The same discourses that were intended to consolidate Mobutu's rule also imposed on the Zaïrian leadership significant limits on how to act and what courses of action were possible.

This chapter's primary focus is on these national identity discourses, for they reflect a coherent attempt by a segment of the Congolese to define and inscribe their own identity in an international context that had heretofore portrayed the Congo in negative terms. Henry Morton Stanley, Leopold II, and the Belgian colonial agents had constructed images of the Congo as a primitive, ahistoric land filled with both riches and cannibals. In response, the Congo Reform movement imagined the Congo as a "Heart of Darkness" where the primordial barbarity of Africa corrupted pseudocivilized white men, resulting in a bloodletting of enormous proportions in the name of rubber acquisition. After the newly independent Congo collapsed into "chaos" and "barbaric anarchy" in 1960, the country became in the eyes of much of the West a symbol of the Africans' supposed inability to rule themselves. As Dietrich Mummendey, a Western reporter and photographer stationed in the Congo from 1960–1965, wrote: "[T]he Congo soon became a catch-word for all that seemed wrong with independent Africa. It became a symbol... [T]he Congo meant premature independence, the clear demonstration of the inability of Africans to govern themselves; administrative incompetence; irresponsibility and savage tribal warfare, capable of wiping out a century of civilisation" (Mummendey 1997, 1). Once again, the Congo became synonymous with backwardness, barbarism, incompetence, tribalism, and savagery.

It was within this context that Mobutu came to power in 1965. Though ostensibly a military coup, Mobutu's government quickly took on civilian trappings, organizing a one-party state around the Mouvement Populaire de Révolution (MPR), becoming what one observer called "the most 'civilian' of tropical Africa's military regimes" (Bustin 1967, 168). This chapter focuses on three distinct albeit interconnected projects: the renaming campaign that began in 1966, the philosophy of *authenticité* and the political/economic program of "Zaïrianisation," also know as the "Radicalization of the Revolution," which began in 1973. However, an important distinction should be drawn between these discourses and what became known as *Mobutisme,* which represented a clear shift toward a cult of personality and was less concerned with articulating a national identity than justifying Mobutu's regime.

Most Western observers have been dismissive of these projects, equating discourses on Zaïrian national identity with mere rhetorical maneuvers to justify the regime's repressive actions. Indeed, there has been a tradition in Western academic studies to regard the national identity rhetoric of the Mobutu government as "absurd" (see Young 1978, 169–85; Young 1994; and Mudimbe 1994). An often-cited example of this "absurdity" was the image of Mobutu descending from the clouds, shown every day on Zaïrian television, implying that Mobutu was a gift from God. While it is somewhat humorous to consider Mobutu a "gift from God," this imagery is not any more "absurd" or "irrational" than American television networks closing every broadcast day with images of fighter planes superimposed over the American flag to the tune of "God Bless America," as they did during my own childhood. National identity discourses must not be taken out of their proper context even if their performative aspects may seem ridiculous.[3] Furthermore, dismissing Congolese discourses continues a troubling trend. Indigenously articulated identity discourses have historically been delegitimized and dismissed by Western powers who have claimed a superior perspective, often with detrimental consequences.

The Politics of Renaming and "Authenticité"

In May 1966, the Mobutu government began the policy of renaming many of the country's major cities, replacing their colonial names with "African" ones. Leopoldville became Kinshasa, Elisabethville became Lubumbashi, Stanleyville became Kisangani, Coquilhatville became Mbandaka, Banningville became Bandundu, and so forth. In most cases, this move represented a "*re*-baptism" because Belgian colonizers had renamed the cities between 1885 and 1935 as signs of monarchist allegiance and exploration glorification (Mudimbe 1994, 134). A few years later, streets in Leopoldville with colonial names were given African ones and statues of colonial icons such as Leopold II and Stanley were removed—sometimes violently.

On October 27, 1971, Mobutu announced that the Congo—both the country and the river—would henceforth be known as "Zaïre." The flag was replaced by the MPR party flag and a new national anthem was written. Continuing this trend, Mobutu proclaimed that all citizens of Zaïre were required to change their names by adopting more "African" ones. Those who refused to do so ran the risk of losing their citizenship. In January 1972, Joseph-Désiré Mobutu changed his own name to Mobutu Sese Seko Kuku Ngbedu Waza Banga.[4] These name changes were justified on the grounds of overcoming the colonial legacy, making the country more authentically African, and removing the negative baggage associated with the "Congo" (Mobutu 1975 and Manwana-Mungongo 1972). There was, however, a fair degree of irony, since the name "Congo" was derived from the Kingdom of Kongo, while

"Zaïre" was the Portuguese rendering of the KiKongo word for "river" *(N'zadi)*, later extended to the surrounding region, including the Northernmost province of modern Angola. It remains curious why Mobutu chose the Portuguese corruption over the more authentic KiKongo form "N'Zadi."[5]

It would be a mistake to assume that this act of (re)naming was an attempt to bring the past back to life. Rather, it was transformative in that it sought to create new knowledge formations: "the naming, the representing, and the claiming are all one; the naming brings the reality of order into being" (Pratt 1992, 33). While the (re)naming by colonizing whites was bound up in the European expansion of capitalism, technology, political domination, and systems of knowledge, the (re)naming of Zaïre by its political elites represented the *self*-invention of the populace they sought to govern.

Mobutu's construction of a national identity for Zaïre was most clearly realized in his *authenticité* campaign. As articulated by the MPR party theorist Kangafu-Kutumbagana, *authenticité* sought to move away from borrowed or imposed ideas toward an increased awareness and privileging of indigenous cultural beliefs and values (Kangafu-Kutumbagana 1973). This was seen as a pivotal act of decolonization, because it restored the dignity of local cultures that were denigrated under Belgian colonial rule. As Mobutu stated: "By the policy of *authenticité*, the return to our sources, I hope to mentally decolonize my people, that is to say, to modify the . . . structures left by the colonizer" (quoted in Du Bois 1973, 13). Many of *authenticité*'s propagandists and theorists were explicit in their desire to challenge the dominant, racist images of Congolese identity and replace them with a more positive and "authentic" Zaïrian identity (see Manwana-Mungongo 1972, 143–47).

Mobutu stated that the central element of *authenticité* was: "Being oneself and not how others would like one to be, thinking by oneself and not by others, and feeling at home in one's culture and country" (quoted in *Salongo*, 5 November 1973, 9). The most explicit goal of *authenticité* was to restore amongst the Zaïrian people a sense of pride in their own traditional culture, which had been taken away by colonialism. As political scientist Kenneth Adelman argued, "Authenticity calls for a self-being, a national consciousness, a collective ethic, and an awareness of the nobility of ancestral values" (1975, 135).[6] Importantly, Mobutu and his agents made it clear that they were not uncritically rejecting Western culture and embracing an idealized past.[7] As Mobutu argued, "The recourse to authenticity does not mean that we should adopt all the practices of our ancestors. We renew our culture while rejecting that which is contradictory to the modern world" (quoted in Adelman 1975, 137).

The underlying domestic goal of these projects was to increase cultural pride in the hope of furthering national unity. As such, they should be regarded as expressions of *nationalism*. Sociologist Anthony Smith has observed that nationalism is "an ideological movement for attaining and maintaining autonomy, unity and identity on behalf of a population deemed by some of its members to constitute an actual or potential 'nation'" (Smith 1991, 73). The dilemma for Mobutu's regime was that there was no "nation" to unify. There were no "national" traditions, beliefs, and values to "authenticate." As the social philosopher Ernest Geller noted: "Nationalism is not the awakening of nations to self-consciousness; it invents nations where they do not exist" (Geller 1964, 168). Such was the case in Zaïre.

It is important to note the extent to which his regime was successful in building an imagined Zaïrian political community. One of the largest obstacles facing the regime was time. Sakombi Inongo, one of *authenticité*'s primary architects, noted that European nations had centuries to construct a national identity (quoted in *Nyoto*, May 1972, 3). Zaïrians had to make do with a few years, and thus the artificiality and forcedness of *authenticité* was more obvious—though no more absurd or irrational—than similar projects had been in Europe and elsewhere. Within its discursive construction of Zaïre, Mobutu's regime was engaged in the process of selecting, plotting, and interpreting the events and characteristics that narrated Zaïrian identity. Thus, the discourses on *authenticité* were engaged in a larger project of *inventing* a national identity, which required the production of a narrative of common precolonial historical memories, myths, and traditions.

In his study on Congolese ethnology, Jan Vansina wrote that "the cultures of the Congo resemble each other strongly when one compares them to other African cultures, and even more if they are compared to other cultures in the world" (Vansina 1966b, 10). This assertion led many, especially within Mobutu's regime, to argue for the existence of a common cultural unity (see Callaghy 1979, 317). While Vansina obviously has a point about the relative similarities among Central African cultures, his argument obscured the significant cultural diversity *within* the Congo. By focusing on a return to traditional cultures, the Zaïrian elites ran the risk of increasingly fragmenting a precariously unstable multicultural country, since the cultural identities at play in the region bore little relationship to the territorially delineated nation state known as Congo. To counter this trend, the regime engaged in trumpeting and, in many cases, inventing commonalties. Indeed, Mobutu and his propagandists spent a great deal of time defining the philosophies, beliefs, and values of "traditional Zaïre." Much of this entailed synthesizing different cultural traditions and beliefs into a single "Zaïrian" discourse.

However, national identities not only are narrated but can also involve performative aspects (Weber 1998). For example, the Mobutu regime would hold extravagant displays of dancing, performances, parades, and other "authentic" displays of national character across the country. These performances of Zaïrian identity were called *animation*, officially defined as "the national consecration of our vital force and our arrival at the national spirit" (*Salongo*, 22 March 1974, 2). *Animation* involved public dancing and singing in which "the words of traditional songs and chants [were changed] so as to praise the President and the national party, rather than the founding ancestors or the goodness of life" (Adelman 1975, 135). At the center of these displays, usually accompanied by numerous women dressed in "national" garb and singing songs of praise to Mobutu, was the leader himself. Bringing these disparate symbols, signs, and acts together in his own personage, Mobutu became the *site*, and *sight*, of an imagined Zaïrian political community. As Ghislain Kabwit described,

> to clothe his authority with an indigenous identity and to appeal more directly to his people, Mobutu introduced a number of African symbols that could be easily recognised and understood by everyone in Zaïre. He began to wear a Tanzanian-style suit with a leopard skin head-dress that symbolised the national "totem" exemplified by the creation of the National Order of Leopard in the Congo. Moreover, he was also seen walking with a cane carved by a village sculptor symbolising the power of the traditional chief (Kabwit 1979, 387).

Thus, Mobutu was gradually transformed into a personification of the body politic. He dressed himself in the accoutrements of *authenticité*, drawing from different cultures around the country. As both the author and symbolic representation of what it meant to be and dress like a Zaïrian, Mobutu became the physical embodiment of Zaïrian national identity (see figure 4.1). The suit itself, however, was an invented symbol, inspired by Nyerere's adaptation of Nehru's and Mao's form of dress. Called *abacos* (an acronym for *à bas le costume* which means for "down with suits"), the two-piece male garment was designed as part of the *authenticité* campaign to replace the European suit and tie.[8] It became mandatory business attire despite its invented nature (Schatzberg 1988, 106).

Mobutu's production of national identity also relied on the narrativization of the country's colonial and postcolonial eras. Through the *authenticité* campaign, Mobutu narrated a national community by selecting, plotting, and interpreting the shared colonial experiences of abuse at the hands of the Belgians.⁹ This was a reversal of the Colonial *Othering:* the postcolonial African *Self* binarily constructed through the remembrance of the white colonial as the *Other.* At the same time, Mobutu and his agents narrated the history of the First Republic as one of communal Congolese (Zaïrians) suffering under the "Imperialists" and corrupt, incompetent rulers. Despite repeated rhetorical moves to "put those years behind us," great attention was paid to the "mistakes" of the postcolonial/pre-Mobutu era in order to solidify shared historical experiences. One of the most interesting discursive maneuvers was the remembrance of Patrice Lumumba, the assassinated first prime minister. Despite the fact that Mobutu led a coup against Lumumba and was implicated in his murder, Mobutu appropriated his image in the name of Zaïrian nationalism (Chomé 1974, 100–10; DeWitte 2001). In a speech on the sixth anniversary of independence, Mobutu officially installed Lumumba as a "national" hero (Mobutu 1975, 97–114). This symbolic gesture was utilized as a unifying theme for Zaïrians. But it also involved an interesting double movement. On the one hand, Mobutu sought to identify himself with Lumumba's nationalist principles, casting himself as the defender and heir to his legacy. At the same time, Mobutu's regime (re)invented Lumumba and his political stances in its own terms, effectively depoliticizing and neutralizing his memory (see Djungu-Simba 1997, 81–91; Leslie 1993, 31).¹⁰

In its invention of common traditions within the narrative of Zaïrian identity, the Mobutu regime emphasized the image and political beliefs of "chieftaincy," reimagined according to their own needs and agendas. In fact, the regime sought to interpret Zaïrian tradition as undemocratic and authoritarian, much as earlier colonial agents had done in the past. For example, the Kinshasa newspaper *Nyoto* proclaimed: "One of the first acts inspired by the recourse to *authenticité* was the suppression of political parties. The notion of political partisanship is foreign to Zaïre and even to all of Africa" (19–21 May 1972, 10). This characterization of Zaïrian traditions coincided with the regime's narration of the First Republic. The *N'Sele Manifesto* of the MPR warned that because individual liberties may lead to anarchy, the authority of the regime could not be questioned (MPR 1967, 71–73). As Mobutu himself said, "Africa with its recent heritage of rule by village chief, cannot accom-

Figure 4.1: An elderly Mobutu with leopard skin hat and carved wooden cane, May 4, 1997. Source: AP/Wide World Photos.

modate European or American-style democracy" (quoted in *New York Times*, 5 July 1970, 4).

Rhetorically exploiting the image of the chief helped Mobutu establish himself as an authoritarian ruler (see Callaghy 1979, 342; Young and Turner 1985, 211). Mobutu's domestic control was intimately tied to the narrative of national identity. By claiming authorship of the Zaïrian political community, Mobutu's regime was able to delineate between legitimate and illegitimate political activity. The discursive reimagining of "chieftaincy" and the invention of Mobutu as the chief among chiefs produced a context within which Mobutu practiced a distinctly nondemocratic form of personal rule that included the banning of all parties but the MPR and the incarceration of political opponents. An important symbolic gesture was made less than a year after he came to power, when his regime publicly hung four political leaders, including Évariste Kimba, who had been appointed prime minister by the previous president. Moreover, the rhetorical imagining of the Zaïrian community as a family with Mobutu as the father figure harkened back to the colonial discourse of paternalism and produced the political dynamic of coercive authoritarianism and violent repression (Schatzberg 1988).

These discursive moves allowed Mobutu and his supporters to construct a "political aristocracy" and to "privatize" the state (Callaghy 1983, 287–309; and C. Newbury 1984). There is a vast literature that examines the various ways in which Mobutu maintained his power. The discourses he and his supporters constructed enabled his regime to employ a wide range of economic and political machinations, from elaborate systems of patron-client networks to manipulation, coercion, and cooption; from economic extraction and (extensive) corruption to pure repression and violence. Yet, what much of this literature overlooks is that these discourses on Zaïrian national identity were produced for *international* consumption as much, if not more so, than for a domestic audience.

Producing Zaïre for Export

> *Congolese nationalism consists, for us, of being constantly present with the necessary spirit of action that contributes to the overall wellbeing of the Congolese citizens, to the overall development of the country by revolutionary methods of action and of thinking, that is to say it breaks radically with the inertia that blemished the first years of our existence as an independent state.*
>
> —Joseph-Désiré Mobutu (1971, 24)

By and large, the nationalist rhetoric produced by the Mobutu regime was aimed at other African and Third World countries in order to alter their views of both the regime and the country as a whole. At first, many Third World leaders viewed Mobutu as a neocolonial creation, put in power and supported by the CIA and other Western political and economic interests. Likewise, the Congo was seen as a symbol of Western intervention and the thwarting of Third World nationalist aspirations, as embodied in the murder of Patrice Lumumba.

Mobutu and his agents actively sought to create "a more Third World image" by appropriating the language, symbols, and discourses of nationalism as understood and employed elsewhere (Young and Turner 1985, 65–66). In fact, his restoration of Lumumba as a national hero had more to do with tapping into Third World sentiments than exploiting domestic memories, as Lumumba remained an ambivalent and ambiguous symbol for most Congolese (see Djungu-Simba 1997). Moreover, many of the symbols of Zaïre's *authenticité*-as-nationalism, such as Mobutu's Tanzanian styled *abacos*, were clearly aimed at resonating more with Third World nationalist audiences than an indigenous "traditional" constituency.

A telling example of Mobutu's production of externally focused discourses was his introduction of *Zaïrianisation*, or the "radicalization of the revolution," announced in 1974.[11] "Radicalizing" the revolution was largely aimed at earning Mobutu's rule (a.k.a. the "revolution") credibility in the Third World. Much of its success lay in the fact that the policy drew from established Third World nationalist discourses, namely from China, North Korea, and, to a lesser degree, radical African states. As Michael Schatzberg has observed: "Aspects of Mobutu's 1974 'radicalization' bore the pronounced imprint of what the president had seen abroad. National pilgrimage points were copied from the North Koreans and, for a time, high-level Zaïrian officials could be observed valiantly trying to pore through the collected works of Kim Il Sung" (Schatzberg 1991, 64; also 1980, 7). Thus, Mobutu and his agents deftly appropriated the language and symbols of Third World nationalism in order to alter their own image. The Congo may have been perceived as a symbol of neocolonial intervention, but Zaïre now projected itself as a leader of Third World nationalism.

The international angle of *authenticité* can be seen in the way it drew from other Third World nationalist philosophies. For example, Kenneth Lee Adelman has examined *authenticité*'s intellectual and symbolic debt to Léopold Sédar Senghor and Aimé Césaire's philosophy of *Négritude* (Adelman 1975, 134–139). Tellingly, the policy of *authenticité* was *not* announced at home. Rather, Mobutu unveiled his foundational philosophy in 1971 in Dakar, Senegal at the National Congress for Senghor's Union Progressiste Sénégalaise (Mobutu 1975: II, 99–111). This was not a coincidence but reflected the fact that *authenticité* had as much to do with Zaïre's international image as it did with the Zaïrian national identity.[12]

Just as Mobutu and his agents borrowed from the rhetoric and symbols of Third World nationalism, they also appropriated Western images of the Congo and Africa and turned them back on the viewer. During this time, Mobutu's regime employed Western popular discourses to construct an identity of "Zaïre" that was acceptable to the West. The primary sources for this project were the works of Belgian scholars, such as Placide Tempels's *Bantu Philosophy* (1948) and Jan Vansina's *Introduction à l'Ethnographie du Congo* (1966), which provided the framework and "evidence" of Zaïre's cultural heritage for proponents of *authenticité*. By employing Western, mainly Belgian, knowledge of the Congo, Mobutu was able to present the West with an image it already understood and accepted as "authentic."

This project was further revealed in Mobutu's appropriation of "traditional" Zaïrian symbols of chieftaincy. Because there was not a common political system in the precolonial era, "traditional" Congolese practices of chieftaincy would not resonate equally among different segments of the population. However, the rhetoric and symbols employed by the regime did carry tremendous currency with Western observers who were accustomed to the idea that the Congolese were too immature and irrational to understand modern Western political practices and institutions, such as democracy. Mobutu's casting himself as the primary "chief" of the Zaïrian "village" served not only to legitimize his rule among the populace but, more importantly, to justify his position to the international community. This approach resonated well with many Western observers. For example, a CIA report on the Congo stated admiringly:

> Mobutu's approach to government derives from the African traditions of chieftainship liberally interspersed with ideas from his favorite political theorist, Machiavelli. Mobutu believes that the Congolese—whom he describes as but one generation removed from the villages—expect a strong chief who must be the unquestioned authority and the sole source of power (CIA, *Special Report: Mobutu and the Congo*, 23 June 1967; quoted in Kelly 1993, 193).

Not only were Western discourses at odds with the notion of Congolese democracy, they were also at odds with images of Africans in Western-defined roles of power. By "re-traditionalizing" power, Mobutu drew on images of Africa that the West "knew" and was comfortable with. For example, Africans were supposed to look "tribal." Therefore, his leopard skin cap and carved (magical?) walking stick were far more acceptable—and "authentically" African—than if he were in a three-piece suit. He was accepted by the West because, in large part, he was not threatening Western notions of the Self while simultaneously reinforcing their notions of the African Other.

Interestingly, Mobutu's justification of his power also drew from the rhetoric and imagery of Belgian colonialism. Mobutu re-employed past discourses used to justify Belgian colonialism in order to justify his own repressive rule. For example, government agents revived the notion that the average Zaïrian could not understand power in abstract terms, and therefore it had to be personalized. Likewise, Mobutu restored the view that the populace were like children in need of a strong authoritarian hand to guide and develop them (see Schatzberg 1988; Callaghy 1979). This was an image well understood in the West, especially in Belgium, where it had been the foundational myth of the Belgian colonial project, aptly referred to as "paternalism." Indeed, much of the anti-Mobutu literature produced by Western scholars has keenly noted how the Zaïrian regime re-employed the rhetoric and symbols, as well as the violent repression, of the Belgian colonial state (see Young and Turner 1985, esp. chap. 6; Schatzberg 1988, 71–98; Naipaul 1975, 19–25; Callaghy 1986a, 221 and 1979, 311). What much of this scholarship misses is the fact that Mobutu's re-employment of colonial discursive elements had international as well as domestic implications.

Significantly, Mobutu's propagandists explicitly framed their presentation of *authenticité* within the works of Western existentialist philosophers, such as Jean Paul Sartre, Albert Camus, and Martin Heidegger. Sakombi Inongo, one of the primary architects of *authenticité*, often openly employed existential philosophical rhetoric in his treatises, the most famous of which is *Authenticité au Zaïre* (n.d.). Kangafu-Kutumbagana's pamphlet *Discours sur l'Authenticité*, a major intellectual presentation of the project, is filled with supporting quotes from Sartre, G. W. F. Hegel, Karl Mannheim, Michel Foucault, and other Western philosophers. Kangafu-Kutumbagana opens his pamphlet with the assertion, taken directly from André Lalande, that *authenticité* means to "act with authority, to be in the proper manner" (1973, 17). Kangafu-Kutumbagana's work, like much of the *authenticité* rhetoric, consciously echoed Sartre's view that authenticity is the "self-recovery of being which was previously corrupted" (Sartre 1956, 70). Though their usage of the rhetoric was different from that of the European existentialist philosophers, the propagandist's employment of Western philosophical discourses suggests that Mobutu's *authenticité* campaign was partly aimed at an international community more versed in existentialist rhetoric than the Congolese populace.[13] Equally telling is the fact that Mobutu decided in 1971 to replace the terms *Monsieur* and

Madame not with titles used in Lingala, KiKongo, or any other indigenous language but with *Citoyen* and *Citoyenne*, taken from the French Revolution (Young and Turner 1985, 117).

Zaïre and Counterhegemony

> *If the ruling class has lost its consensus, i.e. is no longer "leading" but only "dominant," exercising coercive force alone, this means precisely that the great masses have become detached from their traditional ideologies, and no longer believe what they used to believe previously, etc. The crisis consists precisely in the fact that the old is dying and the new cannot be born.*
>
> —Antonio Gramsci (1971, 275–276)

The appropriation and re-employment of established rhetoric and images by the Mobutu government is highly significant because it can be seen to represent a counterhegemonic move in the construction of the identity of the Congo, reimagined as Zaïre. Authorship of the "Congo" had previously resided almost exclusively in the West, an asymmetry that was challenged by Mobutu's nationalism and *authenticité* discourses.[14] In large part because of the discursive space now available to Mobutu's regime, for the first time, a Congolese scripted discourse effectively emerged. There were two primary reasons why Mobutu was able to successfully articulate and circulate his discourses to international audiences. First, he was able to employ discursive tools and platforms that had previously been unavailable. For example, on October 10, 1973, Mobutu was the first Congolese leader to give a direct address to the UN General Assembly. His numerous interviews and speeches were printed and circulated both domestically and internationally via radio, television, and print, including a number of magazines such as *Jeune Afrique* and *Africa Report* that were published in Europe and the United States. Moreover, Mobutu was able to access a discursive space at regional and international conferences, such as the annual meetings of the Organization of African Unity (OAU) and Franco-African leadership summits.

In addition, the rhetoric and representations produced by the regime existed within a "respectable" discursive framework. Whereas the earlier identity discourses of Patrice Lumumba were seen as directly oppositional to Western-scripted "truths" and "knowledge," Mobutu's were acceptable because they drew upon existing elements that were already accepted and popularized in Western societies. As such, Mobutu's construction of a Zaïrian identity needs to be recognized as a "counterhegemonic" maneuver in the Gramscian sense. This is in keeping with Gramsci's discussion of a "war of position" in which an old social order is challenged by constructing a new one within the existing framework (Gramsci 1971, 229–243; see also Gill 1993, 15; Cox 1993; Murphy 1998). To paraphrase the writings of Michel Foucault (1980: 122–123), hegemony consists of the codification of a whole number of power relations that render its functioning possible, while counterhegemony is a different type of codification of the same relations. The hegemonic discourses worked to map or classify specific understandings of the Congo's identity, while Mobutu sought to alter that "horizon of the taken-for-granted."

One of the key elements of Mobutu's counterhegemonic move involved what postcolonial theorists call "mimicry." This activity was discussed in chapter two as one of the tactics Africans used to resist the imposition of colonial authority. Homi Bhaba argues that the "menace of mimicry is its double vision, which in disclosing the ambivalence of colonial discourse also disrupts its authority" (Bhaba 1984, 89). Or, as Jenny Sharpe puts it, a "mimic man is a contradictory figure who simultaneously reinforces colonial authority and disturbs it" (Sharpe 1995, 99). To a certain degree Mobutu operated as a postcolonial "mimic man," providing the "international community" with an image that reinforced its own authority while simultaneously disrupting that authority. Furthermore this was successful whether this discourse addressed radical nationalists within the Third World or Western leaders in three-piece suits. In this way, Mobutu and his propagandists were able to alter how the Congo/Zaïre was imagined at the international level. Like Ali's manager, they "loosened the ropes" to provide greater maneuverability for their identity constructions.

Mobutu's articulation of these new images of Zaïrian identity exploited a number of other discursive openings, the most important fact of which was the historical context of the cold war. Mobutu had long maintained close connections with both the Belgian secret service and the CIA. Both of his coups—in 1960 and 1965—were supported by the CIA. Western intelligence agencies had thrown their support behind Mobutu because they identified him as someone who would serve and protect their interests—an image Mobutu cultivated. The U.S. official position on cold war competition defined it as a zero-sum game, where any gain by the Soviet Union was regarded as a loss for the United States. Once in power, Mobutu deftly exploited these cold war discourses for his own benefit.

Mobutu reappropriated the rhetoric of Congo as an inherently chaotic society, constructing an image of himself as the only possible solution toward stability. Thus, he rhetorically altered the previous equation of "Congo=Chaos" into "Mobutu=Stability," and its important corollary: "Zaïre=Regional Stability" (see Schatzberg 1991, 61–76). The strategic appeal of a stable Zaïre carried significant weight given that the pro-Western, racist regimes in Rhodesia and South Africa were under threat and, more importantly, the neighboring Portuguese colony of Angola was facing defeat at the hands of a Marxist nationalist movement. For several decades, the Congo was, in the Conradian sense, equated with the "Heart of Darkness," embodying the primal, barbaric "nature" of Africa. Mobutu and his agents appropriated and recast this trope to privilege a second interpretation, which located Congo/Zaïre in the *strategic heart* of Africa. The rhetoric of Mobutu's regime thus reimagined Zaïre as a strategic linchpin in the cold war, challenging the view of the Congo as a backward jungle of insecurity. Throughout his rule, Mobutu increasingly emphasized this image of Zaïre's strategic importance and his own role as provider of stability.

Finally, Mobutu manipulated popular images of the Congo as an economic paradise waiting to be exploited and developed, which had long been a theme in the Western imagination since Henry Morton Stanley's earliest exploration of the region. Mobutu's regime employed similar rhetoric to portray Zaïre as a country of enormous untapped resources, both in terms of labor and minerals, to increase foreign investment and raise the strategic importance of the country. The rhetoric of exploiting Zaïre's labor was captured best in the policy of *Salongo* ("community work"), which was an attempt by the state to harness the domestic economic potential of the populace. This was largely a case of regaining control over legitimate labor, given the fact that the official economy had collapsed during the First Republic (while the black market and informal sectors had flourished).[15] Stressing Zaïre's mineral resources and potential wealth was largely designed to increase foreign investment and raise the strategic importance of the country. Mobutu's attempt to rehabilitate the country's economic image was reflected in the hosting of an annual International Trade Fair in Kinshasa, for which the regime constructed buildings, a park, and houses for its exclusive use (Willame 1971, 15). Establishing Zaïre as a potentially profitable country allowed the Mobutu government room to maneuver and increase its capacity for agency in international affairs. Mobutu also attempted to exploit the differences and competition among Western states: namely the United States, Belgium, and France. Mobutu often played these governments off on each other to his own advantage. Furthermore, he exploited the competition between the business communities of these countries, gaining valuable resources from the awarding of key contracts, development projects, mining privileges, and so forth. All this led to an increase in Mobutu's importance as various Western interests vied for his favor.

The International Consumption and Reproduction of Zaïre

> *In the years before independence, the Congo was viewed from abroad as a symbol of the mysteries of Africa, of the perils of Tarzan's dark jungles, of cannibalism, crocodiles and bewildering and bitter rivalries between backwards people with names like Lulua and Baluba.*
>
> *In the years just after independence, she became a terrifying symbol of all that could go wrong in a new land, of tribal savagery and vicious anti-white violence.*
>
> *Now, at the end of a decade of turbulence, many observers in this vibrant capital city [Kinshasa] are saying that those days are past, and that, finally, the time has come for the Congo to become a new kind of symbol for the world.*
>
> —*New York Times*, 5 July 1970, 4

This passage from the *New York Times* illustrates the extent to which American media sources accepted and reproduced Mobutu's rhetoric, particularly the narratives, characterizations, and performative aspects of its constructed national identity. Yet, it would be fallacious to assume that the meaning of these discourses was consumed by the international community exactly as Mobutu and his agents had produced them. Cultural studies theorists have shown that audiences often resist discourse, or read/consume images in ways that might have been unintended by their producers. As Hall notes, the "codes of encoding and decoding may not be perfectly symmetrical" (Hall 1980, 131). The different meanings of Zaïrian discourses were not always "decoded" exactly as they were intended, or consistently by all audiences.

In the case of Belgium, the traditionally conservative press initially expressed hostility toward the Mobutu regime, which stemmed in part from a nostalgia for the more moderate, pro-Belgian, Moise Tshombe. Moreover, the narrative of Zaïrian identity created a paradox in terms of the ways in which it was received in Belgium. On the one hand,

Mobutu's re-employment of colonial portrayals of the supposed "child-like" nature of the Congolese/Zaïrian character resonated well with Belgian common sense, which was familiar with the rhetoric of colonial Paternalism. On the other hand, his negative portrayal of Belgian colonialism and neo-imperialism during the Congo's First Republic was counter to conservative interpretations of the relationship between Belgium and Zaïre. A major issue, however, involved Mobutu's attempt to divest Belgium's Union Miniére of all its mining concessions in favor of the newly created and government-controlled Société Générale Congolaise des Carrières et Mines. The struggle between Mobutu and the Union Miniére resulted in a full-scale diplomatic war, with highly negative and hostile representations of him appearing in the Belgian press. Yet, the incident greatly improved Mobutu's nationalist image in Africa and among the more radical Congolese. After this initial flare-up, Belgian portrayals of Mobutu became somewhat more favorable as the country's political and, more importantly, economic life stabilized (mostly because the eventual settlement of the Union Miniére nationalization dispute turned out to be highly profitable for Belgian interest groups) (see De Villers 1995 and 1994).

By the 1970s, Mobutu's regime succeeded in raising both his and the country's international status. For example, a front page article in the *New York Times* on 5 July 1970 (from which the above quote was taken) lauded Mobutu with praise for reversing the Congo's fortune and, as such, reproduced much of the Mobutu-scripted image of the Congo. The coverage portrayed the Congo as a stable country experiencing national unity under Mobutu's firm but enlightened control. The Congo, it proclaimed, was "back on the path toward what many regard as its intended role as leader in Africa" (*New York Times*, 5 July 1970, 1, 4).[16]

Perhaps the best example of Zaïre's changed image was found in the coverage of the 1974 Ali-Foreman fight. As *Time* proclaimed, "the real winner will be President Mobutu Sese Seko. The ballyhoo for 'The Fight of the Century' has made the proud President's country an international household word" (28 October 1974, 36).[17] While much of the international media coverage noted the poverty of the populace and the excesses of Mobutu's flamboyant lifestyle, these were excused by the numerous achievements credited to Mobutu. The *Washington Post* proclaimed that "once synonymous in Western minds with civil war and anarchy, [Zaïre] has become a fast-growing, stable nation and is now reaching out for African grandeur and international recognition" (28 October 1974, 1). The narrative of Congolese history that the Mobutu regime had authored—depoliticizing the pre-Mobutu past by portraying it as a chaotic state of nature plagued by primordial tribal attachments—resonated well with the established images of the Congo and were duly reproduced in the Western media. Quoting an anonymous Western ambassador, *Time* concluded its coverage of the Ali-Foreman fight by noting that: "This was not a nation until he took over, only an amalgam of bickering regions and tribes. Now there is a national identity that never existed before. The masses don't begrudge Mobutu his luxurious life-style. In fact, they seem to take pride in it" (*Time*, 28 October 1974, 39).

The nationalist rhetoric of the Mobutu regime also struck a chord with many in the American black community, who, frustrated by mainstream resistance to their civil rights movement, often portrayed postcolonial Africa as an idealized homeland. Within this community, there was a move to refer to themselves as "Afro-Americans" in order to highlight their connection with Africa. As such, images of Zaïre and other African countries became idealized. Muhammad Ali, for example, cried out "I'm home" upon landing in Kinshasa and told Zaïrians that they, not he, were truly free.

The rise of Zaïre and Mobutu's international status could also be noted in the increased flurry of high-profile diplomatic activities. Mobutu attended a "good neighbors" conference of East and Central African heads of state in April 1966. He hosted state visits by such esteemed African leaders as Tanzanian President Julius Nyerere and Zambian President Kenneth Kaunda, improving his self-presentation as a Third World nationalist leader. In September 1967, he succeeded in having Kinshasa host the fourth annual summit meeting of the OAU. In June 1970, King Baudouin visited the country for the tenth anniversary of Congolese independence. In October 1973, Mobutu traveled to New York to address the United Nations, where he announced the severing of diplomatic relations with Israel, a move that earned Zaïre major points among Third World nationalists. Equally important was Mobutu's "rose garden" meeting with U.S. President Richard Nixon and his visit to London, where he accompanied Queen Elizabeth II in a horse-drawn carriage. All of these activities, which were previously unthinkable, increased the discursive space available for articulating and circulating the discourse of the new Zaïrian identity. Furthermore, in 1968 he was awarded both the American "Order of Master-Paratrooper" and the Belgian "Great Order of Leopold." On May 30, 1969, the International Peace Academy awarded him the Dag Hammarskjöld prize (Ba 1970, 88). The irony of these awards is truly remarkable.

One of the clearest testaments to Mobutu's success in promoting Zaïre as a leader of Third World nationalism was the emulation of his *authenticité* philosophy. By the mid-1970s, *authenticité* had been adopted as the official ideology in Chad, Equatorial Guinea, Gabon, and Togo (see Nzongola-Ntalaja 1977–78, 115–30). Mobutu gave a series of lectures on *authenticité* at the Sorbonne in Paris and the Presidents of Panama and Uruguay had Mobutu's speeches published and studied by local party officials (Adelman 1975, 137). For many in Africa and the Third World, Mobutu and his reimagined Zaïre became important postcolonial symbols. As Mobutu himself asserted, they provided "dignity for Africa" (Mobutu 1989).

Just as Third World nationalists seemed to accept the narrative of Zaïrian national identity that Mobutu was constructing, so too did Western audiences accept the cold war rhetoric he reappropriated. For example, the *Washington Post* spoke of Zaïre's "excellent position to influence the course of events throughout central and much of eastern Africa" (28 October 1974, 3). Even Mobutu's critics accepted the view that Zaïre was strategically located in the heart of the continent. As René Lemarchand noted, "[w]ithdrawing support from Mobutu is seen by some as the surest way of preparing the ground for chaos or a communist take-over, or both" (Lemarchand 1981, 157–58; see also Minter 1986).[18]

At the same time, Western states and business interests, convinced that Zaïre provided a potential source of wealth, competed with each other to get a piece of the pie. Mining corporations vied for contracts, banking on visions of Zaïre's untapped riches. Within the first decade of Mobutu's rule, Gulf Oil, Standard Oil, Goodyear Tire and Rubber, General Motors, and Rockwell International all sought to establish themselves in Zaïre. The well-worn vision of the Congo's "enormous and untapped" economic potential became a familiar feature in Western discussions. For example, the *Washington Post* quoted a Western economist who argued that "[t]his country has all the stuff the world is running out of—cobalt, copper, gold, uranium, tin, manganese and oil" (28 October 1974, 1 and 3). This was not an unimportant claim in the midst of the 1970s, with the West increasingly obsessed with maintaining its access to such products. In 1973, a group of Japanese banks made a series of loans to Zaïre in the hope of ensuring Japanese access to the country's raw materials. This set off an avalanche of similar loans from American, British, and Belgian banks. As Michael Schatzberg notes: "Their aim was to get a foot in the door because of Zaïre's huge natural endowments and the rosy financial and development future which almost all predicted. These 'brownie-point loans' were . . . designed to create a presence in Zaïre which could be exploited subsequently" (Schatzberg 1984, 300).

There was, of course, a sharp tension between these pro-West rhetorical maneuvers, aimed at increasing or maintaining Western support for the regime, and Mobutu's nationalist rhetoric, aimed at establishing his position as a nonaligned Third World leader. This tension ultimately undermined many of the truth claims he was producing. Yet, for the first few years of his rule, he deftly exploited the rhetoric and imagery of both. In this way, Mobutu capitalized on the discursive spaces open to him, while occasionally testing the limitations. For example, his 1973 state visit to China bolstered his standing among Third World states, yet was not regarded as a threat by Western interests (while a similar move by Lumumba would have been unthinkable). However, on November 30 of that same year, Mobutu announced his *Zaïrianisation* economic policies, which effectively nationalized most of the foreign-held interests in the country (see Mobutu 1975: II, 391–444). Within a short time, it was clear to all that the policy was an economic disaster. Mobutu quickly back-pedaled and foreign investors returned, vying for favor with the regime. While the initial announcement was heralded across the continent as an important blow to neocolonialism, Western governments (with the strong exception of Belgium) remained relatively unfazed. This point is not insignificant, especially given the track record of certain Western governments in intervening in Third World countries to protect their interests in similar situations.

In hindsight, it may be argued that Mobutu was able to achieve this balancing act because Western governments assumed that he was firmly under their control, a view found in much of the neocolonial literature on Zaïre (see, for example, Nzongola-Ntalaja 1982 and Kelly 1993). However, such a position overemphasizes Western influence and denies Mobutu and his regime any agency. During the first decade of his reign, Mobutu frequently acted against the interests of his supposed Western keepers. For example, his relationship with Belgium was rocky and could best be characterized as unstable and potentially volatile. Likewise, the U.S. government was frequently frustrated by Mobutu's actions, belying the image of him as their puppet. Zaïre's severing of its ties with Israel, for example, was unexpected and embarrassing for the United States. Indeed, some Western audiences expected an African leader like Mobutu to be more docile and malleable than he was. For example, the U.S. State Department frequently characterized Mobutu as "impulsive" when his actions contradicted U.S. interests (Kalb 1982, 165–66). This disjuncture between Mobutu's creation of Zaïrian national identity and the assumptions of Western audiences hints at the tensions and struggles between the production and consumption of national identity, an issue which will be explored below in greater detail.

The Invasion of Angola and Shaba I and II

By the late 1970s, Zaïre's image as a bulwark against neocolonialism and symbol of African grandeur was shattered. This was due largely to historical events that exposed the tension between the discourses of Third World nationalism, emphasizing self-determination and independence, and cold war competition, emphasizing the zero-sum struggle between the "West" and the "East." It is exactly in this respect that Mobutu became victim of his own identity construction, in between two conflicting world views, but unable to escape the discourses constructed around him.

By the mid-1970s, Portuguese control of neighboring Angola was increasingly threatened by armed nationalist groups, particularly the Soviet-backed Movimento Popular de Libertação de Angola (MPLA). The rise of the MPLA directly challenged Mobutu's rhetorical self-portrayal as an anti-communist bulwark and stabilizing force in the region. In response to the ascendancy of the Soviet-backed MPLA, the Mobutu regime initially gave aid to one of the MPLA's competing factions, the Frente Nacional de Libertação de Angola (FNLA), headed by Holden Roberto. When the FNLA proved ineffective in thwarting the MPLA, Mobutu's government invaded Angola directly in November 1975. This invasion was part of a larger CIA-sponsored plan to support another Angolan faction, Jonas Savimbi's Uniao Nacional para a Independência Total de Angola (UNITA), a movement also backed by the People's Republic of China. The plan also involved the invasion of Angola from the south by apartheid South African troops. After the invasion—which eventually failed—Mobutu continued his support for the UNITA rebels and the CIA's and apartheid South Africa's destablization of independent Angola.[19]

Mobutu's actions were unacceptable to many Third World leaders. While his actions were informed by, and consistent with, his discursive production of Zaïre's anti-Communist, stabilizing image, these leaders read the actions through the discursive lens of Third World nationalism. The fact that Mobutu had actively supported the U.S. and white-ruled South Africa's invasion against an African nationalist movement fighting a European colonial power was viewed as unconscionable. Mobutu's status among fellow African and Third World leaders was deeply damaged, undermining the carefully nurtured image of himself as a leader of Third World nationalism and anti-neocolonialism. One may consider that such an outcome was inevitable, that Mobutu would be unable to maintain his balancing act in such a hostile cold war climate. For much of the African and Third World audience, Mobutu and Zaïre became regarded as puppets of the West.[20]

Yet, Western governments read the events through the discursive lens of cold war competition as further proof of Mobutu's vital role as an African ally and bulwark against communism and chaos. Western portrayals of Mobutu and Zaïre became characterized by "our boy" and "our ally" rhetoric. In fact, Western (mainly American and Belgian) governments' consumption of his dual representations of Zaïre as chaos without him and as the strategic "heart" of Africa strengthened their support for him. Their support became essential to his survival in the late 1970s, as his government faced two armed incursions.

In the mid-1970s there occurred a rhetorical shift from *authenticité* to *Mobutisme*, signaled in a speech by Mobutu on August 15, 1974. Loosely defined, *Mobutisme* was the "sayings, thoughts and actions" of the "President-Founder" (Mpinga Kasenda 1975, 8–12; Mobutu 1975: II, 524). By the late 1970s, the rhetoric of national identification, exemplified by *authenticité,* had been clearly replaced by *Mobutisme,* which was the rhetoric of regime justification and personal aggrandizement. Thus, discourses on Zaïrian national identity at that time revolved around shared adoration of Mobutu as the "Guide" and "Savior" rather than through shared cultural or historical affinity. One of the effects of this shift was a rise in anti-Mobutu sentiment among the dispossessed. Fueled in part by this sentiment, and reflecting longstanding resistance to the discourse of a unified Congo/Zaïre, armed rebels invaded the southern province of Shaba (formerly Katanga) in 1977 and, again, in 1978.

It is illuminating to contrast the two Shaba uprisings to note the different ways Mobutu's discourses on Zaïre's identity were consumed in the West. Shaba I began when former Katangan soldiers poured into the province of Shaba from neighboring Angola. Mobutu was quick to claim that the governments of Angola, Cuba, and the Soviet Union were behind the invasion. Mobutu's regime portrayed the uprising as a cold war conflict—with regional and international ramifications—rather than as a domestic affair. To this end, he was relatively successful. Two months into the war, the *New York Times* reported:

> Through adroit stage management and political string-pulling [Mobutu] has succeeded in internationalizing what had been primarily a threat to his continuing rule . . . Through diplomatic missions he won over most African governments to his view that the challenge confronting him in Shaba was a challenge for the whole continent, that what was

at stake was the principle of territorial integrity—the pillar on which rests the fragile solidarity of African countries (*New York Times*, 12 May 1977, 1).

Crucial to Mobutu's survival was the material support his government received from the governments of China, Belgium, Morocco, France, and the United States. Mobutu was able to acquire this aid by playing on cold war fears as well as economic concerns. In the case of Belgium and France, Mobutu played each off by capitalizing on their mutual desire to acquire lucrative copper-mining management contracts (see *New York Times*, 12 May 1977, 8; Trefon 1989, 79–81; De Villers 1995, 71–79).

In the United States, however, the disposition of the government had shifted significantly. The new administration of Jimmy Carter—only seven weeks in office at the outbreak of Shaba I—had already signaled its intention to move away from a cold war–framed world view. One of Carter's primary foreign policy goals was the protection and promotion of human rights. As such, the Mobutu regime no longer held such a privileged place in Washington as it had in the past. Yet, the administration still operated within the "Mobutu or chaos" mentality.[21] As Secretary of State Cyrus Vance wrote later: "None of us wished to face the uncertain consequences that might flow from the collapse of his regime and the consequent disintegration of Zaïre into unstable segments open to radical penetration" (Vance 1983, 70). The result was tepid direct support for Mobutu by the administration ($15 million in nonlethal assistance) while insuring that other allies would come to Zaïre's aid

After successfully surviving the first Shaba uprising, Mobutu's regime was threatened again in May 1978 when rebel forces reinvaded. This time they came across the border from Angola and Zambia, quickly controlling the western half of Shaba's copperbelt. Again, the Belgian and French governments were quick to respond. More importantly, this time the Carter administration reacted rapidly to support the Mobutu regime. The difference in the two responses was due to the fact that in Shaba II, Mobutu and his agents were far more successful in convincing the U.S. administration that the uprising was due to Angolan and Cuban intervention (it wasn't) and portraying it as a cold war showdown. In its early stages, Carter held a press conference placing responsibility for the invasion on Fidel Castro (see U.S. Department of State 1978; quoted in Schraeder 1994, 92). Mobutu and his agents exploited Carter's fear of perceived weakness and emasculation in the face of Soviet advances in Africa (Angola, Ethiopia) and elsewhere (Strategic Arms Limitation Talks [SALT] treaty negotiations).

In the wake of Shaba I and II, Mobutu increasingly stressed the dual image of "Mobutu or chaos" and Zaïre as a cold war linchpin for the West (see Schatzberg 1991, 55–59). As noted above, this had the effect of ending Zaïre's positive image among most Third World nationalists. Within the West, however, the image of Zaïre became complicated due to an increase in the number of discursive voices on Zaïre's identity. Claiming authoritative positions, these voices generally came from scholars, government officials, and popular culture. Though this division relies on a fair degree of generalization, it provides a useful approach for understanding the competing images of Zaïre in Western-scripted discourses of this time.

In general, most of the Western scholarship on Zaïre was highly critical of Mobutu and his regime. These critiques sometimes found their way into the mainstream press, enlarging their audience. In Belgium, for example, Jules Chomé produced a scathing indictment of Mobutu in his *L'ascension de Mobutu* (1974), which was well received by a press that was, by and large, anti-Mobutu since the Union Miniére showdown. In France, Benoît Verhaegen, writing under the pseudonym Jean Rymenam, published a highly critical article in *Le Monde Diplomatique* on "La Fiction Zaïroise" (Rymenam 1977). In general these scholars constructed an image of Mobutu as an authoritarian, exploitative tyrant and Zaïre as his besieged kingdom. During a major speech on November 25, 1979, Mobutu spoke of *"le mal Zaïrois"* ["Zairian sickness"] among the population to explain the country's economic and social failures.[22] Mobutu's critics quickly appropriated this term and turned it against him, rhetorically constructing him as the incarnation of *"le mal Zaïrois"* (see, for example, Nguza Karl-i-Bond 1982 and Boissonnade 1990).

This negative portrayal was at odds with the image of Zaïre constructed by Western political and economic leaders. In France, for example, the government of President Giscard d'Estaing openly embraced Mobutu as an ally and friend (Trefon 1989).[23] In fact, the 1982 Franco-African Summit—featuring thirty-seven heads of state including France's Mitterrand—was held in Kinshasa, providing Mobutu with important discursive space (see Mobutu 1983, 71–94). In the United States, the administrations of Carter, Reagan, and Bush continued to produce and subscribe to the image of Mobutu as an important cold war ally and provider of Zaïrian unity (see Schatzberg 1991; Kelly 1993; Weissman 1981; Lemarchand 1981; Leslie 1993). Mobutu made three official trips to the Reagan White House and was the first

African head of state to visit after George Bush's inauguration. In April 1990, U.S. Deputy Assistant Secretary of State Irvin Hicks told the Congress that "we need him" because he "continues to play an important role mediating regional conflicts" (quoted in *New York Times*, 11 April 1990, 7–8). The World Bank and the International Monetary Fund also reproduced the view that Mobutu and only Mobutu could bring stability and order to Zaïre, thus providing the regime with access to resources and legitimacy within the international community (see Schatzberg 1984; Callaghy 1986a and 1986b; Leslie 1986).

Thus, there appeared to be two competing discursive trends: one anti-Mobutu produced by scholars and the other pro-Mobutu produced by government and economic interests. Yet, there was another discursive construct at play, one that provided the backdrop for this contestation. These were the images of Zaïre circulating in Western (mainly, American) popular culture. Taken together, all three discursive trends informed and influenced the others. However, popular cultural images provided the foundational myths upon which the other discourses were built. For example, the popular belief that Zaïre was inherently chaotic due to its primitive nature was central to Western discourses. This image provided the theoretical justification for supporting an authoritarian dictator, thus providing "truth" to the "Mobutu or chaos" image.

This image was, by and large, based on African exoticism and reproduced existing tropes as well as invented new forms of "Othering" Zaïre and the Zaïrians. In general, it was extremely rare for Zaïre to be covered by the mainstream media, except in times of crises, such as Shaba I and II, or global spectacles, such as the Ali-Foreman fight. When the American media spotlight did shine on Zaïre, its rhetoric was deeply rooted in tropes of African exoticism. Take, for example, the Ali-Foreman fight. Dubbing it the "Rumble in the Jungle" reinforced images of Zaïre as a primitive land that time forgot. Ignoring the "modernity" of Kinshasa's city life, the coverage of the fight reinforced primeval images. For example, the *New York Times* asserted: "But the dark jungle of the central Congo is little changed from the 19th century . . . The forests are still largely impenetrable and inhabited by people to whom the 20th century would be a dazzling puzzle" (5 July 1970, 4). The *Washington Post* explained Western intervention in Shaba I and II as "the reluctant acceptance to shoulder once again the *white man's burden* in that ramshackle central African land" (7 June 1978, 21; emphasis added). Coverage by the *New York Times* employed similar rhetoric, noting that violence was a "natural" element of "the explosive and sinister quality of this land, a quality well depicted in such novels as Joseph Conrad's *Heart of Darkness* and Graham Greene's *A Burnt-Out Case*" (3 June 1978, 3; for discussions of each novel, see chapters two and three respectively).

When mainstream American media portrayed Zaïre, it employed and reinforced existing images of the country as a primeval jungle incompatible with history, civilization, or modernity.[24] As the anticipated promises of decolonization faded, Zaïre became (once again) a popular symbol for all that was wrong with postcolonial Africa. Zaïre—symbolizing the failure of Africans to modernize, democratize, and develop—became synonymous with corruption, ineptitude, and unrest. These elements were often personified in representations of Mobutu. Perhaps no other African leader, save for Idi Amin, was more recognizable to Western audiences as symbolic of Africa's postcolonial failures. His leopard-skin cap and wooden staff became seen less as proud "authentic" displays of African heritage than as physical markings of Zaïre's difference and backwardness or as hollow props used to cloak a repressive and exploitative dictator.

Much of these images came together in V. S. Naipaul's popular and critically acclaimed novel, *A Bend in the River* (1979). The novel is a variation on *Heart of Darkness,* reproducing its themes, rhetoric, and even setting (Kisangani, a.k.a. Kurtz's Inner Station). As the country slides backward toward chaos and barbarism, Naipaul asserts that Zaïre's encounter with civilization and modernity was doomed to fail because that civilization was flawed and African primitivism was too strong to overcome (see Gruesser 1992, 45–69).[25] Perhaps more interesting (and more popular) was Michael Crichton's best-selling novel *Congo* (1980). Crichton's novel is an updated version of Haggard's *King Solomon's Mines* with a group of whites (including a "talking" ape) journeying into the primeval jungle of eastern Zaïre to find the lost city of Zinj, home to fabulous wealth and a group of murderous apes. In the novel (and the 1995 movie), Zaïre is portrayed not as a country sliding toward primitivism, but one that is already there. The book is heavy on familiar Africanist tropes: cannibalism ("Old habits die hard" [147]), savagery, unimproved nature, barbarism, anachronistic space, and so forth. At the end of the novel, the whites escape in a rain of poisoned arrows, a volcano eruption covers the lost city, and the talking ape returns to her "natural" habitat of the Zaïrian jungle. The moral of both novels is that Zaïre, with its hostile environment and inherently savage primitivism, is no place for whites or their civilization. The division between Western modernity and African barbarism, we are told, is simply too great to bridge, and we are all better off knowing and staying in our places.

Zaïre as the Quasi-Sovereign Lame Leviathan

By enforcing juridical statehood, international society is in some cases also sustaining and perpetuating incompetent and corrupt governments. Perhaps the best example in sub-Saharan Africa is the international support that has gone into ensuring the survival of the corrupt government of Zaïre.

—Robert H. Jackson and Carl G. Rosberg (1982, 22)

Throughout the 1980s, Mobutu maintained his external support by banking on the "Mobutu or chaos" imagery and promoting Zaïre as a strategic cold war ally for the West. Mobutu's regime exploited the discursive space and the system of signs offered up by the cold war. However, with the collapse of superpower competition, this space closed and these signs and symbols lost much of their currency. The strategic importance of the "Mobutu or chaos" rhetoric was devalued, especially as "democratization" and "development" increasingly came to dominate Western discourses toward Africa. Yet, American discourses on Zaïre had already shifted dramatically prior to the end of the cold war. A second discursive trend had emerged by the 1980s— informed by the "development" and "democratization" discourses— that measured the ability of non-Western societies to conform to American-defined notions of sovereignty and the state. Thus, at the end of the cold war, American discourses on Zaïre's identity included explicit discussions on its *sovereignty* and ability to function like a Western-scripted *state*.

Perhaps the most influential work on the sovereignty of African states during this time was by Robert H. Jackson and Carl G. Rosberg (1982). These authors argued that Africa's weak states persisted because their leaders were able to exploit the "juridical" attributes of statehood conferred on their governments by the international community (1982, 22). This was closely tied to the notion that African states only possessed "negative" sovereignty—the legal claim to noninterference in their domestic affairs—a point Jackson developed further in his work *Quasi-states: Sovereignty, International Relations and the Third World* (1990, 24). Jackson's basic argument was that African states possessed neither the internal coherency nor the credible governments needed to be granted the status of full sovereignty.

Jackson (and Rosberg) adopted the view that sovereignty was a gift bestowed by the "international community" (i.e., the West) upon Africans who had subsequently abused it. Rhetorically, this represented a return to the conception of independence and sovereignty articulated by the Belgian and American governments during the 1960s crisis. While the work of Jackson (and Rosberg) has been severely critiqued—most eloquently by Roxanne Doty (1996, 147–56), Naeem Inayatullah (1996, 60–77), and Siba Grovogui (1996 and 2000)—it did garner wide acceptance in Western scholarship. Jackson's insight was his realization that African conceptions and practices of sovereignty were different from the Westphalian/Western ideal. However, this led him to conclude that African sovereignty is *inferior* to "positive" (i.e., Western) sovereignty, due to the inability of Africans to master modern political practices and norms. What he failed to realize was that "sovereignty" is a social construct (Biersteker and Weber 1996) that is historically contingent and contextual (Bartelson 1995). Rather than questioning the conceptual nature of sovereignty, Jackson used it as an idealized marker of African difference and inferiority—a theme that was picked up in larger discourses on Africa and Zaïre.

Mobutu and his regime constructed and employed sovereignty in at least two ways. During the earlier stages of his rule (1965 to the late 1970s) Mobutu rhetorically constructed Zaïrian sovereignty to mean noninterference in its domestic affairs and territorial integrity. In order to maintain the country's territory (threatened by the 1967 mercenary mutiny and Shaba I and II), Mobutu articulated this definition of sovereignty, as was illustrated by his appeals to the OAU and UN. In fact, the Mobutu government was willing to forgo some of its domestic control in order to maintain Zaïre's territorial integrity.[26] This is somewhat in line with what Jackson derogatorily refers to as "negative" sovereignty.

By the 1980s, however, the Mobutu regime was employing sovereignty in different and more complex ways. Zaïrian sovereignty increasingly became constructed as a shield behind which power was generated and practiced; where international affairs were conducted and legitimized. As political scientist William Reno observed:

> As formal state bureaucracies collapsed under Zaïre's president Mobutu Sese Seko (1965–97), the country's ruler increasingly exercised authority through control over markets, rather than bureaucracies. Control became less territorial and more centered on domination of an archipelago of resources that could be used to generate income and attract powerful

allies... Rather than providing security to citizens, the regime held on to power through opposite means. Even outsiders' recognition of Zaïre's sovereignty has become contingent to what are violent, essentially private commercial arrangements as a means of exercising authority (Reno 1998a).

Rather than illustrating "supreme authority" within a territory, sovereignty became primarily important in helping to legitimize deals with foreign firms and creditors. The practice and production of sovereignty allowed nonstate actors, primarily foreign firms, to hide their partnerships behind a legal facade, simplifying questions "concerning legitimacy of contracts, insurance, and adherence to laws in the firm's home country" (Reno 1998a). For the international community at large, the production of Zaïrian sovereignty was essential because it "leaves in place an interlocutor who acknowledges debts and provides a point of contact between foreign state officials and strongmen without raising politically disturbing questions of recognition" (Reno 1998a).

While Mobutu and his agents redefined and reinscribed the concept of sovereignty in order to protect and enrich their regime, Western observers maintained the myth that Western practices of sovereignty were somehow more "natural" and "positive." Thus, instead of exploring the myriad ways in which sovereignty was constructed and performed, Western ideals were reified and differences were portrayed as evidence of Zaïre's inability to master modernity.

A similar trend was occurring in the related literature on the Zaïrian state, which focused on how the Zaïrian state (not just the regime) was different from the Westphalian ideal. This seemed to inspire a cottage industry among academics as each author tried to come up with new, more inventive ways of categorizing the state. For example, political scientist Thomas Callaghy repeatedly invented new terms to characterize the Zaïrian state: "early modern," "patrimonial-bureaucratic authoritarian" (1979), "aristocratic" (1983), "absolutist" (1984), and "lame Leviathan" (1987). This reflected a growing trend in the African state literature. For example, Richard Sandbrook referred to Zaïre and other African states as "fictitious" (Sandbrook 1985, 35–36). Joel Migdal (1988) labeled African states "weak," while Donald Rothchild (1987) called them "soft." Taking a different tack, Colin Leys (1976) characterized them as "overdeveloped" and "centralized," while Larry Diamond (1987) used the term "swollen."

It is not important which of these numerous labels best categorized the Zaïrian state. The main point is the realization that the Zaïrian state was different from what Western theories expected and accepted. As was the case with the literature on sovereignty, many of these authors assumed that an idealized Western state provided the ahistoric baseline for judging a country's "stateness." Instead of using African experiences to critically interrogate the conception of the "state," much of this literature reified Western notions of the state and constructed African states, particularly Zaïre, as an example of a failed Other. For them, the failure of the Zaïrian state to look and act like the Western ideal was seen as further evidence of African's failure to master modernity.

What this literature does show is the fact that the Zaïrian state was not the hegemonic social force within its territorial demarcation. It should be recalled that previous attempts by the Belgian colonial state to achieve dominance—monopolizing the legitimate means of coercion, for example—had failed. The point is that there never was a "hard" hegemonic state to begin with. The "state" in the Congo/Zaïre was constantly transforming itself as it came in contact and competed with other social forces; that is to say, it was consistently being (re)constructed and (re)constituted. These transformations will have important ramifications in the late 1990s, as the next chapter shows.

Mobutu placed great emphasis on the performativity of the state. By most accounts, the central government's power did not extend beyond the major cities and, by the 1980s, that zone had effectively shrunk to the area in and around Kinshasa. Yet, the Mobutu regime still emphasized the performative aspects of the state, in large part, to access international resources. For example, many of the development projects, such as the Inga dam and power grid, can be regarded as grandiose presentations of "stateness." These performances brought international grandeur to Zaïre, reified state power, and provided the political and economic elites with valuable (and often illicit) resources.

In conclusion, it should be recognized that Mobutu and his agents were appropriating Western discourses on sovereignty and the state to justify their power while simultaneously redefining and reinscribing these discourses. It is important to realize that simply because Mobutu's power gradually shrank to areas around the capital, one should not assume the rest of the country was in chaos. Other sociopolitical forces and networks were at play, challenging, co-opting, and often replacing the state. There were complex and myriad forms of sociopolitical networks throughout the country, illustrating the limitations of Western-centric, state-centric approaches. Rather than using the Zaïrian case as an opportunity to reconceptualize sovereignty and the state, most Western observers clung to the myth of linear state development with the Western state at its apex. Thus, they argued that Zaïre "proved" the failure of modernity (i.e., Western "civilization") in

Africa. Such rhetoric gained increased currency and circulation throughout the 1990s, the implications of which are examined in the next chapter.

Chapter Five

Cancer, Kabila, and the Congo: Central Africa at the End of the Twentieth Century

> They call it a country. In fact it is just a Zaïre-shaped hole in the middle of Africa. It has been sold, bought, appropriated, stolen. Equally, to describe it as corrupt implies some health somewhere . . . The virus infecting this carcass of a could-be state is the president himself, Mobutu Sese Seko.
>
> —*Economist*, 8 July 1995, 37

The Cancer of Mobutu

By the mid-1990s Mobutu was dying from prostate cancer. As the above passage illustrates, Mobutu's cancer-ridden body became a metaphor for Zaïre: two hollow, diseased bodies in the final stages of life (see also *Newsweek*, 12 May 1997, 40; and 26 May 1997; *Time*, 25 November 1996 and 26 May 1997, 45–46). Toward the end of his life, he spent more time in France and Switzerland undergoing treatment than he did in his own country.

The cancer metaphor was employed by his detractors in at least two ways. First, as the disease progressed through his body, Mobutu was portrayed as a cancer on the Zaïrian body politic. Pressured in large part by his Western backers, Mobutu made tentative moves to "democratize." On April 24, 1990, he announced the end of his own regime and a move toward political pluralism. A National Conference was convened, but Mobutu retained control—artfully exploiting divisions in the opposition, co-opting dissidents, and occasionally unleashing the army. Economically, Zaïre was officially in shambles. Its formal economy shrank more than 40 percent between 1988 and 1995. Its foreign debt in 1997 was around $14 billion. At $117, its 1993 per capita gross domestic product was 65 percent lower than its 1958 pre-independence level (Collins 1997b, 592). It has been estimated that Mobutu and his close friends pillaged between $4 billion and $10 billion of the country's wealth, siphoning off up to 20 percent of the government's operating budget, 30 percent of its mineral export revenues, and 50 percent of its capital budget (Collins 1997a, 277–278). Physically, Mobutu's control effectively ended a few hundred kilometers outside of Kinshasa, while the rest of the country operated through a web of complex power relations. Regional "Big Men" had always been at the heart of the political system but were largely obscured by Mobutu and his international backers' employment of traditional discourses of state sovereignty. As these discourses underwent dramatic changes in the 1990s and formal government structures withdrew and imploded, these regional forces were revealed in the full glare of publicity (see De Boeck 1996; Reno 1997 and 1998b; Turner 1997).

Second, Mobutu and Zaïre were increasingly portrayed by neighboring countries as a cancer on the region. The country's economic condition had regional implications, not the least of which was the thriving black market trade across its highly porous borders.[1] Politically, the Mobutu government was in general regarded as a pariah in the region. By 1996, the only neighboring government on friendly terms with Kinshasa was in Khartoum, Sudan. Mobutu's unpopularity was largely attributed to his open support for a rebel group attempting to overthrow the Angolan government and the fact that eastern Zaïre was being used as a base of operations by rebels fighting the regimes in Burundi, Rwanda, and Uganda.

Interestingly, few Westerners discussed the "origin" of the "cancer" or the causes of its "growth." However, within Zaïre and Central Africa, much more attention was paid to this aspect of the metaphor, and, by 1996, numerous anti-Mobutu interests had converged. While the doctors in Switzerland sought to remove the cancer from his body, a rebellion broke out in the eastern part of the country. In less than a year, the rebellion had succeeded in overthrowing Mobutu's regime and placing Laurent-Désiré Kabila in power. On September 7, 1997, Mobutu died from the cancer. A year later, history seemed to repeat itself as Kabila was faced with another rebellion from the eastern part of the country, a rebellion that continues at the time of this writing.

In the closing years of the twentieth century, the country underwent two rebellions, invasions from several of its neighbors (some welcome, others not), a change in leaders, a change in its name (back to the Congo), and re-emerged yet again as a symbol of contemporary Africa—the embodiment of all the continent's woes. What is apparent is that the region as a whole is in flux. At the center of these changes are ongoing conflicts over identity, authority, resources, and sociopolitical structures. As such, approaches based on cold war frameworks or state-centric perspectives are incapable of adequately reflecting or analyzing the region's complexities.

Recent events illustrate several of this book's key points. The state in which the people of the Congo now find their country can be directly traced back to historical constructions of their identity. Those past imaginings have cumulatively helped make the current situation possible. This underscores the point that discourses on the Congo/Zaïre's identity are linked to political dynamics. They frame the cognitive map of actors, shaping the possibility of action. Even during the closing years of the twentieth century, the ways in which the Congo/Zaïre was reimagined authorized certain actions and not others. During these years, a greater multiplicity of discursive voices emerged in the construction of the Congo/Zaïre. In addition to the Mobutu regimes and the governments of the United States, France, and Belgium, neighboring regimes such as Uganda, Rwanda, Burundi, Angola, and Zimbabwe, as well as numerous nonstate entities, actively scripted alternative and competing truth claims. This increase in the number of discursive voices was due primarily to two factors. On the one hand, these disparate groups were able to employ new forms of technology to access discursive space. For example, interviews and speeches by many of the primary participants in the armed conflicts were available on the Internet, thus allowing them to articulate and circulate their ideas and opinions. On the other hand, changes in how the governments of the United States, France, and Belgium imagined the region increased the discursive space available to these regional voices. These changes were related in large part to decreased relevance of the discourses of cold war competition in the wake of the Soviet Union's 1989 collapse. However, these Western powers' perceptions of the region became further rooted in the persistent images of the Congo as a chaotic, backward space. As such, these changes offered both opportunities and limitations for alternative voices from the region.

Moreover, the events on the late twentieth century illustrate the complexity in the relationship between political actors and the images they adopt, create, and reinforce, especially as new images compete with old in changing historical contexts. Finally, these events illustrate how persistent imaginings of the Congo as a chaotic space inhabited by "backward" and "uncivilizable" people not only shape how external actors understand the events in the region but also fundamentally shape the events themselves.

This chapter is divided into four sections. The first provides a brief overview of recent historical events. The second examines the regional discourses employed by various agents to define "reality" and justify a course (or courses) of action. The third section explores how the Western *"troika"*—United States, France, and Belgium—read/wrote the collapse of Mobutu's regime. In the conclusion, I examine the discursive themes in the West's coverage of the current anti-Kabila war. Given the recent and ongoing unrest in the region and the inability to access key sources of information and archives, my arguments are somewhat speculative. However, I believe that clear discursive trends are evident. Though my arguments in this chapter are tentative, the rhetoric and representations employed by the various actors are illuminating nonetheless.

From Zaïre to the Congo: A Brief Narrative

Avant moi le chaos, après moi le déluge.

—Mobutu Sese Seko

There is some disagreement among scholars as to when and where to trace the roots of the late-1990s rebellions. Some, such as David Newbury (1998), argue that Central Africa experienced several separate and distinct historical phenomena that happened to converge. Others, such as William Cyrus Reed (1998), view the regional events of the 1990s as intimately intertwined. Peter Rosenblum (1997), for one, traces the roots of the rebellions to the 1994 Rwandan genocide. Mel McNulty argues that their origins reside in the emergence of "Congolese nationalism and its campaign against Mobutu which dates back to 1965" (1999, 55). The events behind the recent instability in the region have a long history, and claiming an originary moment is often impossible and arbitrary. In this section, I provide a very brief historical overview of recent events.[2] In the next section, I focus on the discursive elements that informed, framed, and influenced these events.

What should be stressed at the outset is that Zaïre was best conceived of as a complex web of regional and local sociopolitical networks, some of which were "engaged" with the central government in Kinshasa, most of which were not. One of the elements that made the 1990s dramatically different from previous decades was the undermining of the discourses utilized by the Mobutu regime to provide legitimacy for an imagined sovereign state called "Zaïre." Many authors speak of the 1990s as a time of Zaïrian "state collapse" (Zartman 1995; Clark 1998; Villalón and Huxtable 1998). Yet, it is more illuminating to talk not of "state" collapse (for no such mythical state ever really existed) but of the alteration of discourses on "stateness" (both at the international and local levels). What occurred in the 1990s was the removal of the guise of the "sovereign state" and the exposure of the complexities of Zaïrian "realities." The complexities and contestedness of these realities became apparent after President Mobutu's 1991 decision to hold a National Conference.

One of the results of the National Conference was the ability of many local NGOs and elements of Zaïre's so-called civil society to access officially sanctioned discursive space. As scholars such as Peter Rosenblum have noted, Zaïrian civil society—the informal economy, churches, local NGOs, human rights groups, and development organizations—had long been instrumental in "mitigating the abuses of the state, mediating conflict, rendering services, and creating opportunities" (Rosenblum 1997, 202; also Collins 1997a, 278).[3] At the same time, the National Conference also exposed the numerous tensions in Zaïrian society, not the least of which stemmed from ethnicity and social identity. For example, the representatives from North and South Kivu provinces in the eastern part of the country used the National Conference as a forum to attack the Kinyarwanda speakers in the regions, referred to as Banyarwanda and Banyamulenge. The Kivu representatives sought to rescind the citizenship of these groups under the 1981 Zaïrian Nationality Act and force them to return to Rwanda and Burundi. This highlighted ongoing and complex tensions in the Great Lakes region. By 1993, armed groups began attacking Banyarwanda in North Kivu. Soon, the killings were in full swing, paralleling actions in neighboring Rwanda. By mid-1994, thousands were dead in North Kivu and thousands more had sought refuge in Rwanda and South Kivu (Prunier 1997, 195).

On April 6, 1994, a plane carrying Rwandan President Habyarimana and Burundian President Ntaryamira was shot down over the Rwandan capital of Kigali. This provided the spark for several months of killing and fighting, now commonly referred to as the 1994 Rwandan genocide.[4] The hundred-day killing spree resulted in the murder of at least 800,000 Rwandans, the overthrow of the Rwandan government by Paul Kagame's Rwandan Patriotic Front (RPF), and the exodus of over 2 million Rwandans to refugee camps inside Zaïre. These refugees were a mix of civilians, Interahamwe (the militia largely held responsible for the genocide), and members of the defeated Rwandan army (Forces Armées Rwandaises, FAR). The refugee camps quickly became controlled by the Interahamwe and FAR. Over the next two years, these groups (with the blessing of Mobutu's central government and, more importantly, regional strongmen) reorganized and rearmed. Soon, they began launching attacks from the camps into neighboring Rwanda and against the Banyamulenge in South Kivu. After their requests for assistance were ignored by the international community, the Rwandan government and local Banyamulenge decided to take matters into their own hands by attacking their attackers.

The rebellion in eastern Zaïre slowly began to take shape in August and September 1996 with the rebels launching a multiprong attack against the refugee camps, Interahamwe, and Zaïrian army (Forces Armées Zaïroises, FAZ). Orchestrated and assisted by the RPF regime in Kigali, the rebels quickly moved from south to north, gaining control of the 300 miles of Zaïre's eastern frontier and capturing the cities of Uvira on October 24, Bukavu on October 30, and Goma on November 1. The refugee camps were attacked and disassembled. An enormous human wave moved westward, made up of refugees, Interahamwe, and FAZ, all of which were fleeing from the advancing rebels. Quite unexpectedly, thousands of refugees suddenly stopped and turned around. During the week of November 10 to 17, the largest refugee repatriation in history occurred as the bulk of refugees walked back into Rwanda.[5] By this time, the rebellion had acquired a name, Alliance des Forces Démocratiques pour la Libération du Congo (AFDL), and a leader, Laurent-Désiré Kabila. Kabila was a former supporter of Lumumba and a member of the 1965 rebellion who had since survived as a small-time career rebel ensconced in the east and engaged in gold smuggling and the occasional armed attack.[6] Kabila seems to have been plucked out of relative obscurity by the Ugandan and Rwandan regimes in order to give a "Zaïrian" face to the rebellion.

Mobutu returned to Kinshasa on December 17, 1996, and tried to organize a counteroffensive in early 1997, aided by Serbian and other mercenaries. As the rebels moved westward, they were joined by other anti-Mobutists. Their external supporters included the regimes in Rwanda, Uganda, and Burundi (and some logistical support from the United States). Mobutu's counteroffensive collapsed as Kisangani fell to the rebels on March 15. By April the rebels gained control of the mineral-rich provinces of Kasai and Shaba, thus robbing Mobutu and his power elite of a major economic lifeline. As the rebels moved toward Kinshasa, Angolan government troops poured across the border to assist them in the overthrow of Mobutu, who was being aided by the

Angolan rebel group UNITA (Uniao Nacional para a Independência Total de Angola). By May 17, 1997, Kinshasa had fallen and Mobutu and his entourage had fled. Soon afterward, Kabila proclaimed himself the new president, renamed the country the Democratic Republic of the Congo (DRC), reintroduced the flag and the currency unit originally adopted at independence, banned political parties, and began to consolidate his power.

Within a year of Kabila's victory, his relationship with his regional allies, as well as the international community, had soured. Various international organization and foreign donors threatened to cut off aid and assistance because of Kabila's refusal to allow investigations into alleged human rights abuses—specifically the massacre of Rwandan refugees that had been carried out by his allies in the Rwandan army. More importantly, his relationship with the regimes in Rwanda, Uganda, and Burundi had become increasingly hostile. On August 2, 1998, a new rebellion broke out in the eastern part of the country, exactly where the original rebellion had occurred. The nominal leader of the new rebellion was Ernest Wamba-dia-Wamba, a professor on leave from the University of Dar es Salaam.[7] However, it quickly became apparent that the rebellion was being directed by the regimes in Uganda, Rwanda, and (to a lesser extent) Burundi. In the western part of the Congo, anti-Kabila forces were assisted by UNITA troops. The rebel line-up also included numerous unreformed Mobutists and disenfranchised Kabila supporters. The rebellion quickly swept through the east and by early 1999 more than a third of the country was in rebel hands.

Kabila's regime was rescued by the governments of Angola, Zimbabwe, Namibia, and, to a more limited extent, Sudan and Chad. After several months of fighting, it appeared a military solution was untenable for either side. Negotiations began, but by the summer of 1999, the rebel front had splintered into three groups backed by different foreign sponsors and fighting had broken out between the Rwandan and Ugandan contingents occupying different portions of the Congo. After complex diplomatic negotiations, a ceasefire was finally signed by most of the combatants. However, as the region entered the new millennium, foreign troops remained in the Congo and fighting continued in what appears to be a protracted war.

The Rise of Regional Voices

The big mistake of Mobutu was to involve himself in Rwanda. So it's really Mobutu who initiated the program of his own removal. Had

> he not involved himself in Rwanda, I think he could have stayed, just like that, as he had been doing for the last thirty-two years—just do nothing to develop Zaïre, but stay in what they call power, by controlling the radio station, and so on.
>
> —Ugandan President Museveni (quoted in Gourevitch 1998, 324)

The previous summary illustrates at least three points: (1) the complexity of the situation; (2) the inadequacy of a traditional state-centric approach to capture and adequately explain those events, in large part because discourses of the state and sovereignty were being redefined and reinscribed by African actors[8]; and (3) the increased discursive space available to regional (i.e., Central African) forces. While there is nothing new about African states intervening in neighboring countries, the 1990s signaled a significant shift. Not only did the influence of regional actors rise, but their discourses gained increased circulation and status within the international arena. That is to say, their interpretations of "reality" were given a degree of currency unheard of beforehand. This was due in large part to two factors. First, new technologies allowed these actors greater access to international discursive space (see Morley and Robins 1995). For example, speeches by Kabila, Wamba-dia-Wamba, and other actors were readily available on numerous Internet sites, as were regional newspapers and opinion pieces by African scholars. Satellite connections and mobile telephones allowed actors in the "bush" to conduct interviews with the international media, particularly on the British Broadcasting Corporation's (BBC) World Service programs. These technologies allowed a multiplicity of actors the opportunity to articulate and circulate their discourses and narratives of events in the region. Second, as the next section will show, increased discursive space was also provided by the United States, France, and Belgium—the so-called Western *troika* backing Mobutu—because of their changing perceptions of Central Africa. In this current section, it is impossible to discuss all the regional forces involved or provide a detailed analyses of these discursive constructions. However, I concentrate on those groups, rhetorical maneuvers, and representational practices I regard as most relevant.

Central African regional groups were engaged in producing competing discursive images of "reality" that shaped and guided their actions. For most of these forces, established (i.e., Western-imposed) discursive constructions were dismissed or redefined. This referred not only to notions of the state and sovereignty, but also to the social identities of individuals. As such, conceptions of "Zaïrian," "Congolese," "Rwandan," and so forth were reimagined. It is important to note that the social identities of the Africans living in this region become increasingly important, often to a level of life and death. As these social identities became more politicized, they also became more contested. These two developments are not, of course, unrelated.

Finally, it has been wisely suggested by several scholars that one needs to understand recent African developments through an appreciation of "the politics of borderlands" (Clapham 1999; Nugent and Asiwaju 1996). There has recently been much insightful scholarship in this direction, particularly in addressing issues of "deterritorialization" (the selective coverage of a territory by a government), the loss of governmental control and political loyalty in borderlands, and the cultural and political implication of Africa's porous borders (Bach 1995; De Boeck 1996; Davidson 1992; Richards 1996). As such, one could conceive of Central Africa as a region without "meaningful" state borders: the flow of people, weapons, goods, and resources is largely unrestricted. Yet, we need to move beyond considering only state borders and engage in examinations of other forms of boundaries (see Shapiro and Alker 1996; Barnes and Duncan 1992; Morley and Robins 1995; Pile and Keith 1997). Taking another perspective, Central Africa is a region enmeshed in a complicated web of socially constructed borders: linguistic, political, ethnic, cultural, economic, and so forth. At the end of the twentieth century, these boundaries were more important than the borders of so-called sovereign states. As such, this analysis will consider the construction and political implication of those boundaries. To a certain extent, most Central Africans live in a "borderland" where, as Clapham has noted, the two major factors are conflicting sources of authority and the unequal distribution of resources (1999, 62).

Mobutu and Zaïrian Patriotism

Mobutu had long established himself as a political survivor, in part by playing off and co-opting his opposition. When faced with the 1996 Kivu rebellion, Mobutu's regime presented a dual image of the situation. Its international response was largely informed by a traditional "state security" framework. Kinshasa claimed that the rebellion was actually an irredentist maneuver by the Museveni government in Uganda and its protégé in Rwanda (see McNulty 1999, 53). As such, Mobutu employed "sovereignty" to mean protection of Zaïre's territorial integrity. However, this was questioned by most foreign observers who held that his government was incapable of claiming authority within that territory. At home, Mobutu explicitly played the ethnicity card by portraying the conflict as one pitting "Zaïrians" against "Tutsi foreigners." As such, he was reconstructing Zaïrian identity through the exclusion of ethnically defined easterners. This reflected a long-standing utilization of "ethnicity" by the Mobutu regime to garner domestic power.[9] Throughout the 1990s, the Mobutu government had manipulated the ethnic tensions in the Great Lakes region, contributing to the outbreaks of violence and genocide. As the Bishop of Goma, Monsignor Faustin Ngabu, observed: "the authorities, which should be coming to the aid of the victims of violence, seem on the contrary to wish to feed the flames" (quoted in Evans 1997, 45–46). As Museveni's earlier quote suggested, Mobutu's exploitation of ethnic hatred eventually led to his own downfall.

It has been suggested that resistance to the Kabila rebellion was due to "Zaïrian patriotism." Yet, the situation was far more nuanced than that. The social identities at play were not foregrounded in the nation-state. Rather, they were based on the construction and maintenance of other forms of boundaries, such as linguistic and ethnic divisions. Thus, while there was clearly some resistance to Kabila and his supporters, this should not be mistaken for a defense of the Zaïrian nation-state.

Social Memories and Ethnic Divisions in the Great Lakes

There has been a long history of socially constructed ethnicity in the region, such as between "Hutu" and "Tutsi."[10] Yet, precolonial distinctions between "Hutu" and "Tutsi" were fairly blurred and porous prior to European intervention. As David Newbury observes:

> The social identities we now associate with Rwanda long preceded colonial rule, but they were not primordial; they have changed over time. In short there are histories of ethnicity, for not only has the nature of ethnic perception changed over time, but the different identities each has its own history . . . Here as elsewhere, ethnic identities are not rigid, unchanging, or universal categories. But neither are they entirely ephemeral, fluid, and individual; they are socially-produced categories, not identities freely chosen (1998, 83).

However, under Belgian colonial rule,[11] the division between the two groups became increasingly reified and politicized. The distinction was formalized in 1933–34, when the colonial government issued "ethnic" identity cards in Ruanda-Urundi. Though greatly outnumbered in both countries, the "Tutsi" elite had maintained its power for centuries (in fact, membership in that elite was a basic determinant of "Tutsi" identity). However, following the introduction of mass political participation—and with tacit Belgian support—a violent social revolution occurred in Ruanda from 1959–62, replacing the "Tutsi" political elite with a "Hutu" one. Ten years later, a "Hutu"-instigated rebellion broke out in Burundi, leaving thousands of "Tutsi" dead. The uprising failed to unseat the "Tutsi" political elite in Burundi and, in the ensuing repression that lasted from April to November 1972, between 100,000 and 200,000 "Hutu" were killed—making this the first genocide in the Great Lakes region (Lemarchand 1998a; Lemarchand 1995).

The 1972 genocide led to an increased politicization of social identities. One of its direct outcomes was the seizure of power in Rwanda by Juvenal Habyarimana and his "Hutu" extremists. In Burundi, the "Tutsi" political elite continued to retain power until democratic elections were held in 1993. The result was the election of Melchior Ndadaye, a "Hutu," to the presidency. However, Ndadaye was assassinated a few months later during a failed military coup. His murder set off a killing rampage by "Hutu," many of whom feared a replay of the 1972 genocide. Between October and November 1993, some 200,000 "Tutsi" in Burundi were murdered. The Burundian military responded by killing an equal number of "Hutu" and driving even more into Rwanda, where many became involved in the genocide of "Tutsi" the following year.

In an insightful article, René Lemarchand has pointed out how ethnically defined social memories have produced different historical myths and conceptual frameworks between the region's "Hutu" and "Tutsi" (Lemarchand 1998a). The remembrance and anticipation of genocides have served as formative elements for social cognitive maps. Lemarchand writes: "Genocide . . . leaves a profound imprint on the processes by which people write, or rewrite history, on what is being remembered and what is forgotten. What is being remembered by many Hutu is an apocalypse that has forever altered their perceptions of the Tutsi, now seen as the historical incarnation of evil" (Lemarchand 1998a, 7) and, in the wake of the 1994 Rwandan genocide, many "Tutsi" construct similar images of "Hutu." Lemarchand also notes a tendency among many "Tutsi" (and I would suggest "Hutu" as well) to substitute collective guilt for individual responsibility (Lemarchand 1998a, 8). Thus, both sides affix the label *génocidaire* to the other community collectively.[12]

The rebellions in Congo/Zaïre took place within this context: Social memories of genocide informed the perception of many actors. In 1996, the Rwandan regime of Paul Kagame defined its "reality" as such: Thousands of Hutu *génocidaires* were openly being hosted, aided, and assisted in eastern Zaïre. From the refugee camps that they controlled, these *génocidaires* (Interahamwe, FAR, and their local supporters) were engaged in attacking Tutsi in the region.[13] This perception did not rest on conceptions of social identities tied to nation-states; labels "Zaïrian" and "Rwandan" were relatively meaningless. Furthermore, traditional conceptions of sovereignty and stateness held little currency. Sovereign state borders mattered little, except in providing international protection for the *génocidaires*. Moreover, the Zaïrian "state" was virtually nonexistent in the eastern part of the country. Regional strongmen and "warlords" were the primary forms of sociopolitical power, and the majority of these had aligned themselves with the *génocidaires* in order to advance their own political agendas. Thus, within their discursive construction of "reality," it was in the RPF's interest to close the refugee camps and eradicate the *génocidaires*. As Lemarchand argues, "anticipation of genocide becomes justification for killing the potential genocidaires" (1998a, 10).

Arguments that the RPF's involvement in the Kabila rebellion was an attempt to ensure the security of the Rwandan sovereign state—or its regime—are highly misleading. If one cannot speak of a Zaïrian sovereign state in the traditional sense, then neither can one speak of a Rwandan state. The RPF's authority barely stretched beyond Kigali, the capital. Moreover, the Kagame regime was not motivated by the protection of the Rwandan population—many of whom were incarcerated or wanted for their role in the 1994 genocide. Rather, the RPF was interested in the preservation of the "Tutsi" community writ large—a community whose boundaries did not correspond to recognized state borders. Protection of "sovereignty" referred not to states but to ethnically defined communities. Tellingly, RPF troops have become known locally as *"soldats sans frontiéres"* (soldiers without borders) (Collins 1998, 112–113).

A similar discursive "reality" was constructed by the regime in Burundi. Many members of late President Ndadaye's Front Démocratique du Burundi (FRODEBU) had sought refuge in eastern Zaïre, where they joined Leonard Nyangoma's National Council for the Defense of Democracy (CNDD) and its armed wing, the Front for the Defense of Democracy (FDD). From their bases inside Zaïre, they engaged in a war of attrition against "Tutsi" in Burundi, as well as in South Kivu. The Burundi regime engaged in a project where, "by projecting the 1994 Rwanda genocide into Burundi a new version of the country's history emerges, in which one genocide is 'forgotten' (1972), and another invented (1993)" (Lemarchand 1998a, 7). Thus, the regime in Burundi joined the Rwandan regime, as well as Banyamulenge leaders in South Kivu, in producing an image of impending genocide against "Tutsi" to justify their involvement in the 1996 rebellion. To reiterate, traditional notions of the Zaïrian state were dismissed and the rhetoric of "sovereignty" and "security" was now employed with reference to the "Tutsi" community.

As already noted above, the numerous "Hutu" groups operating in eastern Zaïre (Interahamwe, FAR, FRODEBU, CNDD, and FDD) were involved in constructing their own historical myths and social memories. Drawing from the 1972 Burundi genocide and 1993 repression, these groups produced a distinctively different cognitive map, one which justified a continued armed struggle against the "historical incarnation of evil" (Lemarchand 1998a, 7). The rhetoric employed by the "Hutu" leadership before, during, and after the 1994 Rwanda genocide has received considerable attention (see Gourevitch 1998). Using the radio, printed media, and popular music, so-called "Hutu Power" resorted to the long-standing portrayal of "Tutsi" infiltrators as *"inyenzi"* (Kinyarwandan for "cockroaches") and expanding it to cover all "Tutsi" as in need of extermination. Several scholars have already noted how these discursive constructions of "Tutsi"/"Hutu" social identities were instrumental in the realization of the 1994 genocide, where average citizens became implicated in the murder of friends and neighbors. As Cyprian F. Fisiy writes: "it is worth mentioning the pivotal role played by *Radio Milles Collines* in mobilizing Hutu sentiments against the Tutsi. The Tutsi were stereotyped and dehumanized as cockroaches in broadcasts, with the effect that when they were killing Tutsi, the *Interahamwe* saw them as cockroaches, not human beings" (1998, 21). Such rhetorical constructions continued throughout 1995 and 1996, with many local Zaïrian groups joining in.

The events of 1996 also illustrate the complex forces involved in identity formation and the role of mass communication in that process. For example, the social identities of the refugees based in Zaïre were shaped by at least three different forces. Given Western conceptions of refugees, the international humanitarian community treated these individuals as victims, regardless of their role in the 1994 genocide. At the same time, the Interahamwe and FAR who controlled the camps and used the refugees as human shields reinforced (and enforced) a "Hutu" identity tied to the violent repression of the "Tutsi" Other. Furthermore, because many "Tutsi" ascribed collective guilt rather than individual responsibility, the refugees' flight from Rwanda was read as evidence of their guilt and, thus, their identity as *génocidaires*. Fisiy notes the important role played by the international media in "homogenizing" cultural identity: "People who were seen crossing over to Goma or to Bukavu (in what was then called Zaïre) were all seen as

Hutu who were collectively responsible for genocide. They automatically acquired a Hutu identity even if they were not all Hutu" (Fisiy 1998, 18).

Thus, the "reality" imagined by these forces was not grounded in Western discourses of national identity, the state, or sovereignty. These regional discourses were spatially and temporally different from those produced by Western forces over the past hundred years. Yet, it is important to recognize the contexts in which these discourses were being produced, lest one fall prey to deterministic assumptions about "ethnic hatred" being universal, apolitical, and ahistoric. Such readings of these discourses are untenable and highly misleading. On the one hand, these discourses are neither irrational or apolitical; quite the contrary. As Fisiy notes, the "centrality of social memory lies in the ability of political entrepreneurs to manipulate it in the construction of a collective identity to support their own agendas" (1998, 20; see also Lemarchand 1994). Furthermore, we need to return to the recognition of violence as a discourse, mentioned in previous chapters. When alternative outlets are closed off, some individuals seek expression through bloodshed. Violence can be seen as a tool in the authoring and policing of socially constructed identities and memories, particularly for the dispossessed. With reference to the Great Lakes region, Lemarchand notes: "With the growing polarization of ethnic feelings, extremists at both ends of the spectrum . . . make their voices heard, most of the time violently" (1998a, 10).

Ridding the Region of Mobutu

The motivations of the Museveni regime in Uganda were quite different than those in Burundi or Rwanda, though the end result was similar. Prior to the 1996–97 rebellion, Museveni had a relatively hostile relationship with the Zaïrian government. This was largely due to Mobutu's inability and possible unwillingness to suppress rebel groups attempting to overthrow Museveni.[14] For his part, Museveni was involved in destabilizing the government of the Sudan. He was doing this by supporting the southern Sudanese rebel movement (the Sudan People's Liberation Army, SPLA), which was headed by his former schoolmate John Garang. For that reason, the Sudanese regime in Khartoum had joined other Zaïrian local strongmen in supporting to varying degrees the Lord's Resistance Movement, the West Nile Bank Front, and the Allied Democratic Front—three armed groups battling Museveni's regime from bases outside of Uganda.

Museveni's involvement in the 1996–97 rebellion was motivated by several considerations. The first was preservation of his regime's security. By aiding Kabila's AFDL rebels in Zaïre, he hoped to clear the area of bases utilized by the Ugandan rebels, especially the Allied Democratic Front. Supporting the AFDL in their drive to Kinshasa would also remove Mobutu, a continuing thorn in his side. Museveni, like the leaders in Rwanda and Burundi, hoped that a central government headed by their ally Kabila would prove to be more friendly and capable of exerting control in the eastern part of the country. At the very least, they hoped Kabila would be willing to look the other way while they were doing the job themselves. Finally, by actively supporting Kabila, Museveni was also increasing Uganda's regional hegemony and his own status as an African leader. Indeed, the rise of Uganda and Museveni in regional affairs was greatly resented by Mobutu, whose own importance had largely faded in the aftermath of the cold war.[15]

The MPLA (Movimento Popular de Libertação de Angola) government in Angola also harbored long-standing resentment of Mobutu. Not only had Zaïre (backed by the United States and apartheid South Africa) invaded Angola in the 1970s, but the Mobutu regime had continued to provide invaluable assistance to the UNITA rebel group, even after the end of the cold war. Over the years, UNITA had established itself as a "shadow state" whose existence greatly relied on Mobutu's support and on Zaïre as a conduit for arms and the smuggled diamonds used to bankroll its war (see De Boeck 1996; Malaquias 2000; Hawthorne 1999). With Kabila's forces rapidly moving westward, the MPLA regime saw an opportunity to rid themselves of Mobutu and strike a (hopefully) fatal blow against UNITA's base and supply lines inside Zaïre. As Kabila moved closer to Kinshasa, MPLA troops poured across the border and aided in the final capture of the capital.

In the case of the Ugandan and Angolan regimes, little concern was given to notions of Zaïre's sovereignty and territorial integrity. The political space of the region was conceived as concentric circles of diminishing political control—for example, as MPLA space, UNITA space, Museveni's space, Mobutu's space, and so forth. These cognitive "maps"—reflecting the political complexities and contradictions on the ground—framed the actors' conceptions of "reality" far more than established state boundaries. Moreover, the identities of the people on the ground were much less defined in terms of "Zaïrian," "Angolan," or "Ugandan" than by other social divisions, such as language and ethnicity. Events in the 1990s merely brought these African cognitive maps to the forefront of international relations, challenging those maintained in Western capitals. In fact, some observers assumed that the events unfolding in Central Africa would lead to a redrawing of the map of Africa (Clapham 1999; Makau wa Mutua 1994). Yet, this cartographic change did not (and probably will not) come to pass precisely because the existing state borders have long been regarded less as barriers than as conduits and sources of opportunities.

In an interesting but not wholly surprising development, South African interests became involved in the 1996–97 rebellion. At one level, the government of Nelson Mandela sought a diplomatic settlement to the rebellion, with Mandela playing a personal role in the negotiations. Mandela's involvement reflected his own self-defined role as regional statesman. Yet, Mandela's government was also motivated by domestic concerns, mainly the interest of the South African business community. For, at another level, South African diamond mining companies were deeply involved in Zaïrian politics. DeBeers had long dominated diamond purchasing in Zaïre under Mobutu (Collins 1997b, 593). When, as Edouard Bustin puts it, "the moribund Mobutu regime, in its desperate need for ready cash, seemed ready to sacrifice all national assets," South African mining ventures increased their interest in the mineral resources of southern Zaïre (Bustin 1999, 84–85). Though many of these mines had virtually collapsed in the closing years of Mobutu's reign, South African companies viewed them as "salvageable"—building on the long-held vision of wealth derived from Zaïre's untapped resources. When it became apparent that Mobutu's army would be ineffective in protecting the mines from Kabila's rebels, these same South African (and other multinational) mining groups quickly moved to cut deals with the AFDL (see Reno 1998a; Gray 1998). Who controlled the region was a far greater concern than who occupied the statehouse in Kinshasa.

Kabila and a New Congolese Identity?

As the AFDL swept across the country, regional strongmen had to decide whether to back their distant patron in Kinshasa or throw their support behind Kabila. Responses varied, but what became most evident was the ineffectiveness (and often unwillingness) of the Zaïrian army to combat Kabila. For his own part, Kabila was generally distrustful of those leaders who had "supped at the devil's [Mobutu's] table." Casting himself as a Congolese "revolutionary," Kabila claimed to be "liberating" the country from Mobutu. Even before assuming power, Kabila's articulation of a new Congolese identity was grounded in the construction of a shared social memory: the suffering of the "people" under Mobutu's neocolonial rule. He drew particular attention to the role of Mobutu's international backers (United States, France, and Belgium) and foreign economic interests. After coming to power, Kabila proclaimed: "We created the AFDL as a movement for the liberation of our country, which was ruled by an 'anti-people state,' a state whose essential task was to defend foreign interests and to keep the exploited Congolese populations down so that those foreign interests could bleed the Congo white" (Kabila 1999). Grounding his construction of a new Congolese identity in the rhetoric of nationalism, Kabila's regime sought to revive, redefine, and appropriate the memories and images of Patrice Lumumba, Pierre Mulele, and other "revolutionaries" (see Kabila 1998).

Yet, Kabila's popularity was limited by his refusal to deal with established opposition and civil society groups, his banning of political parties, his appointment of several ex-Mobutists (most notably Dominique Sakombi Inongo, a key architect of *authenticité*),[16] and his perceived heavy reliance on Rwandans and Banyamulenge. Kabila soon took steps to distance himself from his eastern backers and combat his image as a "Rwandan puppet." A few months after his victory, Kabila began to replace his Rwandan advisers and the Banyamulenge in his cabinet. This move exacerbated tensions between himself and his erstwhile sponsors. As these tensions grew, Kabila proved himself increasingly willing to exploit anti-Rwandan and anti-"Tutsi" sentiment within the Congo.

By mid-1998, it had become apparent that Kabila had established close links with the Interahamwe and FAR militia still operating in the Congo. Echoing the radio broadcast in Rwanda that preceded the 1994 genocide, Kabila urged listeners of the Congolese state radio to use "a machete, a spear, an arrow, a hoe, spades, rakes, nails, truncheons, electric irons, barbed wire . . . to kill the Rwandan Tutsi" (*Financial Times*, 1 September 1998; *The Guardian*, 31 August 1998; reprinted in *World Press Review*, November 1998, 14–16). The result was a witch hunt against all eastern Congolese and perceived foreigners, often judged exclusively by facial appearances (McNulty 1999, 55; Bednarek 1999, 38–41; *Le Monde*, 6 August 1998, 2; 7 August 1998, 4; and 28 August 1998). Thus, Kabila's construction of a "Congolese" identity moved beyond the promotion of shared social memories to one of shared ethnic hostilities. This move was to have important repercussions.

If at First You Don't Succeed . . .

The Kabila government had failed to achieve its anticipated goal of bringing security to the eastern part of the country. More importantly, Kabila denied the Rwandan and Ugandan regimes the latitude to create the kind of security zone they wanted. This was partly because Kabila's power was relatively limited to the area around Kinshasa and the mineral-rich regions in the south. Power and authority in the east remained fragmented and diffused. The rebel groups attacking the regimes of Uganda, Rwanda, and Burundi had not been completely wiped away. Ironically, the 1996–97 rebellion had succeeded in driving many of these armed groups *into* those countries, heightening the levels of violence and insecurity. Viewing their erstwhile ally as ineffective and increasingly hostile, the regimes in Rwanda, Burundi, and Uganda decided to directly intervene in the Congo again.

Though Kagame's regime in Rwanda initially denied any involvement, it was the primary force behind Wamba-dia-Wamba's Rassemblement Congolais pour la Démocratie (RCD). Its motivations—and those of the Burundi regime—were similar to their motivations in 1996. Both regimes imagined the spatial dimensions of Central Africa primarily in terms of ethnic divisions rather than sovereign state delineations. Facing increased attacks by Interahamwe, FAR, and FDD, as well as the growing hostility of the Kabila regime to "Tutsi" (loosely defined), the regimes of Burundi and Rwanda produced a perception of imminent genocide, drawing on the social memories and imagery of 1994. Such discursive constructions provided the justification for aiding Wamba-dia-Wamba's RCD. At the same time, the regimes sought to rhetorically construct an image of Kabila as a neo-Mobutu. This served the purpose of portraying the rebellion as a "domestic" affair.

A similar situation existed for the Ugandan regime. The initial intervention had merely shifted the rebel bases into Uganda itself. Moreover, the Kabila government was unable to extend its control over the northeastern section of the Congo, where regional leaders continued to provide support for Ugandan rebels, particularly the Allied Democratic Front. Worse, it soon became evident that the Kabila regime had established significant links with the Sudanese government in Khartoum, with whom the Museveni regime had been engaged in a mutual war of attrition. Following Kagame's lead, the Museveni government intervened on behalf of Wamba-dia-Wamba's RCD. The policy of intervention was sweetened for the Museveni regime by prospects of tapping into, if not controlling, resources in northeastern Congo, from gold mining to the smuggling of coffee, timber, and minerals (*New Vision,* 18 April 1999, 14 December 1998, and 18 December 1998; *Africa Confidential,* 20 November 1998).

However, by late 1998, the anti-Kabila rebellion began to fragment. In November, a new group (Mouvement pour la Libération du Congo, MLC) headed by businessman Jean Pierre Bemba surfaced in the Equateur province of northeastern Congo. Since this was an area controlled by the Ugandan army (Ugandan People's Defence Forces, UPDF), it has been generally assumed that the Museveni regime is Bemba's primary supporter.[17] In April 1999, the RCD split into two with Wamba-dia-Wamba leading a splinter faction in Kisangani (also the headquarters of the UPDF) and Emile Ilunga leading the Goma group. The division within the RCD reflected a growing rift between the Museveni and Kagame regimes, with the former supporting Bemba and Wamba-dia-Wamba and the latter Ilunga. Reviewing the rhetoric available, it appears that the break between Museveni and Kagame was primarily motivated by the desire of each to play the role of regional hegemon as well as to exploit the mineral resources of occupied eastern Congo (*Africa Confidential*, 10 September 1999; Braeckman 1999).

The anti-Kabila rebellion was also supported by UNITA, which sought to restore the privileges it had enjoyed under Mobutu. Though the Kabila government had failed to both drive UNITA out of the Congo and effectively cut off its access to resources, the MPLA regime in Luanda decided that its interests would best be served by maintaining Kabila in power. Thus, when the anti-Kabila rebellion broke out and a western front briefly opened up as rebels threatened to take Kinshasa, the MPLA responding by sending in troops to shore up Kabila's regime.

The biggest and most important defender of the Kabila regime turned out to be the Mugabe government in non-neighboring Zimbabwe. Rhetorically, Mugabe has justified his support for the Kabila government in the principles of the Southern African Development Community (of which the "new" Congo had become a member, while Mobutu's Zaïre had consistently been denied admission), a view also reiterated by the MPLA regime in Angola and the governments of Namibia and South Africa. This was an interesting development in that the principles of state sovereignty were being defended by an organization aimed primarily at regional economic integration.

Highly unpopular at home—the casualty figures are a state secret and the cost is estimated to be around U.S. $1 million a day—Mugabe's intervention appears to be motivated by many factors. Rebel leader Wamba-dia-Wamba has referred to Mugabe's interest in the Congo as "basically a mercantilist intervention" (Wamba-dia-Wamba 1999, 14). This economic enrichment appears to solely benefit the ruling elite. By late 1998, it was revealed that members of Mugabe's ruling party, top military officers, and member's of the president's own family had lucrative contracts with the Kabila government (*Economist*, 7 November 1998, 46; Block 1998, A1; *MRB*, February 1999, 1–5; *Le Monde*, 13 January 1999; *Africa Confidential*, 20 November 1998). Yet, prestige and hegemonic aspirations also appear to play an important role. On one level, Mugabe has used the situation to promote himself as a regional leader, pushing South Africa's Nelson Mandela into the background. On a more interesting level, Mugabe has rhetorically constructed Kagame and Rwanda as small-time players who have overstepped their boundaries. In heavily gendered language, Mugabe has justified his intervention by claiming that Zimbabwe could not let "little" Rwanda push it around: "Do they think a country as vast as the [Congo] could ever be subject to the wiles and guiles of little Rwanda, or even Uganda? It's absolutely stupid" (Barrell and Wetherell, 16 October 1998).[18]

For their part, the rebels rhetorically constructed an image of Kabila as "Mobutu redux" to justify their actions. In interviews and press releases, both Wamba-dia-Wamba and Bemba portrayed Kabila as a repressive dictator, explicitly drawing parallels between him and Mobutu (Wamba-dia-Wamba 1999; *The Monitor*, 26 August 1998; *The East African*, 19 July 1999). While this rhetorical maneuver was echoed by certain elements in the international press, the sanctimoniousness of the rebel groups was compromised by the inclusion of many unreformed Mobutists. For this and other reasons, the anti-Kabila rebellion appeared to have relatively little popular support in the Congo. Some have credited this to Congolese nationalism (Braeckman 1999; Mamdani 1998). As one observer noted, "The sense of Congolese patriotism or aggrieved national pride triggered by the rebellion and its perception as a foreign invasion was surprisingly strong" (Bustin 1999, 90). However, this "new" Congolese identity was grounded primarily in xenophobia, ethnic exclusion, and renewed internal regionalism. As the primary author of that identity, Kabila appeared content in using ethnicity as an instrument of political mobilization for his regime's survival, souring any tentative sense of populist nationalism that may have emerged in the last few decades. This exclusionary rhetoric, and the fact that the three rebel leaders (Bemba, Wamba-dia-Wamba, and Ilunga) all pledged to respect the Congo's "territorial integrity," illustrates the complexities and contradictions at play in the construction of a "new" Congolese identity.

The *Troika* Looks On

> [A]n alarming number of Western commentators took cynical solace in the conviction that this state of affairs was about as authentic as Africa gets. Leave the natives to their own devices, the thinking went, and—Voilà!—Zaïre. It is almost as if we wanted Zaïre to be the

> *Heart of Darkness;* perhaps the notion suited our understanding of
> the natural order of nations.
>
> —Philip Gourevitch (1998, 284)

> The situation in the Great Lakes region not only shocks the
> conscience. It also defies intelligence.
>
> —Sennen Andriamirando in *Jeune Afrique* (20 November 1996, 22)

The discourses produced by actors in Central Africa became more pronounced in the 1990s, shaping regional political dynamics to a tremendous extent. Indeed, many commentators proclaimed that Africans were solving African problems without the meddling of outside interference (the point that many of those commentators were from the West was enough to make one suspicion of such claims). But the question remains: Why, after decades of Western interference in Congolese affairs, did the *troika*—the United States, France, and Belgium—*appear* to spend the 1990s on the sidelines? There seems to be two related answers. First, the end of the cold war saw a change in Western discourses of intervention that influenced their policies toward Africa in general. Second, and more importantly, this rise of regional influence was facilitated by a reimagining of the Congo/Central Africa in which discursive space was open to these regional voices.

Political economist Chris Allen (1997) has noted that Western interest in postcolonial Africa had three principal goals. The first concerned the protection of cold war geostrategic interests. The second goal consisted of exercising control over the nature and development of African economies. The third goal was based in self-defined "national interests" of Western powers. In the case of France, its governments had long sought to establish a *chasse gardée* (private estate) in postcolonial Africa. This *chasse gardée* provided these governments with an arena to act as a global power. Since 1975, Paris actively incorporated the former Belgian colonies into that sphere of influence (see Trefon 1989; Bach 1986; Smith and Glaser 1992; Marchal 1998). Central Africa became a space into which France projected its own self-identity through the performance of its diplomatic, economic, and military strength.

The end of the cold war, however, significantly altered the West's relationship with Africa. With the 1989 collapse of the Soviet Union, the Western powers lost one of the key elements of its African policy: the containment of Communism. Indeed, after the MPLA held democratic elections in Angola, that regime shed its pariah status with

Washington, thus depriving Mobutu of his trump card. Furthermore, with the fall of Communism, Western business interests became more focused on Eastern Europe and the former Soviet Union. In the case of Africa, economic control was increasingly achieved through international financial institutions (IFIs), such as the World Bank and the IMF.

As Allen notes, "The discourse of intervention has changed too, concealing older goals behind assertions of the need to promote democracy and human rights, and to secure humanitarian goals" (1997, 166). In the early 1990s, this meant that increased pressure was placed on the Mobutu regime to "democratize" and clean up its dismal human rights record. Though Mobutu's staging of the National Conference did provide the regime with some leeway, his obvious manipulation of the National Conference increased the ire of his backers, primarily the United States and Belgium. Despite his flaunting of the "democratization" process and increased human rights abuses, the *troika* was unwilling to impose multilateral sanctions on Mobutu. What is more, the 1994 Rwandan genocide—a humanitarian crisis virtually ignored by the West—provided Mobutu with a golden opportunity. Now hosting over a million refugees, Mobutu exploited the West's new rhetorical focus on "humanitarian" issues (as well as its guilt for inaction during the genocide) to provide himself with increased maneuvering space and regional power (Reno 1997, Reed 1999). However, when those same refugees provided the impetus for the 1996–97 rebellion, Mobutu found himself with little to no support from his former Western backers. What happened?

On the one hand, the dominant discourses of state sovereignty had also changed in the 1990s. As Allen notes, the achievement of humanitarian goals meant that state sovereignty, "once a convenient cornerstone for ignoring human rights abuses on the part of cold war allies, is now—no less conveniently—ignored" (Allen 1997, 166). By 1996, Belgian and American governments had adopted the perception that Mobutu was the cause of, not the solution for, most of the humanitarian problems in the region. Zaïre's sovereignty was rhetorically (re)defined and ignored, much like Yugoslavia's sovereignty was during the 1999 NATO war over Kosovo. In the case of Zaïre, the (re)defining and (re)inscribing of its state sovereignty had already begun before the 1996–97 rebellion. As illustrated at the end of the previous chapter, African states were increasingly seen as subpar states, lacking in the attributes (and thus the prerogatives) of Western stateness. Western notions of sovereignty, autonomy, and territorial integrity were seen as being less relevant to Africa, and therefore less of a diplomatic concern in discussions of intervention. Thus, actors in the West were less inclined to come to the defense of the Zaïrian "state" or its "sovereignty" because both of those concepts had become highly suspect within Western discourses.

Yet, this provides only part of the picture. Western powers had altered their perceptions of Zaïre (and Central Africa) during the 1990s. These (re)imaginings provided different discursive frameworks by which each of the three governments pursued similar policies of relative inaction during the 1994 genocide, the 1996–97 rebellion, and the current anti-Kabila war. On the one hand, these discursive shifts enabled regional actors greater space in which to voice their own discourses. On the other hand, however, this multiplicity of voices reinforced the perception of the region as inherently chaotic, a cacophony of unintelligible and incomprehensible discourses.

France

Of the three Western powers, France remained the friendliest to the Mobutu regime during the 1990s. While the Belgian and U.S. governments moved to isolate the Mobutu regime, the French government remained its most important international supporter—even after French Ambassador Philippe Bernard was killed in January 1993 when Mobutu's troops strafed the embassy. Yet, France had few investments in Zaïre and French trade was far behind that of Belgium and the United States. At $71 million in 1996, French trade with Zaïre was a third of its 1990 level (Huliaras 1998, 604; Buchan 1997). Their support for Mobutu—and the Habyarimana regime in Rwanda—was intimately tied to their desire to maintain their *chasse gardée* in Central Africa. The "loss" of either regime was seen as a blow to France's self-image as a global player.

As the international community belatedly recognized the scope of the genocide in Rwanda, the French government took the lead in proposing an interventionary force. Stonewalled by the U.S. and Belgian governments, France finally acted unilaterally, sending in troops under Opération Turquoise in June 1994. The intervention in Rwanda fulfilled the French-drafted UN mandate of stopping the genocide, protecting refugees, and laying the groundwork for a future UN presence.

However, France was increasingly seen as complicit in the genocide, given its established support of "Hutu Power" and training of the Interahamwe (Evans 1997; Gourevitch 1998; McNulty 1997). In fact, Opération Turquoise was an attempt to stall an RPF victory and protect the retreat of the former Rwandan government, its army, and the Interahamwe. Accordingly, the regional and international reputation of France was severely damaged. As McNulty notes, "*Opération Turquoise* discredited France as a force for any form of regional peacemaking to the extent that, when faced in late 1996 with a rebellion in Kivu province which would escalate to threaten Zaïre itself, no further intervention was possible" (McNulty 1999, 71).

As Kabila's rebellion gathered strength, the French government demanded that Mobutu's regime be salvaged. Employing the "Mobutu or chaos" theme, Paris argued that Mobutu was the only leader that could "save Zairians from themselves and the inevitable ethnic bloodbath that would follow" (McNulty 1999, 73). France's Foreign Minister, Hervé de Charette, claimed that Mobutu was "undoubtedly the only person capable of contributing to the solution of the problem" (quoted in Huliaras 1998, 596). However, France's legitimacy within the region and the international community had already been severely compromised. It had lost the discursive authority it had once enjoyed. Despite the will to intervene, France's past record and damaged reputation meant that its hands were tied. Even the French press openly questioned the government's humanitarian motives and viewed Mobutu as a lost cause (*Libération,* 14 March 1997; *Le Monde,* 19 March 1997)

In the late 1990s, the major French discursive maneuver was its portrayal of the Kabila-led rebellion as part of an "Anglo-Saxon" conspiracy. The French government and many French newspapers argued that the United States and its proxies in Uganda and Rwanda were attempting to spread their hegemony into France's former *chasse gardée* (Huliaras 1998; Prunier 1995; see also *Jeune Afrique,* 20 November 1996, 18–25 and 16 December 1997; *Le Monde,* 11 February 1997; *Newsweek,* 2 December 1996, 46; and 12 May 1997, 40–41).[19] As Jean-Claude Willame has noted: "France's behavior and its 'reading' of Zaïrian evolution was based less on actual dynamics than on France's obsession with the supposed American ambition to supplant French influence" (Willame 1998, 27).

France's image of events in Central Africa was largely shaped by this "Fashoda syndrome,"[20] with the region depicted as "a cultural, political and economic battlefield between France and the Anglo-Saxons" (Prunier 1995, 104–8; Huliaras 1998; Evans 1997, 63–64).[21] However, after Kabila's victory, French policy toward Africa began to change significantly. The new socialist government moved to reduce its military and economic commitments in Africa and began to downsize the Ministry of Cooperation, traditionally the center of France's African policy. In February 1998, Prime Minister Lionel Jospin announced the dismantling of the ministry and its incorporation into the Foreign Ministry. The scholar Asteris Huliaras has observed that, at the end of the twentieth century, "French foreign policy is in an era of transition, in search of a new identity, in quest of a new role in the post-bipolar world" (1998, 609; see also R. Marchal 1998).

Belgium

By the early 1990s, the Belgian government had already distanced itself from Mobutu's regime.[22] In fact, Belgian society became increasingly focused on its own domestic concerns, further marginalizing its interest in its former African colonies. Evidence of this waning interest came on April 10, 1994, when the government decided to withdraw its troops from the UN force in Rwanda. This action has been seen by many as a major factor in the realization of the genocide there. It is argued that, had the Belgian troops remained, the genocide may have been averted. In the wake of the Rwandan genocide, Belgian society reflected on its own complicity with a mixture of silence and polarizing introspection (Willame 1998, 27; Verwimp and Vanheusden 1999).

Memories of the Rwandan genocide informed the way Belgians viewed the 1996 rebellion in Zaïre. An official government investigation on Belgium's role in Rwanda was undertaken and facts were slowly revealed to the media in mid-1996, just as the Kivu rebellion began. In the aftermath of the Rwandan crisis, the Belgian prime minister announced that the country would never again send troops to its former colonies. Thus, as the rebellion swept across Zaïre, the Belgian government was generally without the will or confidence to intervene on Mobutu's behalf. Competition between personalities and departments also fueled a policy of inaction (Verwimp and Vanheusden 1999). After over a hundred years of intervention, Belgium had virtually removed itself from being an external player in Central Africa. Much of this had to do with a crisis of confidence and Belgium's perceptions of Mobutu (as highly corrupt and embarrassing) and Central Africa (as inherently chaotic).

United States

Most scholars on U.S. foreign policy toward Africa argue that it is largely reactive, driven by responses to crises rather than coherent long-term strategies (Schraeder 1994; Clapham 1996, 134–142). For decades, Western media presented Africa almost exclusively through stories of famine, drought, military coups, and "tribal" violence. In the early 1990s, Americans rediscovered Africa as images of the humanitarian crisis in Somalia (a former cold war ally) filled their television screens. In response, President George Bush authorized the use of military force to protect the delivery of humanitarian aid in that country. However, in September 1993, Somali militia downed a U.S. helicopter and the bodies of the dead soldiers were dragged through the streets of Mogadishu. The event and corresponding images horrified the American public, souring it on its new-found enthusiasm for humanitarian intervention. Rhetorically, the "lessons" of that failure appeared to be that African problems were just too complex, intractable, and/or irrational to comprehend. As Gourevitch notes, "a stubborn misconception . . . had dominated Western attitudes toward post–Cold War Africa—that Africans generate humanitarian catastrophes but don't really make meaningful politics" (Gourevitch 1998, 326).

When world attention finally turned to the genocide underway in Rwanda the following year, American perceptions were heavily influenced by the memory of their so-called failure in Somalia. The U.S. press presented it as yet another case of Africa's inherent savagery that was beyond rational understanding. On November 14, 1996, as media reports from eastern Zaïre raised fears of another genocide, the Clinton administration belatedly gave its approval to UN Resolution 1080, authorizing a multinational force to intervene on behalf of the refugees. Hours after the announcement, Kabila's Rwandan allies attacked the largest refugee camp at Mugunga, provoking a mass repatriation of refugees. The U.S. government and the international community breathed a collective sigh of relief as they tabled their plans to intervene.

As late as 1993, the U.S. government's discourse on Zaïre still reflected the "Mobutu or chaos" mentality. According to an interagency memo, the government was concerned about Zaïre's role as the "linchpin of regional stability" and as a source of strategic mineral wealth (quoted in Collins 1997a, 284). By the outbreak of the Kabila rebellion, however, Washington was less committed to protecting its long-time cold war ally. In a telling statement, the U.S. ambassador to Zaïre stated in December 1996 that the Mobutu government was "a decadent regime sustained by France" (*Le Monde*, 5 December 1996; quoted in Huliaras 1998, 596). This was an interesting rhetorical maneuver, for it erased the United States' own complicity in sustaining Mobutu and put the onus on Paris. In fact, many read the U.S. government's initial silence about the rebellion as implicit support. It was not until early 1997 that the U.S. ambassador to Kinshasa publicly denounced the rebellion as a foreign invasion. Many of the government's mixed signals can be credited to divisions within the State Department, namely between the embassies in Kinshasa and Kigali (Rosenblum 1997, 205; Collins 1997a, 284–285).

As Kabila's rebels swept across Zaïre, the U.S. government's rhetoric was grounded in the dual issues of democratization and human rights—reflecting its new "discourse of intervention" (Allen 1997). In a February 1997 statement before a House Subcommittee, Secretary of State Madeline Albright asserted that U.S. interests in Zaïre were "to encourage a halt to factional violence, ensure respect for human rights, and create stability based on democratic principles throughout the country" (Albright 1997a, 13). Promoting a negotiated settlement, the Clinton administration made a half-hearted, last-minute attempt to salvage the Mobutu regime. Once Kabila seized power, the U.S. government increasingly called for assurances that the new regime would quickly democratize—and establish an open market economy (Albright 1997b, 1998a, and 1998b; Richardson 1997). Moreover, much attention was paid to suspected human rights violations by Kabila's forces during the war (see Human Rights Watch 1997). Protecting his RPF backers, Kabila refused to allow a foreign investigation to look into these accusations, thus spoiling what little credit he had amassed among Western leaders for toppling Mobutu. In the first year of Kabila's reign, the U.S. government—and other international actors—withheld support to the new government and threatened to suspend aid and debt relief until Kabila addressed these humanitarian and democratization issues. This was in direct opposition to the tack taken with the previous regime, where the *troika* had turned a blind eye to Mobutu's abuse for decades. This new approach probably had more to do with a shift in the "discourse of intervention," an attempt to make up for past ills, and a desire to restore the self-image of the United States as protector of human rights than a concerted attempt to unseat Kabila.[23]

Thus, the Clinton administration's responses to the Great Lakes crises were influenced by both a post-Somalia shift away from seeing the United States as full-time "world's policeman" and the post–cold war shift toward the rhetoric of democratization and human rights. However, this only partly explains U.S. (in)action, particularly when contrasted to its intervention in Haiti and Kosovo in the following years. Why intervene there, but not in Zaïre/Congo? The answer has much to do with American popular perceptions of that country. In his discussion of the Great Lakes crises, historian David Newbury observed: "This is a region not well known in the west, but one nonetheless enveloped in a century of powerful imagery—ranging from the 'Heart of Darkness' to the 'Noble Savage.' In other words, it is an area that outsiders feel they 'know' well" (Newbury 1998, 76). What was "known" was that Zaïre/Congo was a land of AIDS, the Ebola virus, inherent savagery, and barbarism, an apolitical chaos beyond the rational comprehension of the "civilized" West.

This (re)constructed trope has become known as the "New Barbarism" thesis and has been applied to numerous African contexts, including Sierra Leone and Liberia. The basic tenet of this thesis is that Africa is an inherently wild and dangerous place, plagued by politically meaningless violence brought about by culture and the environment (Richards 1996, xiii-xv). One of the foremost proponents of this perspective has been Robert Kaplan, particularly in his 1994 *Atlantic Monthly* article "The Coming Anarchy." Kaplan paints a picture of the world going to hell in a hand basket, often using Africa as his "evidence." The continent, he suggests, is undergoing a breakdown of its social fabric because, well, it is Africa. If his subtly racist stance is missed in his article, it is clearer in his follow-up book, where he proclaims that Africa is sliding back to the "dawn" of time. In one memorable passage, Kaplan asserts that "Africa's geography was conducive to humanity's emergence, [but] it may not have been conducive to its further development" (1996, 7). In the rhetoric of "New Barbarism," Africa simply can not sustain basic elements of civilization. What should the U.S. response be? "Insulation rather than intervention is the rational response of the major powers" (Richards 1996, xiv).

Western, particularly American, responses to the events in Zaïre and the Great Lakes were largely informed by this trope. Throughout the 1990s, media coverage was steeped in the language of "New Barbarism"—employing the rhetoric of "chaos," tribalism, and irrational African violence (*Time*, 25 November 1996, 24 March 1997, and 12 May 1997; *Newsweek*, 2 December 1996, 31 March 1997, 21 April 1997, and 12 May 1997; *Economist*, 8 July 1995, 15 February 1997, 24 May 1997). Zaïre was represented as wallowing in the "law of the jungle" (*New York Times*, 17 March 1997). There was a clear attempt to conjure up images of a society that had reverted to a prehistorical condition. This appears literally as an image of Zaïre—and Africa—going "down the drain" (see figure 5.1). In an extremely telling example, *Newsweek* greeted the collapse of Mobutu's regime with a headline lifted directly from Conrad's *Heart of Darkness*: "The Horror, The Horror" (31 March 1997).

This rhetoric performed the important function of erasing past interventions and actions by Western powers in Congolese affairs. The "New Barbarism" trope "explained" the situation in Central Africa in terms of a Congolese identity that is presented as fixed, static, and ahistoric. This maneuver effectively erased American/Western involvement in the creation of the colonially imposed state, the erasure and degradation of African sociopolitical beliefs and practices, the scuttling of its democratic institutions at the time of independence, and the imposition and administration of a dictator for over thirty years. All of these historical events were obscured by essentializing a savage Congolese identity and a mythical "law of the jungle."

At the same time, the familiar vision of the Congo as an untapped source of wealth gained renewed currency. Secretary Albright spoke of "unlocking the Congo's vast potential" (Albright 1998a, 2; see also Albright 1997b, 10; and 1998b). *Newsweek* proclaimed: "The new Zaïre offers a bonanza to US investors" (*Newsweek*, 12 May 1997, 41). Foreign gold and diamond mining corporations, especially American Mineral Fields Incorporated (AMF), engaged in what some saw as another "scramble" for Congo's wealth (Reno 1998a; Collins 1998; French 1997; McKinley 1997). As one observer wryly commented, war made good business sense for the mining corporations (Gray 1998).

Thus, employment of the "New Barbarism" discourse allowed for political "isolation" on the part of the West, with maintenance of its economic extraction of Congolese resources. This isolationist stance effectively opened up discursive space for regional voices. Western media and government officials heralded the use of "African solutions" in solving "Africa's problems." It appears that Western confidence in its past authorship had been shaken. More to the point, it had lost its confidence in its ability to "civilize" and "develop" Africa. At the heart of the "New Barbarism" perspective was the image of an Africa too inherently savage and backward to progress toward "modernity." It was, to a certain extent, a renunciation of the "civilizing mission"— "You Africans are beyond hope; we give up." It also signaled a shift to the "privatization" of Western policies toward Africa, in which intervention is now being left (or subcontracted) to private sector agencies such as mining interests, "security" providers and consultants, NGOs, and so forth.

The Rhetoric of "Africa War One"

The Western *troika* seemed to greet the anti-Kabila rebellion with moderated inaction. This can partly be explained by examining the ways in which the war was (and continues to be) discursively constructed in the West. In general, there appear to be three basic themes. First, there was an interesting move to label the war "Africa War One"—an allusion to Europe's own "World" War I. Second, many observers regarded the war as illustrative that Africa was going "back

Figure 5.1: Africa going down the drain
Source: Bado, *Le Droit*, Ottawa, Canada, November 1996.

to the future." Finally, the events were portrayed as further evidence of the "New Barbarism" thesis.

The label "Africa War One" is often used to capture the war's complexity and regional scope (see *New York Times*, 6 February 2000, 1, 8–9). To date, the war has involved actors from Angola, Zimbabwe, South Africa, Congo-Brazzaville, Chad, Namibia, Sudan, Burundi, Rwanda, and Uganda. While it is a misnomer to call this conflict the first multistate war in Africa, allusions to World War I are problematic for other reasons.

Analyses based on this "Africa War One" trope tend to be highly state-centric, focusing on the *realpolitik* that is supposedly driving African state leaders. Yet, as this chapter has illustrated, such a perspective is highly limited and limiting. It is based on an understanding of international relations that tries to comprehend Africa solely within a Western historical framework. This is reflected in other analyses that attempt to make contemporary Africa "knowable" by references to a European past. Take, for instance, Philip Gourevitch's view that "I often found it helpful to think of central Africa in the mid-1990s as comparable to late medieval Europe"—a perspective echoed by other writers (Gourevitch 1998, 325; Buzan 1998). The Africa of today is clearly not the Europe of 1914 or 1614. Moreover, arguments grounded in the rhetoric of the past tend to fix Africa on a Western-scripted evolutionary ladder. The implication is that Africa is currently undergoing "growing pains" as it "matures" into something more recognizably European.

Political scientist Christopher Clapham wryly asserts that "I have lost count of the papers and lectures called 'Back to the Future,' though a more precise description would be 'Forward to the Past'" (Clapham 1999, 61). Such rhetoric has frequently been used in relationship to the current war in the Congo. At best, this rhetoric implies that the colonially imposed political, social, and economic structures in Africa are being replaced by ones that better reflect the "reality" of African life. A corollary of this thesis is a rediscovery of precolonial African political systems (see Davidson 1992). At worst, it is a portrayal of Africans "de-evolving" into what Kaplan calls "re-primitivized man" (1994, 73). As such, it is reminiscent of the image of Africa sliding back to the "dawn" of time. Moreover, it implies that Africa and "civilization" or "modernity" are incompatible.

Yet, the more dominant theme in Western portrayals of the current Congolese conflict is to use it as "proof" of the "New Barbarism" thesis. The rhetoric and imagery of the Congo as a chaotic land ruled by the "law of the jungle" remains prevalent. Or, as *Time* put it, the Congo is the "Bleeding Heart of Africa"—enduring violence that is beyond rational comprehension (15 March 1999, 62–63). Further "evidence" of the "coming anarchy" emerged in March 1999 when Interahamwe forces murdered eight Western tourists along the Uganda-Congo border. Coverage of the attack employed familiar tropes of African barbarism and tribalism. Ignoring the political motivation behind the attack, many used the event—which occurred in a national park renowned for its mountain gorillas—to portray the Africans as animals (*The Commercial Appeal* [Memphis], 15 March 1999, 9; see also, *Newsweek*, 15 March 1999; *Time*, 15 March 1999).

One can see the re-employment of past images and rhetoric in Western discourses on the Congo. In the first two cases—"Africa War One" and "Back to the future"—there is a reinvention of the evolutionary, temporal rhetoric used by the colonial agents a hundred years ago. The Congo is imagined as existing either outside of time or further down an evolutionary ladder. In the "New Barbarism" thesis, there is a clear re-employment of the rhetoric used by Stanley and others to imagine the Congo as chaos and the Congolese as savage barbarians. During that time, these discourses produced a "knowable" Congo that necessitated its conquest, repression, and exploitation by Western "civilization." Today, these discourses produce a "knowable" Congo that allows Western nonintervention and isolation.

These discourses effectively erase the West's role in the past one hundred years of Congolese history. On one level, by reifying the "Congo," these discourses provide the illusion that a "Congolese" entity and identity existed prior to Western contact. On another level, discourses portraying the Congo as chaos and the Congolese as savages work to fix that identity in such a way as to "explain" the current situation. The Congo is the way it is today, we are led to believe, because of its "inherent" nature. Thus, these discourses work to combine environmental determinism and cultural essentialism in such a way as to erase the political, economic, and social history of Western contact. These discourses remove any notions of Western responsibility while allowing Western business interests to continue to exploit the Congo's promised "potential" through economic extraction in the name of "development."

Yet, the discourses external actors have constructed about the Congo's identity have fundamentally shaped the events that make it what it is today. The mere fact that one can speak of the "Congo" at all is due to the colonizing discourses of Stanley and Leopold II, who imagined it as a unified political entity and engaged in political activities that reified that perception: constructing a colonial state and coercively shaping the inhabitants into a cohesive "Congolese" population. By persistently employing images of the Congo as chaotic, backward, and uncivilized/uncivilizable, external actors worked to forcefully replace existing sociopolitical practices and systems of knowledge with Western-scripted notions of sovereignty, stateness, and development. This erasure/imposition was done either directly, through interventions such as those in the 1960s, or indirectly, through the promotion and support of Mobutu's repressive dictatorship of thirty years. Alternative and competing discourses were frequently stamped out and/or portrayed as illegitimate. At the beginning of the twenty-first century, the extent to which the people within this country find themselves violently fragmented, preyed upon by external actors, and marginalized by international attention can be directly traced back to the long-term discursive constructions of their identity, past imaginings that have cumulatively helped make this current situation possible.

Chapter Six

Taking Inventory

Let us end where we came in. On the afternoon of January 16, 2001, while sitting in his office, Congolese President Laurent-Désiré Kabila was gunned down by a bodyguard. His assassination ended his short but tumultuous reign in the renamed Democratic Republic of Congo, a reign largely dominated by a protracted war that, at the time of his death, had claimed at least 100,000 lives (*New York Times*, 6 February 2000, 8). I have argued that to understand these recent events, one needs an examination of the Congo's origins and the forces that have produced and defined them. Such a genealogical approach examines how specific relations of power have arisen, become dominant, and affected politics over the course of time. In order to do this, I have explored how the Congo has been imagined over time: how it has been defined, by whom, and to what ends.

By choosing to begin and end this study with the assassination of Laurent Kabila in the midst of violent regional war also provides an interesting fulcrum point by which to expose the intricacies of international relations in general. The war in the Congo provides a moment of rupture that exposes the tenuous and contradictory discursive underpinnings of the Westphalian state system. What emerges is the realization that the Westphalian state system is a myth, an aspiration of state elites, maintained by multiple and conflicting discourses within the international and domestic arenas. In this conclusion, I will briefly draw out a few of the overarching themes of this work, suggest a few of the implications it poses for International Relations (IR) theory, and reflect on a rather interesting cultural phenomenon that took place while I was researching and writing this book.

Narratives and Themes

A central theme of this work has been that the current war in the Congo has been shaped by long-term discourses on its identity—images and ideas authored not only in the West, but within the Congo and Central Africa as well. The political actors in the Congo today operate within these discursively produced frameworks that help define themselves, their interests, and the meanings given to other social subjects and objects. Within this book's excavation of the idea of the Congo, a number of possible narratives have emerged. Here is but one:

> Over one hundred years ago, Henry Morton Stanley—a man who was always "inventing" his own self-identity—traveled through Central Africa on a mission of civilization, exploration, and subjugation. He laid the groundwork for King Leopold II's Free State, a political entity that violently destroyed existing social, political, and economic structures and systems. In the names of God, Reason, and Commerce, Stanley portrayed the "Congolese" as savage, childlike beings who needed to be subjugated and forced into labor for their own well-being. One-third to one-half of the population perished during that civilizing encounter.
>
> Over the next several decades, Belgian colonial agents continued the process of constructing a "modern" state and society for the inhabitants, who they continued to regard as inferior and childlike, and who were denied access to higher education, political organizations, and forums for political expression. In 1960, the Belgian colonial "fathers" decided that the Congolese were developed enough to engage in "modern" political practices. Independence was granted, many political institutions Africanized, and Congolese political leaders elected to public office. Yet, within days, Western powers intervened to forcefully thwart Congolese actions, dismissing the institutions and leaders as illegitimate and irrational. In order to "protect" the Congolese from themselves, Western powers sought to remove the Prime Minister, Patrice Lumumba.
>
> Instead of bringing peace to the region, Western interventions contributed to the country's violent political unrest for the next five years. The Western powers helped install a dictator, deciding that it would be the only way the Congo could experience stability in their absence. With direct backing of the U.S., Belgian, and French governments, Mobutu Sese Seko ruled the country for the next thirty years. Under his rule, the Western powers continued to enrich themselves from the country's mineral wealth, ensuring their control of the natural resource markets. Protected by his Western patrons, Mobutu and his cohorts bled the country of millions as the infrastructure crumbled, state social services collapsed, and the official economy sank into ruins. To sustain their rule,

> Mobutu and his supporters played on the increased fragmentation of the country, exploiting ethnic and regional divisions and even helping to facilitate a genocide in the mid-1990s.
>
> After a hundred years of direct and indirect intervention by the West, the Congo exists today as a much-abused entity. Robbed by a dictator, its mineral wealth largely controlled by external powers, the Congo now faces a multifaceted war threatening to topple its shaky central government. The indicators of economic growth and social well-being are low, while the levels of human insecurity are high. It is a situation many Western observers find incomprehensible and evidence of the Congolese inherent barbarism and inability to "civilize."

Yet, this is merely one narrative embedded in the genealogical unpacking of the idea of the "Congo." I present this narrative to draw attention to the political implications involved in a century of external imaginings of the Congo. Over a century of Western representations and practices have produced the current situation in central Africa. This is because discourses and imagery on the Congo's identity have directly influenced political policies toward the Congo. Representing the Congo as a primitive, chaotic, "heart of darkness" has made certain things happen in the political world. The long-term implications of these discourses and actions are now evident. The extent to which the people within the Congo now find their country violently fragmented, preyed upon by external actors, and marginalized by international inattention can be directly traced back to historical constructions of their state's identity. Those past imaginings have cumulatively helped make the current situation possible.

There are other narratives embedded in this genealogy. I might just as easily have begun this conclusion presenting a narrative of African resistance to these Western interventions. Or, I could have constructed a narrative of Congolese sovereignty and its continuous redefinition and reinscription, or a narrative of the Western-imposed state and the numerous discourses of stateness within the Congo over the past century. Even yet, I could have presented a narrative of discursive space and its utilization by numerous actors. Instead, due to my own normative prerogative, I chose to articulate a narrative of Western intervention in the Congo, a narrative of the cumulative effects that Western-scripted discourses have had on the Congo's identity. Mine is a narrative of some of the political dynamics those discourses have engendered over the past one hundred years.

The larger purpose of telling this narrative, in fact, of constructing this genealogical study, is to examine the ways in which political effects have been produced within the project of imagining the Congo. In this, I am drawing from Roxanne Doty's *Imperial Encounters* (1996), which itself draws from Edward Said's reading of Antonio Gramsci's *Prison Notebooks*. Gramsci writes that the starting point of critical elaboration is the interrogation of how subjects are products of historical processes that seemingly do not leave traces. Gramsci argues that the first step of critical inquiry is to compile an inventory of the "traces" left by these historical processes (Said 1978, 25). By focusing on the historical processes involved in imagining the Congo, a number of themes have emerged. Perhaps most obviously, this project has illustrated how similar rhetoric used to define the Congo has been employed in different ways at different times. The image of a "chaotic" and "barbaric" Congo has authorized different courses of action within different historical contexts. Within the colonizing discourses of Stanley and Leopold II, these images enabled the brutal conquest of the region and the forceful "ordering" of its space and society within the prescribed frameworks of accepted European models. At the end of the twentieth century, these images are taken to be "natural" characteristics of the Congo and are used to explain why the region is currently undergoing such economic and political turmoil. Within this contemporary framework, the history of foreign intervention is erased and a posture of nonintervention is prescribed with the dual accompaniment of hand-wringing and hand-washing by Western powers.

This work illustrates not only the power of discourse production but also the circulation and consumption of those discourses. As such, this project has underscored the importance of accessing discursive space. Over the past one hundred years, not all actors have been able to access discursive space equally in order to articulate and circulate their discourses of the Congo's identity. Often times, access to discursive space has been forcefully closed off by external powers. Such was the case when the Congo's first democratically elected leader was denied the ability to address the country's parliament, largely because the U.S. government feared the parliament might openly support its leader. The U.S. administration—via its Congolese allies—also denied Lumumba the ability to speak directly to the populace by barring him from the radio station in Leopoldville. Through its diplomatic maneuvering, the United States also succeeded in keeping Lumumba's delegation out of the UN General Assembly. Finally, they were either directly or indirectly responsible for physically removing Lumumba by assassination. Rumors abound about Lumumba's body allegedly being dissolved in a bathtub of acid by Belgian and CIA agents. Whether true or not, the myth speaks to the intensity of the U.S. and Belgian governments' desire to completely erase the threat posed by Lumumba.

In addition to the accessibility of discursive space, another theme that has emerged is the historical malleability of discursive space. While there are numerous physical sites from which to access discursive space—the floor of the UN, the front page of the *New York Times,* and so forth—recent technological advances have provided new modes of accessing that space. There is tremendous power to be gained by delineating and sanctioning the "acceptable" dimensions of discursive space and performing the role of gate-keeper to that space. However, as this project has also shown, there are always options available for resistance, in large part because of the infinite dimensions to discursive space. Moreover, the history of Congolese resistance has illustrated the potential for articulating counter discourses through the practices of appropriation, mimicry, revaluation, and, of course, violence. By focusing on the ways in which discursive power has been produced, exercised, and resisted over the past century, this project has attempted to avoid totalizing and tautological explanations frequently found within the field of international relations, particularly regarding North-South relations.

Exposing the Myth of the Westphalian State System

The myth of the Westphalian state system rests on the notion of autonomous and sovereign states. But the state and sovereignty must be constantly reified through representational practices. As IR theorist Cynthia Weber has argued, "Sovereign foundations are produced as signified in order to make representational projects possible, in order to allow sovereignty and the state to refer to some original source of truth" (Weber 1995, 123). For Weber, the production of sovereignty and state discourses are most clearly seen through the practices of intervention. These representational practices are also everyday occurrences necessary for maintaining the myth of the state and the Westphalian state system. On a daily level, we see the making and the remaking of global affairs via the discursive production of state identities (as well as nonstate identities that frequently challenge and/or reinforce the Westphalian myth). When these identities become highly and publicly contested, as they are during foreign interventions or warfare, then the discursive underpinnings of the myths are exposed. A genealogy of the

Congo illustrates the fact that the state is not sovereign, autonomous, or the primary social entity in the region. The mobility of peoples, ideas, goods, and images, as well as competing social identities, plays against the moves by state elites and IR theorists to construct the world as being divided into separated and sovereign spaces. The necessary myths underpinning the Westphalian system—the autonomy of sovereign states and abstract levels of analysis—are territorializing discourses that seek to create specific understandings of space and identity, and pass them off as stable and representable. The ongoing war in central Africa ruptures these conceptions and assumptions about space, movement, and identity and exposes them as being arbitrary, constructed, and counter to the lived experiences of most of the region's inhabitants.

But this is not to imply that these discourses of the Westphalian state are inconsequential. Quite the contrary. Despite their constructed nature, these discourses have had tremendous impact on the region and its inhabitants. The exportation of the Westphalian state system and the extractive economic system that accompanied it during the colonial project ensured that a global system of exploitation was created and maintained for generations. The imposition of these discourses, and the practices they engendered, invoked tremendous violence within the lived experiences of individuals, then and now. Just as the Belgian imposition of Western institutions and practices was achieved through horrific violence, currently countless Africans fall victim to violence inflicted in the name of maintaining and protecting these myths, particularly the sovereignty and security of ideas such as the Congo, Rwanda, Uganda, and so on. In the twenty-first century, through the complicated evolution of the global/local nexus, individuals in the region are experiencing brutal violence, as well as opportunities for enrichment and resistance. As with all expressions of power, these are multiple and rife with contradictions.

But what does that mean for how we theorize international relations or Africa's relation with external forces? A central aspect of this project has been to problematize concepts we use in our discussions of world affairs. Within this project, the reified concepts and categories that traditional international relations theorists often accept as solid structures—such as identity, interest, state, and sovereignty—are shown to be constructed through repeated patterns of human practice. Thus, this approach emphasizes identity-making, interest-making, state-making, sovereignty-making and so forth. In so doing, this project makes explicit the past machinations that have made the present situation in the Congo possible. To return to Gramsci's point, they provide an "inventory" of the historical processes that have produced the present.

This is a significant change in how we think about international relations in general and the Congo in particular. From a scholarly perspective, focusing simply on, say, factors of "economic materialism" or "strategic interests" ignores the more foundational elements of the Congo's international relations of the past century—how it has been imagined from both within and without. Conducting a genealogy of the idea of the Congo is thus a necessary first step in a critical exploration of that country's current situation and its relationship with the international community.

The Future and the Past: The Imagining Continues

In the wake of the assassination of Laurent-Désiré Kabila, his son and Army Chief of Staff Joseph Kabila was appointed as his successor. Whether or not the younger Kabila will succeed in establishing peace remains to be seen. However, the first months of Joseph Kabila's reign seemed to offer more than a glimmer of hope. On the day he assumed office, Joseph Kabila gave a speech in which he promised to relaunch the Lusaka peace accord, establish an inter-Congolese dialogue, liberalize the economy, and open up the political system for the realization of democracy. A few months later, he lifted the ban established by his father and announced that political parties would be allowed to organize and take part in future peace talks (Onishi 2001, 6). By the end of March 2001, the first UN observers were in place, though there were many obstacles in the months that followed, from a ridiculously small contingent of UN military observers to heightened hostilities between the Kabila and Rwandan governments.

Unable to rely too heavily upon the army or a domestic political power base, Joseph Kabila has proven adept at engaging external representations of the Congo for his own ends. Hardly a week after his inauguration, he traveled to France, the United States, and Belgium. These trips had the immediate effect of increasing his legitimacy and status at home and abroad. While aware that his ascendancy and survival so far have rested on the shoulders of his Angolan and Zimbabwean allies, Joseph Kabila has shrewdly sought to extend his circle of friends to include the Western powers his father had snubbed, particularly the United States and Belgium. These overtures seem to have earned him valuable points in Western capitals. In fact, *The Guardian* (Manchester) dubbed Kabila the "new young darling of the

West" (Denselow 2001, 1). While such a label bodes well for Western economic interests in Congo, it does little to ensure that Joseph Kabila will not construct strategies for survival at the expense of Congolese well-being, as his father did (Dunn 2002).

While war has been raging in the Congo and I have been researching and writing this work, an interesting phenomenon has emerged simultaneously: the remembrance of the Congo in the Western imagination. While in Central Africa, the (re)imagining of the Congo performs important political work for the various combatants involved in the war—from claiming to be a successor of Lumumba to maintaining the fiction of a sovereign and autonomous Congo entity—(re)imagining the Congo also performs interesting ideological work for Western audiences. At the end of the twentieth and beginning of the twenty-first centuries, there has been a tremendous outpouring of books on the Congo and Congolese history. In 1998, HoughtonMifflin published Adam Hochschild's *King Leopold's Ghost*, a rather sensationalized story of the conquest and brutalization of the Congo by Leopold and his colonial agents. What is interesting is that, though Hochschild does not uncover anything that was not already well known, his book sold extremely well. It seems his retelling of colonial brutality struck a chord among Western readers. Pagan Kennedy followed a few years later with *Black Livingstone: A True Tale of Adventure in the Nineteenth-Century Congo*. Kennedy's work retells the story of William Sheppard, an African American Presbyterian missionary in the Congo who helped expose the violence of Leopold's colonial system (Kennedy 2002).

The same year Hochschild published his historical account, novelist Barbara Kingsolver produced *The Poisonwood Bible* (1998). The bestselling novel is set in the Congo during 1960 and is the story of a self-involved American missionary who takes his wife and four young daughters to save Congolese souls in the "heart" of Africa. The nonfictional events of 1960 that provide the novel's backdrop include the granting of Congo's independence by Belgium, the breakdown of the newly independent state structures, the direct intervention by the United States and Belgium, and the overthrow and murder of Patrice Lumumba. The novel's protagonists are unable to understand the dynamics or implications of these events within their Western-defined worldviews because their perceptions of the Congo and Congolese are firmly rooted in colonially scripted images of African backwardness and primitivism. In its way, it is simultaneously a re-employment and reinvention of the "heart of darkness" trope, where the "civilizing mission" is turned on its head and "going native" can lead to salvation. The historic events providing the backdrop of the novel were closely examined a few years later in Ludo De Witte's *The Assassination of Lumumba* (2001). De Witte, a Belgian sociologist, argues that the Belgian government was directly involved in Lumumba's murder. Originally published in Belgium, the book helped lead to a parliamentary inquiry and the eventual official apology from the Belgian government for Lumumba's death.

Recent books have also revisited the era of Mobutu's Zaïre. Perhaps the most interesting, in part because it openly re-employs the "heart of darkness" trope, is Michela Wrong's *In the Footsteps of Mr. Kurtz: Living on the Brink of Disaster in Mobutu's Congo* (2001). This journalistic account is presented, in the words of one reviewer, as "a bit of a romp" through Mobutu's misdeeds (Fisher 2001, 16). Wrong's narrative was released alongside other books that also recount details from Mobutu's reign: from Bill Berkeley's *The Graves Are Not Yet Full* (2001) to *A Doctor's Story* (2001) by William T. Close, Mobutu's personal physician.

This resurgence in Western interest in the Congo has not been restricted to the printed word. Raoul Peck released his cinematic portrayal of the fate of Patrice Lumumba in his 2001 film *Lumumba*. The infamous "Rumble in the Jungle" boxing match between Ali and Foreman in Kinshasa was reintroduced to a whole new generation of Americans when the documentary *When We Were Kings* was finally released in 1996. The Congo also became an important signifier in Western advertisement campaigns, most notably for the Bronx Zoo. Announcing their gorilla display, the zoo took out a full-page advertisement in the *New York Times* urging people to "come to the Congo this season." Of course, at that moment there was a violent war raging throughout the Congo. But the "Congo" the zoo was conjuring up was not the image of a contemporary political state but the image of a depopulated idyllic state of nature inhabited solely by African animals.

What accounts for this resurgence in interest in the Congo? What ideological work is the Congo performing within these works?

Given that the majority of these works were produced by white, upper-middle-class, Western authors, one may well wonder what function the Congo is serving for them. On one level, I suspect that the Congo acts as a sort of personal totem for some of these authors. For Hochschild, an examination of Western brutality in and exploitation of Africa fits into his ongoing examination of his own subjectivity, especially as a member of a family whose fortune was largely amassed by extracting minerals and exploiting labor in Africa—a topic he addressed in his engaging 1987 biography *Half the Way Home: A Memoir of Father and Son*. For Pagan Kennedy, she believed that the story of William Sheppard "held a key to [her] own history" (2002, xiv). It turns out that a distant relative of hers was also a Presbyterian missionary to the Congo, knew Sheppard, and was instrumental in getting his story out during his own lifetime. For Kennedy and her distant relative, the Congo became a place where they sought to resolve the racism of their own American social environment. Thus, the Congo continues to be employed as a space in which internal demons can be excised and wrestled with. Telling the story of white misdeeds or black heroics seems to be an important practice for dealing with Western privilege and racial angst at the start of the new millennium.

On another level, I suspect that part of the answer lies in the fact that most of these works were produced after the 1994 Rwandan genocide and represent an attempt to come to grips intellectually with that tragedy and the Western response to it. In many of these cases, attention is focused on how the Congo—either as Leopold's Congo or Mobutu's Zaïre—fits within a genealogy of genocide. Such a task may take on even greater importance in the shadow of the (apocalyptic?) millennium.

But whatever the personal motivation of the people behind these productions, the Congo continues to do important ideological work within the Western imagination. Often times it does so by drawing upon established tropes such as "heart of darkness," the Congo as chaos, and the "civilizing mission." But within the postcolonial era, these tropes are sometimes re-employed against the logics they have historically represented. That is, they simultaneously reinforce and undermine the ideological undercurrents from which they spring. Clearly, the Congo continues to be employed as a marker for "evil," whether the evil committed by the West upon Africa (in the cases of Hochschild, De Witte, and Peck) or the evil committed by Africans upon Africa (in the cases of Berkeley, Wrong, and Close). It also retains its status as a marker for the exotic, the unknown, and the unknowable. Often, the Congo is presented not just as a place of backward "Otherness" but as the antithesis to the West, a marker for the antimodern as much as the nonmodern. While in some cases this serves to reinforce a superior sense of the modern self, it has also been employed (perhaps most deftly by Kingsolver) to question such assumptions and attitudes.

In short, the Congo continues to be employed as a signifier—a symbol and an idea—within the Western and African imaginations. And the meanings and characteristics of that signifier continue to be contested, invented, and reinvented. At the beginning of the twenty-first century, the Congo remains a powerful idea and an ideologically saturated image both in the minds and actions of people around the world. There are few signifiers within international relations that have performed as much ideological work for as many actors as the Congo has over the past century. One can only assume that the Congo—as an entity, idea, and symbol—will continue to be employed, re-employed, redefined, and contested for years to come.

Notes

Chapter One

1. This narrative of events is taken from the official government report, as reported in the Ugandan newspaper *The Monitor* (18 January 2002, 13).
2. For good discussions of Kabila's life and his early career as a rebel leader, see Kennes 1999 and Wilungula 1997.
3. Hall also notes that: "Precisely because identities are constructed within, not outside, discourse, we need to understand them as produced in specific historical and institutional sites within specific discursive formations and practices, by enunciative strategies. Moreover, they emerge within the play of specific modalities of power" (Hall 1996, 4).
4. My use of discourse and discourse analysis is drawn from the works of Michel Foucault, Jacques Derrida, Ernesto Laclau, and Chantal Mouffe, who accept that a discourse is a relational totality of signifying sequences that together constitute a more or less coherent framework for what can be said and done.
5. Enunciating this Gramscian interpretation, Stuart Hall argues: "It becomes the horizon of the taken-for-granted: what the world is and how it works, for all practical purposes. Ruling ideas may dominate other conceptions of the social world by setting the limit to what will appear as rational, reasonable, credible, indeed sayable or thinkable, within the given vocabularies of motive and action available to us" (Hall 1988, 44).

Chapter Two

1. Mehmed Emin Pasha, a German explorer, was the governor of an Egyptian province in the Sudan, but had been cut off from contact with Europe by a Mahdist revolt. Stanley left from Zanzibar with over eight hundred men and, after months of forced march and hunger, found Emin Pasha. However, Emin Pasha no longer wanted rescuing and Stanley had to forcibly persuade him to leave the Sudan, but was unsuccessful in bringing Emin Pasha back to Europe.
2. Leopold II ascended the Belgian throne in 1865 at the age of thirty. The king was almost as old as the country itself. Belgium, born in 1830 after a popular uprising against the Dutch, was not a homogenous nation. There were significant cultural,

linguistic, religious, and class divisions within the country. In fact, it has been noted that the small state owed its existence to various international norms and regimes (Grovogui 2000; Clapham 1996, 32). In order to ensure the continental balance of power at that time, the dominant European powers guaranteed Belgium's right to self-determination and sovereignty for its pledge of neutrality. The new country of Belgium established itself as a constitutional monarchy and chose a German prince as its first king, Leopold I. Yet, it was his son who would thrust the small country onto the stage of international politics because of his obsession with acquiring colonies. For Leopold II any populated region of the globe would do, as long as it was his/Belgium's possession (Slade 1962, 36).

3. The claims I make in this section derive from my readings of many of Leopold II's writings and speeches, as well as work produced by his colonial agents operating in the Congo, Europe, and the United States. I have also studied the three popular colonial publications: *La Belgique Coloniale, Le Congo Illustré,* and *Le Mouvement Géographique.* These materials are available at the Bibliothèque Africain, housed in the Belgian Foreign Ministry in Brussels. For a good discussion of *Le Mouvement Géographique* in particular, see Brugailliere 1993.

4. The diversity of the social, cultural, political, and linguistic groups in the region that became known as the "Congo" has been documented best by Jan Vansina's *Kingdoms of the Savanna* (1966a).

5. As V. Y. Mudimbe has noted, "the explorer's text is not epistemologically inventive. It follows a path prescribed by a tradition. Expedition reports only establish a very concrete, vivid representation of what paintings and theories of social progress had been postulating since the Baroque period. In what the explorer's text does reveal, it brings nothing new besides visible and recent reasons to validate a discipline already remarkably defined by the Enlightenment. The novelty resides in the fact that the discourse on 'savages' is, for the first time, a discourse in which an explicit political power presumes the authority of scientific knowledge and vice-versa. Colonialism becomes its project and can be thought of as a duplication and a fulfillment of the power of Western discourses on human varieties" (Mudimbe 1988, 15–16).

6. For example, David Hume (1711–1766) justified European imperialism, slave trade, and colonialism with a racial argument of European superiority, stating: "I am apt to suspect the Negroes and in general all other species of men to be naturally inferior to Whites. There never was a civilized nation of any other complexion than White, nor even any individual eminent either in action or speculation" (quoted in Gould 1981, 40–41). In France, Montesquieu (1689–1755) asserted that humans evolved from the state of nature at a different pace, depending on their mastery of reason. The Europeans had achieved such a mastery, while others had not. Thus, non-European societies could not be regarded as equal. Referring to Africans, he wrote "It is impossible that we suppose that these people are humans; because, if we suppose that they are humans, we would start thinking that we are not Christian ourselves" (quoted in Grimsley 1974, 12). Meanwhile in Germany, Immanuel Kant (1724–1804) divided the world up into enlightened and nonenlightened, where the former enjoyed rights and privileges while the latter did not. Kant and his German counterparts followed other European thinkers in holding that the salvation of (unenlightened) Africa depended entirely on its subordination to Europe (Grovogui 1996, 34).

7. This summary is an obvious oversimplification of complex intellectual currents across several centuries. For more detailed treatments of the non-European *Other*

in European thought, see Pieterse 1992; Mudimbe 1988; Lorimer 1978; Said 1978; and Hammond and Jablow 1970.

8. For good recent biographies, see John Bierman's *Dark Safari* (1990) and Frank McLynn's *Stanley: The Making of an African Explorer* (1989).
9. For a good discussion of the invention and evolution of the concept of "race," see Hannaford 1996. For an excellent discussion of "race" in international relations, see Doty 1993.
10. Jan Nederveen Pieterse (1992) has noted that the use of the cannibal image has historically served as a marker of cultural difference. McClintock observes that for whites, "the fear of engulfment expresses itself most acutely in the cannibal trope ... [through which they] attempted to ward off the threat of the unknown by naming it, while at the same time confessing a dread that the unknown might literally rise up and devour the intruder whole" (McClintock 1995, 27).
11. One of his contemporaries, Samuel Baker, wrote: "African savages is [sic] quite on the level with that of the brute, and not to be compared with the noble character of the dog. There is neither gratitude, pity, love, nor self-denial; no idea of duty; no religion; but covetousness, ingratitude, selfishness, and cruelty" (Baker 1866, 152–3).
12. The 1894 World's Fair in Antwerp was the first to feature Africans. An "authentic" village was built and sixteen Africans were brought for display. Three died during the fair and four fell seriously ill. At Tervuren, seven Africans died.
13. In terms of gender, the colonial project turned on a definition and performance of Belgian masculinity. The Congolese were cast as effeminate, helpless victims that needed rescuing, while the African environs was imagined to be an inhospitable testing ground for the strength, courage, and virility of the white male. Belgian masculinity was intimately tied to the conquest and colonization of the Congo and Congolese. Thus, gendered elements were central aspects of the Belgian-Congolese relationship from its inception.
14. It should be noted that support for the colonial project was not universal by any means. There was strong domestic opposition to Belgian colonialism from many quarters, including the Labor Party.
15. As Pratt notes: "From the point of view of their inhabitants, of course, these same spaces are lived as intensely humanized, saturated with local history and meaning, where plants, creatures, and geographical formations have names, uses, symbolic functions, histories, places in indigenous knowledge formations" (Pratt 1992, 61).
16. William Connolly refers to this as the "civi-territorial complex" (Connolly 1993 and 1996). Kennan Ferguson summarizes it as "the location and creation of civilization in a specific consumption of the land, as well as the subsequent delegitimation of those with different conceptions of it. The use of land in a particular way . . . justifies the claim of civilization and forms the foundation for denying the nomadic people previously occupying the land claim to the earth. It is cultural judgment realized through the imaginary of terrain" (Ferguson 1996, 169).
17. As John Agnew and Stuart Corbridge have argued: "The system of territorial states developed important legal and economic underpinnings as a wide range of spatial practices became more and more bounded by state-territorial limits. Through a social process of recognizing other spaces as potentially 'developed' and 'modern' insofar as they acquired the trappings of territorial statehood (armies, judiciaries, etc.), the state-territorial form of spatial organization came to encompass in some degree most of the world's population" (Agnew and Corbridge 1995, 14).

18. Stanley's invention of his Western identity was grounded in his simultaneous performance of "whiteness" and "manliness." As Gail Bederman argues in *Manliness and Civilization:* "During the decades around the turn of the century, Americans were obsessed with the connection between manhood and racial dominance ... [M]iddle-class Americans found [a multitude of ways] to explain male supremacy in terms of white racial dominance and, conversely, to explain white supremacy in terms of male power" (1995, 4). Stanley epitomizes this impulse, existing at the historical turning point between what Bederman sees as white middle-class American males' construction of "manliness"—with its connotations of sexual self-restraint, moral character, and strong will—and the newly invented term "masculinity"—glorifying ideals of aggressiveness, physical force, and male sexuality (Bederman 1995, 17–19). Stanley embodied both positions simultaneously, reflecting the shift from one stage to the other. For an excellent discussion of Stanley's use of gender, race, and other social markers in his narratives, see Torgovnick 1990, 10–41.
19. An interesting example of this can be found in Ludwig Bauer's amusingly titled *Leopold the Unloved: King of the Belgians and of Money* (1934).
20. There is a distinction between rubber produced on plantations and rubber gathered from wild vines and trees. At this time, most of the rubber accumulated in the Congo was from the harvesting of wild rubber. This was important because, as a nondomesticated resource, it could be extracted without any large-scale investment or infrastructure at a time when little money was flowing into the Congo and the colonial treasury was badly depleted by the cost of securing "effective occupation" of the territory, as demanded by the Berlin agreements.
21. Henry Ward was part of the infamous "Rear Guard" in Stanley's disastrous Emin Pasha rescue mission.
22. Later, after he had relinquished control of his colony to the Belgian state, Leopold II continued to voice this position. For example, in a speech at Antwerp on June 12, 1909, Leopold II stated: "If these vast Congo territories, many of which as yet unoccupied and unproductive, were exploited would they not furnish us with the resources required for many things? ... Is it not legitimate that the unworked lands of the Congo should contribute to ensure our general prosperity? If we desire that our colony shall enrich the Belgian working man we must leave none of its riches untapped" (quoted in Morel 1909, 290–291).
23. For representative examples, see 6 November 1895, 157–159; 27 August 1893, 138–139; and August 1892, 130–131.
24. For a good discussion of the colonial implications of Western knowledge production, see Cohn 1996.
25. These reports came primarily from the American Baptist Missionary Union and the (British) Baptist Missionary Society (Marchal 1996: II, 54–69). However, there were considerable divisions between and within missionary societies (see Slade 1955, 1957, and 1959).
26. The *Heart of Darkness* is the subject of endless literary criticism. Perhaps the most insightful in this context have been Benita Parry (1983), Chinua Achebe (1988), Frances B. Singh (1988), and Edward Said (1993).
27. For example, the British film *Saunders of the River* and the serial novels from which it derived.
28. This point reflects the argument made by Cynthia Weber: "When intervention practices occur, they are accompanied by justifications on the part of an intervening state to a supposed international community of sovereign states. In offering

justifications for their intervention practices, diplomats of intervening states simultaneously assume the existence of norms regulating state practices and an interpretive community that will judge intervention practices in accordance with these norms" (Weber 1995, 5).
29. These themes can be found in other anti-Leopold II writings. For example, H. R. Fox Bourne, secretary of the Aborigines Protection Society, painted a vivid picture of the Congo's state monopolistic practices that were antithetical to free trade (1903, 132–140). In one passage, Bourne states: "The 'civilisation' brought, by ways for which the missionaries are scarcely responsible, and which they cannot control, is almost wholly uncivilising, and its purpose is principally, if not altogether, the conversion of King Leopold's share of Congoland into a monopolist field for exploitation in the exclusive interests of those seeking temporary and unjustifiable profit from their unscrupulous investment" (1903, 301). The same year, Capt. Guy Burrows wrote: "Truth to tell, King Leopold and the Congo clique have never made any really earnest effort to civilise the Congo savages, for civilisation, as generally understood, would mean free commerce, resistance to despotic rule, and other serious impediments to the continued maintenance of a strict monopoly" (1903, 205).
30. On paper, Leopold II had previously agreed to bequeath the Congo to Belgium after he died, largely because the Free State was heavily mortgaged to Belgium in consideration for the large sums of money lent to Leopold II over the previous decades.

Chapter Three

1. After World War I, Belgium became the trustee of Ruanda-Urundi (modern day Rwanda and Burundi), a portion of the former German colonies.
2. Between the 1897 Tervuren Expo and the 1958 Brussels Expo, Belgium hosted at least five major Universal and International Exhibitions. Central features of each were the display of Congolese artifacts and a presentation of the colonial vision. For a good review of these Expos, see Cockx and Lemmens 1958.
3. I maintain that social action and agency result because people are guided to act in certain ways and not others, "on the basis of the projections, expectations, and memories derived from a multiplicity but ultimately limited repertoire of available social, public, and cultural narratives" (Somers 1994, 614). That is to say, they act in ways defined by their sense of *Self* and *Other* defined at that particular place and time.
4. The films, remaining parts of the "Congorama" display, and various other features of the 1958 Congo Section are housed in the Musée Royal de l'Afrique Centrale in Tervuren, which also contains a collection of secondary scholarship on the 1958 Expo.
5. Paternalism represented a grand vision for remaking Congolese indigenous societies from top to bottom. British scholar Thomas Hodgkin wrote that the policy drew from three perspectives: "the Catholic conception of society as a hierarchy, in which the ruling element is responsible for providing the conditions for a 'good life' for the ruled; the large corporation's idea of workers' welfare as a means to good industrial relations and maximum output; and the colonial

Government's view—that it is desirable and politic to concentrate upon the effort to increase the material prosperity of the mass, and to equip them, through education, to play a useful, if subordinate, part, in modern society, before any moves are made to train an African élite or grant political rights" (Hodgkin 1956, 51).

6. Importantly, the first section of the book, devoted to the articulation of Belgian Paternalism, rests on the acceptance of certain representations of Congolese identity (i.e., as lazy children), which is the focus of the entire second half of the book.
7. Perhaps the best work on the colonial state in Africa has been done by Crawford Young (1994 and 1965). See also Davidson 1992; Willame 1972; Anstey 1966; and Lemarchand 1964.
8. The Belgian colonial state prided itself with providing primary education to much of the population. There were solid economic reasons for this, as a 1949 colonial document notes: "The better educated a person is, the stronger his economic performance, and thus the higher his income. Mass education will have a beneficial effect on the population's productivity" (*Plan décennal pour le développement économique et social du Congo*, 1949, 62; quoted in Willame 1972, 13). Yet, as a matter of policy, Congolese were denied access to higher (secular) education. They were kept out of Belgian universities until the early 1950s, with the first Congolese university student graduating in 1956 (Slade 1960, 31).
9. As such, a "Congolese" literature emerged made up of novelists (André-Romain Bokwango, Maurice Kasongo, Louis Mabiala, Paul Lomami-Tshibamba), poets (Antoine-Roger Bolamba, Jean-François Iyeky, Augustin Ngongo), playwrights (Justin Disasi, Albert Mongita, Albert-Joseph Malula), and essayists (Michel Colin, Patrice Lumumba, Antoine Munongo), who produced numerous Congolese discourses on their self-identity. See Ngandu Nkashama 1972 and Quaghebeur et al. 1992.
10. By November 18, 1958, the Belgian government had already declared: "Under the protection of our Kings, the Congolese people, after more than half a century of civilization, have reached a degree of evolution which opens the way to new progress ... Belgium intends to organize a democracy in the Congo which will be capable of exercising the prerogatives of sovereignty and of deciding upon its independence" (*Belgian Congo To-Day*, January 1959, 5).
11. Pierre Ryckmans stated: "The whole history of Africa before the arrival of the white man is that of an appalling tyranny, and if he left there would be a return to the old situation. At the present stage the native peoples would not administer themselves" (quoted in *Belgian Congo To-Day*, January 1955, 38).
12. A representative example of this sentiment is found in the writing of Raymond Scheyen, member of the Belgian Parliament and former Finance Minister for Congo and Belgium (in succession). In response to the U.S. government urging European powers to decolonize, he argued: "Is it too much to hope that in the light of recent developments [i.e., the "Mau Mau" emergency in Kenya] the statesmen in Washington, taking account of reality, will finally understand that in giving a premature autonomy to peoples who are too young for it, they may do more harm than good in putting them at the mercy of communism?" (Scheyen 1956, 109–110).
13. While there were some divisions within the Belgian government on its approach to the Congo—namely between the Foreign Ministry, on one hand, and the Defense

Ministry and the Ministry of African Affairs, on the other—Katanga was clearly its main focus. As Ernest Lefever has noted, the latter two ministries "had a deep stake in preserving Katanga as a going concern, even if it meant disaster for the rest of the Congo" (1965, 29).

14. Perhaps the most interesting, if complex, example of these representations during the 1960 crisis concerned the alleged rape of white women. The threat/fear of rape was an important component in the language of Belgian intervention, for it played upon one of the society's greatest fears: miscegenation. George Siberia of the United Press International (UPI) reported on July 8, 1960, that "Rumors [of rape] drove the whites—mostly Belgians—to fury. Men with clenched fists shouted unconfirmed reports that African mutineers were raping white women. The reports flew around the city, sometimes embellished . . . The word rape was all over the European section of Leopoldville" (quoted in Kitchen 1967, 21–22). In order to help justify their intervention after the fact, the Belgian government published *A Preliminary Report on the Atrocities Committed by the Congolese Army against the White Population of the Republic of the Congo before the Intervention of the Belgian Forces* (Belgian Government Information Center 1960), citing 290 alleged cases of reported rape of white women by Congolese. The outrage in this document, and related media reports, appears not to focus so much on the occurrence of rape (though that surely was an issue) but rather on interracial sex, with all the cultural interpretations that carried: perceived cheapening of women, violation of the white man's property/domain, and fear of disease from unclean blacks.

15. Dismissing Africans for their lack of "sobriety" has been a common rhetorical maneuver since the writings of Stanley. During Belgian colonial rule, native access to alcohol was regulated and restricted. Arguing that they were unable to hold their liquor or were partial to drinking was a move to paint them as uncivilized. Yet, this characterization was not simply about alcohol consumption but also about the "seriousness" and "maturity" of the Congolese. Statements questioning the sobriety of Africans represented claims about their development and aptitude. Such rhetorical maneuvers against Lumumba should be viewed within this tradition.

16. Campbell continues: "The identity that is enframed refers to more than just the characteristics of individuals or national types; it incorporates, for example, the form of domestic order, the social relations of production, and the various subjectivities to which they give rise. In the context of the United States, the identity has often been disciplined by rhetoric associated with freedom of choice for individuals, democratic institutions, and a private enterprise economy" (1992, 158).

17. During the crisis, the United States viewed Kasavubu and Mobutu as acting "impulsively" whenever they did not check in with U.S. embassy *before* making decisions (Kalb 1982, 165–166).

18. For example, in an official report, Ambassador Timberlake adds as an afterthought: "*Parenthetically*, Belgian troops and civilians are behaving similarly [to the Force Publique] and worse in the streets of Leopoldville . . . a white civilian [killed a Congolese] on the street . . . without any provocation . . . Some Belgians . . . particularly the military, have become completely irrational and in many instances have behaved worse than the worst Congolese" (U.S. State Department, "Policy Paper," January 25, 1961, 12–14; quoted in Orwa 1985, 61; emphasis added).

19. *Time*, 13 June 1960, 24; 27 June 1960, 25–26; 4 July 1960, 23; 18 July 1960, 17; 1 August 1960, 22; 22 August 1960, 18; 5 September 1960, 21; 19 September 1960, 28; 26 September 1960, 30–31; 17 October 1960, 35; 24 October 1960, 32; 14 November 1960, 32; and 28 November 1960, 24. Note also the shift away from "Prime Minister" to the more Soviet-styled label of "Premier" in a clear attempt to associate Lumumba with Communism. Similar rhetoric was used in other major American publications, such as *Life*, *Newsweek*, *US News and World Report*, and the *New York Times*.
20. The coverage of Lumumba also had an interesting element in its recurring link between Lumumba and cars. In May, *Time* reported that "the man to beat [in elections] was Patrice Lumumba, 34, the tall, goateed radical from Stanleyville who last week was storming through the back country in a cream-colored convertible" (*Time*, 30 May 1960, 23). During his visit to the United States, much attention was paid to his visit to a Cadillac showroom: "High on his list was a visit to a Cadillac-Oldsmobile agency, where he tested doors, poked seat cushions, asked prices—but in the end, bought nothing" (*Time*, 8 August 1960: 30). This focus may touch on a white American cultural unease with blacks and new cars as symbols of wealth, access, class, and power. In effect, it was a revision of the early trope (discussed in chapter two) that constructed images of Africans in European clothes to ridicule the idea of Africans as "evolved" or "civilized."
21. An earlier report stated that, "Since Lumumba will not remain in one place long enough for his political coloration to show, most Leopoldville observers eye dubiously the three men closest to him, all of whom have obvious Red leanings" (*Time*, 1 August 1960, 22).
22. The U.S. policy was also shaped by the recent "loss" of Cuba. Cuba and Castro became common analogies in the discourse around the Congo and Lumumba. CIA chief Allen Dulles regarded Lumumba as "a Castro, or worse" (quoted in U.S. Senate Report 1976, 57). In an early CIA cable, the station chief in Leopoldville reported: "Embassy and station believe Congo experiencing classic communist effort takeover government . . . Whether or not Lumumba actually commie or just playing commie game to assist his solidifying power, anti-West forces rapidly increasing power Congo and there may be little time left in which take action to avoid another Cuba" (CIA Cable, Leopoldville to Director, 16 August 1960).
23. *Time* asked: "What indeed could anyone do to transform Patrice Lumumba's Congo into a reasonable facsimile of a civilized state?" (*Time*, 5 September 1960, 22).
24. Rostow's "Non-Communist Manifesto" was a clear product of the intellectual currents engendered by twentieth-century American "enlightenment" and modernity. Rostow's argument was that there are five evolutionary "stages" of economic growth a society/state goes through. In his words, this growth involved "maturity" from "traditional" (read "backward" or "immature") society to one of "high mass-consumption" (read "developed") (Rostow 1960, 4–16). This approach fixed the Congo and the Congolese population in a specific reading of space and time within an evolutionary narrative dictated by Western/modernist values of the individual and the market. This had several important implications. Viewing economic activity through a state-centric lens, it privileged the Westphalian state structure and system. Moreover, it unquestioningly accepted the superiority of Western economic policies and practices. As such, existing economic practices, systems of exchange, relationships with the environment, and so forth were cast as illegitimate

and dismissed. More than that, as "traditional" effects, they were regarded as obstacles to "development" and actively opposed. This rhetoric was to have important implications for rural communities and women, who were cast as oppositional figures within this discourse (see Scott 1995, esp. 23–41).

25. Roxanne Doty writes, "the discourse of development constitutes a background of preunderstandings, of given assumptions regarding types of individuals and societies, change, progress, and the desirability of particular kinds of social arrangements. While the discourse of development has for the most part not been a major element in international relations as an academic discipline, it has in important respects formed the basic 'knowledge base' about the 'third world' and the take-off point, so to speak, regarding the place of the 'third world' in international society" (Doty 1996, 157–158).

26. As Adlai Stevenson wrote: "To finish the work well which the West has begun demands more effort and more help and generosity than have yet been given. But to finish it badly would mean that Western man, coming to the most innocent of all continents, would have achieved nothing there, but the destruction of the old gods and the frustration of the new. Such an indictment of the efficacy of our civilization would imperil every confident claim on our part to be the wave of the future" (Stevenson 1960, 48, 54; quoted in Weissman 1974a, 120–121).

27. It would be a mistake to presume that the UN spoke with one voice during the crisis. My focus here is not on the General Assembly or Security Council, but the UN administration: the offices of the Secretary-General and his representatives within the Congo. While there was frequent division between various offices, I will pay particular attention to common elements of the various discourses with emphasis on the Secretary-General.

28. However, it should be stressed that the UN occasionally did go against U.S. interests. The best example of this being a report issued by UN Special Representative Rajeshwar Dayal that was highly critical of Mobutu and the Belgians (see also Dayal 1976).

29. The Organization of African Unity (OAU), the first continent-wide regional organization, would not be created until 1963.

Chapter Four

1. The "Rumble in the Jungle" was Ali's bid to reclaim the world championship title, of which he had been stripped after he had refused to fight in Vietnam, and to restore his image after numerous years of exile from the boxing world. The fight's promoter, Don King, deciding that the two African American fighters should make history by competing in the first major boxing event held on African soil, transformed the fight into an elaborate entertainment event. For an excellent source of information on the fight, see the documentary *When We Were Kings* (Dir. Taylor Hackford and Leon Gast, 1996).

2. Ali was the overwhelming favorite among the local population, in large part because of the association of Foreman with (neo)colonialism. For example, Foreman landed in Kinshasa with a German shepherd, the dog used by Belgian colonial forces. In fact, many Zaïrians had assumed Foreman was white, a point exploited by Ali who referred to him as a "Belgian imperialist." As Suruba Ibumando

Wechsler remembers: "The whole nation felt they had won something much more important than a boxing match, it felt as if we had somehow been liberated once again from the Belgians and all those who had colonized and humiliated Africa" (Wechsler 1999, 198).

3. Taken out of context, the numerous festivals in Belgium (one entailing the throwing of oranges by men with ostrich feathers on their heads) or re-enactments of mythical narratives concerning George Washington and Johnny Appleseed would undoubtedly seem ludicrous to outside viewers.
4. Thomas Callaghy has noted that there are at least two translations for Mobutu's new name. The Ngbandi translation reads, "the warrior who knows no defeat because of his endurance and inflexible will and is all powerful, leaving fire in his wake as he goes from conquest to conquest." In Tshiluba, the name translates to "invincible warrior, Cock who leaves no chick intact" (Callaghy 1979, 341).
5. The name "Zaïre" had been used as an anachronistic and romantic metaphor for the Congo during the colonial period. Mobutu's rejection of the label "Congo" may also have been motivated by his desire to avoid using for the whole country the traditional name of one of its parts, particularly given that deposed President Kasavubu was still identified by many as a Kongo "nationalist."
6. For Mobutu's articulation of the ten fundamental principles of *authenticité*, see Manwana-Mungongo, *Le Général Mobutu Sese Seko* (1972, 31–69). The best primary sources on *authenticité* can be found in Kangafu-Kutumbagana's *Discours sur l'authenticité* (1973) and Sakombi Inongo's *Authenticité au Zaïre* (n.d.).
7. Mobutu stated that, "for us Zaïrians, authenticity consists in taking an awareness of our personality, of our inherent values . . . it doesn't act as a retrograde concept that would shut us in a shell, forbidding us to enjoy some blessings of science and technology" (quoted in Kangafu-Kutumbagana 1973, 27).
8. In June 1973, women's Western dresses, skirts, and "hot pants" were banned by the Zaïrian government (Kabwit 1979, 391).
9. As Mobutu proclaimed: "Faith in the power of our Country, in the certainty of its near development in natural unity and cohesion, kindled by common memories of losses in human life that plunged our families into mourning and that made our hearts weep, by common memories of glorious fights for regaining our rights, and finally, by common remembrance of our martyrs, who died on the fields of honour so that our Country might live, all this represents for us Congolese, the most solid of shields against the onslaught of imperialism" (quoted in Ba 1970, 102).
10. The restoration of Lumumba was rather short lived. A national monument to his memory, situated on the outskirts of Kinshasa, was never finished, and official references to him decreased rather quickly.
11. For a fuller discussion of Zaïrianisation, see Schatzberg 1980.
12. This point is further illustrated by the regime's decision to hold an *international* colloquium to elaborate *authenticité* in 1973.
13. Although the philosophers cited cannot be held responsible for the appropriation of their arguments by Mobutu's regime, this appropriation is an indication of the popularity of existentialist rhetoric at the time. In his critique of existentialism, Theodor Adorno asserted "this philosophical perspective became an ideological mystification of human domination—while pretending to be a critique of alienation" (Adorno 1973, xiii). Mobutu's production of an "authentic" national identity illustrates Adorno's warning that the jargon of authenticity "puts forth as truth what should instead be suspect by virtue of the prompt collective agreement" (9).

Echoing the language of Adorno, a critic of Mobutu argued "The theory of authenticity has also been invoked to justify the authoritarian political system. To this end, an effort has been made to create the myth of Zaïre as an image of some idealistic, pre-colonial African village living in harmony and arcadian bliss under the benevolent authority of a strong-willed chief represented by General Mobutu" (Kannyo 1979, 61).

14. This is reflective of what Roxanne Doty calls "imperial encounters," where "the South has been discursively represented by policy makers, scholars, journalists, and others in the North . . . [to produce] regimes of 'truth' and 'knowledge'" (Doty 1996, 2).

15. For good analyses of the state and its political/economic elite's exploitation of the domestic economy during the early years of Mobutu's reign, see Peemans 1975; Nzongola-Ntalaja 1977–78 and 1982; and MacGaffey 1987.

16. As Michael Schatzberg observed, "when Mobutu proffered the image of a strong, unified, financially sound Zaïre—a country destined to rendezvous with prosperity by 1980—few could disagree" (Schatzberg 1991, 36).

17. Other major Western magazines and newspapers echoed this sentiment. For example, *Newsweek* proclaimed "the bout was a remarkable achievement for Zaïre, winning it global attention and respect" (*Newsweek*, 11 November 1974, 71). Only the liberal publication *The Nation* voiced dissent, publishing an article by Stephen Weissman on the neocolonial nature of the regime and Mobutu's financial investment in the fight (Weissman 1974b, 558–559).

18. For example, the *Washington Post* spoke of Zaïre's "excellent position to influence the course of events throughout central and much of eastern Africa" (*Washington Post*, 28 October 1974, 3).

19. For a detailed description of Zaïre's invasion of Angola, see Kelly 1993, 220–223. For an insightful discussion of Mobutu's role in the CIA and apartheid South African war against the MPLA, see Stockwell 1978.

20. See, for example, Tanzanian President Julius Nyerere's scathing criticism of Mobutu and the West during Shaba II, as reported in the *New York Times* (9 June 1978, 1, 27).

21. For an excellent treatment of the "Mobutu or chaos" mentality in U.S.-Zaïrian relations, see Schatzberg 1991. See also Leslie 1993, esp. 138–164.

22. Peter Schraeder makes the interesting suggestion that this speech may have been intentionally patterned after President Carter's "American malaise" speech (Schraeder 1994, 90).

23. *Le Soir*, covering a presidential visit to Kinshasa, sarcastically commented: "between the Citizen President Mobutu and Mr. Giscard d'Estaing, there is quite a romance; each passing hour enables the two men to praise each other" (9 August 1975; quoted in Trefon 1989, 69).

24. These images also found cultural expression in contemporary films. Interestingly, the late 1970s and 1980s saw the movie industry reproducing earlier Africanist films, such as *Tarzan* (1972, 1981, 1984) and *King Solomon's Mines* (1976, 1985, 1987). There were important counterdiscourses being produced from within the Afro-American community. Take, for example, the lesser-know sequel to *Shaft* (1971), *Shaft in Africa* (1973).

25. See also Naipaul's article "A New King for the Congo" in the *New York Review of Books* (26 June 1975, 19–25). In this scathing critique of Mobutu, Naipaul employs the familiar tropes of flawed colonialism and flawed African primitivism. In an interesting rhetorical move, Naipaul argues that Mobutu's success is due to the

populace's primitivism and void mentality (24). As Gruesser notes, "Modern African and the minds of Africans, asserts Naipaul, have become blank spaces" (1992, 53).

26. In one striking example, the Mobutu government allowed the Belgian mercenary Jean Schramme free rein over the area around Maniema. As Crawford Young notes, "his detachment of mercenaries and Katanga auxiliaries became a kind of private army, and the utter weakness of civil authority in this zone made it possible for him to become a veritable warlord holding sway over a fiefdom of Leopoldian dimensions" (Young 1967a, 14). This arrangement eventually crumbled when Schramme joined forces with Bob Denard to lead a failed mutiny by mercenaries against Mobutu in 1967.

Chapter Five

1. It is important to recognize the extent to which Zaïre was simultaneously fragmented regionally while being bound to international markets by means of clandestine trade. As Janet MacGaffey has noted: "Northeastern Zaïre is part of a regional area extending eastwards to the ports of the Indian Ocean and north to the Sudan, but only as far west as Kisingani. Shaba is tied to Zambia and South Africa and its trade in smuggled imports penetrates to Kasai and Kivu. Lower Zaïre forms a regional trading area with the Democratic Republic of the Congo [Brazzaville] and Angola, including Cabinda. Beyond all these regions, trading ties for some commodities extend much further afield: to Europe, South and West Africa, India, and the Far East" (MacGaffey et al. 1991, 23).
2. For more detailed accounts of Mobutu's final days, see Reno 1997; Turner 1997; McNulty 1999; and Bustin 1999. For a review of the events leading up to the anti-Kabila rebellion, see Reyntjens 1999.
3. Much attention has been paid to the informal sector by scholars of African studies, often with glorified visions of communal redistribution (see Harbeson, Rothchild, and Chazan 1994; Rothchild and Chazan 1988). This "populist myth" is belied by the case of Zaïre/Congo, where the political elite exploits the "second" economy for their own further enrichment. Most citizens engage in the informal sector "out of desperation rather than choice" (MacGaffey et al. 1991, 154; also Bach 1999, 10).
4. For in-depth discussions of the 1994 Rwandan genocide, see Longman 1998; Gourevitch 1998.
5. Much about this episode remains unclear. Estimates on the numbers range from 200,000 to 600,000 refugees. Moreover, it is unclear how many of these returnees did so voluntarily and how many were escorted back under force of arms.
6. For a good discussion of Kabila's career as a rebel leader, see Wilungula 1997.
7. Wamba-dia-Wamba was a longtime critic of Mobutu and had written on African social movements and "emancipative politics" (see Wamba-dia-Wamba 1993).
8. For instance, there is a forthcoming collection of essays edited by Howard Adelman that examines the international politics of the Great Lakes crises. While an important contribution, the book's greatest limitation appears to be its adherence to a state-centric perspective.
9. As Bustin has noted, "even if the regime's well-oiled policies of 'ethnic balancing' had ostensibly been designed to produce a thin, oligarchic 'national' veneer, such policies were, first and foremost, co-optive by nature, and (governed as they were by

an open concern for ethnicity) bound to exacerbate an issue which they purported to exorcise" (Bustin 1999, 88).

10. For several centuries, Western coverage of Africa has been grounded in the rhetoric of "tribalism," in which ethnic divisions were assumed to reflect ahistoric, natural animosities. In order to draw attention to the constructedness of social identities and avoid cultural essentialism, I will put quotation marks around the labels "Hutu" and "Tutsi" throughout this work. For a good discussion of the use of ethnicity as a discourse and practice, see Lemarchand 1994.

11. Rwanda and Burundi, originally colonized by Germany, were governed as a Belgian mandated (later trust) territory (Ruanda-Urundi) until 1962.

12. These categories of identity have become increasingly defined by social myths of revenge and, as Wendy Brown has noted, "revenge as 'reaction,' a substitute for the capacity to act, produces identity as both bound to the history that produces it and as a reproach to the present which embodies it." She goes on to note that "This past cannot be redeemed *unless* the identity ceases to be invested in it, and it cannot cease to be invested in it without giving up its identity as such, thus giving up its economy of avenging and at the same time perpetuating its hurt" (Brown 1995, 73). Yet, rather than essentializing a monochromatic revenge-based identity, it is important to realize that the "Hutu"/"Tutsi" classification is but one of a multitude of identity narratives individuals in the region employ.

13. For a fuller discussion of the RPF's agenda in Zaïre, see Winter 1999.

14. It should be noted, however, that this hostility was somewhat tempered by the convergence of mutual economic interests between the Zaïrian and Ugandan regimes. Uganda had long proved itself willing to be an important transit point for illicit exports of Zaïrian coffee, gold, and ivory carried out by members of Mobutu's entourage, with Ugandan officials receiving financial "compensation" for their assistance.

15. Importantly, the rise of Museveni's regional status was aided by the U.S. government as part of their calculated policy of destabilizing the "Islamist" regime in Khartoum.

16. Sakombi, now a born-again Christian, claimed that he authored Mobutisme while "under the influence of Satan" and that God had sent Kabila as "his instrument to liberate the Congo." See Misser 1998, 26; Sakombi 1997, 38–39.

17. Bemba, the son of one of the Congo's richest businessmen, has little military or political experience. As Belgian journalist Colette Braeckman has rather scathingly noted: "Bemba is more familiar with the restaurants in Brussels, however, than the bush in his own country, his only weapon is a mobile phone, and he relies on the Ugandan army to conduct any military operations" (Braeckman 1999).

18. Many Zimbabweans refer to the Congo intervention as the "Viagra" war, asserting that Mugabe, who recently remarried a significantly younger woman, is using the war to prove his virility.

19. French claims were seemingly supported by the fact that the United States had trained many of the officers in the Ugandan army and the RPF, including Paul Kagame, in the early 1990s. Furthermore, as soon as the RPF seized power, it immediately sent 114 officers to the United States for training (Allimadi 1998, 914).

20. In July 1898, a French military expedition reached the Sudanese settlement of Fashoda in an attempt to extend French colonial reach further into Africa. However, their arrival was soon followed by the appearance of more than twenty thousand Anglo-Egyptians led by Lord Horatio Kitchener. A tense diplomatic crisis ensued, with the French eventually withdrawing in humiliation.

21. For an insightful discussion of this phenomenon, see Huliaras 1998. He argues that French perception of the "Anglo-Saxon conspiracy" can be explained by six factors: "the post–Cold War identity crisis of France's foreign policy; Franco-American rivalry in other geopolitical areas; a perceived threat to French exclusivity in francophone Africa; the 'Fashoda syndrome'; changes in United States foreign policy; and bureaucratic resistance within the French foreign policy decision-making system" (1998, 597–598).
22. Willame writes that "Belgian disinterest and disinvestment in Africa began when it was realized that external affairs were no longer really profitable for Belgium's balance of payments, but mattered only to smaller mining interests" (Willame 1998, 27). By the 1990s, the Belgian government, academic community, and popular press were all increasingly hostile to Mobutu. For a good example of this, see Colette Braeckman's 1992 book on Mobutu and her numerous articles for *Le Soir*.
23. However, the patronizing stance the United States had taken toward Zaïre continued, as is evident in *Newsweek*'s unironic claim: "America is willing to do business with Kabila's new government—providing he manages to behave better than Mobutu ever did" (26 May 1997, 38).

Works Cited

Achebe, Chinua. 1988. "An Image of Africa: Racism in Conrad's *Heart of Darkness.*" In Conrad, *Heart of Darkness: Critical Edition.* New York: W.W. Norton and Co.
Adelman, Kenneth Lee. 1975. "The Recourse to Authenticity and Négritude in Zaïre." *Journal of Modern African Studies* 13(1).
Adorno, Theodor W. 1973. *The Jargon of Authenticity.* Trans. by Knut Tarnowiski and Frederic Will. Evanston: Northwestern University Press.
Africa Confidential. (London).
Africa International. (Paris).
Agnew, John and Stuart Corbridge. 1995. *Mastering Space: Hegemony, Territory and International Political Economy.* London/New York: Routledge.
Albright, Madeline. 1997a. "Promoting America's Interests and Ideals Through Diplomacy." *US Department of State Dispatch* 8(2). February.
Albright, Madeline. 1997b. "Sustaining Principled and Purposeful American Leadership." *US Department of State Dispatch* 8(4). May.
Albright, Madeline. 1998a. "A New Chapter in US-Africa Relations." *US Department of State Dispatch* 9(1). January/February.
Albright, Madeline. 1998b. "US Policy Toward Africa." *US Department of State Dispatch* 9(3). April.
Allen, Chris. 1997. "Zaïre, South Africa: Moving Forward?" *Review of African Political Economy* (72).
Allimadi, Milton. 1998. "The US Connection." *West Africa,* 21 December.
Anderson, Benedict. 1991. *Imagined Communities.* Rev. Ed. London: Verso.
Anstey, Roger. 1966. *King Leopold's Legacy: The Congo Under Belgian Rule 1908–1960.* London: Oxford University Press.
Arendt, Hannah. 1968. *Totalitarianism: Part Three of the Origins of Totalitarianism.* San Diego: Harvest.
Ashley, Richard. 1988. "Untying the Sovereign State: A Double Reading of the Anarchy Problematique." *Millennium.* 17.
Ba, Boubacar. 1970. *Mobutu: L'Homme et L'Oeuvre/The Man and His Work.* Kinshasa(?): Editions Afrique Consortium.
Bach, Daniel C., ed. 1999. *Regionalisation in Africa: Integration and Disintegration.* London/Bloomington: James Currey/Indiana University Press.
Bach, Daniel C. 1986. "France's Involvement in Sub-Saharan Africa: A Necessary Condition to Middle Power Status in the International System." In Amadu Sesay, ed. *Africa and Europe: from Partition to Interdependence or Dependence?* London: Croom Helm.
Bach, Daniel C. 1995. "Frontiers versus boundary-lines: Changing patterns of state-society interactions in sub-Saharan Africa." Paper presented at the APSA Annual meeting, Chicago, September.

Baker, Samuel. 1866. *Albert N'Yanza*. London: Macmillan.
Balakrishnan, Gopal, ed. 1996. *Mapping the Nation*. London: Verso.
Ball, George W. 1961. *The Elements in Our Congo Policy*. Washington, D.C.: US Government Printing Office.
Banning, Emile. 1877. *Africa and the Geographical Conference*. Trans. by Richard Henry Major. London: Sampson Low, Marston, Searle and Rivington.
Barnes, Trevor J. and James S. Duncan, eds. 1992. *Writing Worlds: discourse, text and metaphor in the representation of landscape*. London: Routledge.
Barrell, Howard and Iden Wetherell. 1998. "Rebels advance after fall of Kindu." 16 October. Mimeo in CEDAF archives, Brussels.
Bartelson, Jens. 1995. *A Geneology of Sovereignty*. Cambridge: Cambridge University Press.
Bauer, Ludwig. 1934. *Leopold the Unloved: King of the Belgians and of Money*. London: Cassell.
Bederman, Gail. 1995. *Manliness and Civilization: A cultural history of gender and race in the United States, 1880–1917*. Chicago: University of Chicago.
Bednarek, Jerzy. 1999. "La 'marionette' Kabila rebondit sur l'ogre rwandais." *Africa International*. December/January.
Belgian Congo 59. Brussels: The Belgian Congo and Ruanda-Urundi Information and Public Relations Office.
Belgian Congo To-Day. Brussels: InforCongo.
Belgian Government Information Center. 1959. *The Political Future of the Belgian Congo*. Brussels: InforCongo.
Belgian Government Information Center. 1960. *A Preliminary Report on the atrocities committed by the Congolese Army against the white population of the Republic of the Congo before the intervention of the Belgian Forces*. New York.
La Belgique Coloniale. (Brussels).
Bennett, Norman, ed. 1970. *Stanley's Despatches to the New York Herald 1871–1872, 1874–1877*. Boston: Boston University Press.
Berkeley, Bill. 2001. *The Graves are Not Yet Full*. New York: Basic Books.
Bhaba, Homi. 1984. "Of Mimicry and Men: The Ambivalence of Colonial Discourse." *October* 28, pp. 125–33.
Bhaba, Homi. 1993. "The World and the Home." *Social Text* (summer).
Bierman, John. 1990. *Dark Safari: The Life behind the legend of Henry Morton Stanley*. New York: Knopf.
Biersteker, Thomas and Cynthia Weber, eds. 1996. *State Sovereignty as Social Construct*. Cambridge: Cambridge University Press.
Blanchard, Pascal et al., eds. 1995. *L'Autre et Nous "Scènes et Types."* Paris: ACHAC.
Block, Robert. 1998. "General Partner: Zimbabwe's Elite Turn Strife in Nearby Congo Into Quest for Riches." *Wall Street Journal*, 9 November.
Bøås, Morten, Marianne Marchand, and Timothy M. Shaw, eds. 1999. *Third World Quarterly* 20(5) (special issue: "New Regionalisms in the New Millennium").
Boisseau, T. J. 1996. *The African Adventures of May French-Sheldon*. Ph.D. diss. Binghamton University.
Boissonnade, Euloge. 1990. *Le Mal Zaïrois*. Paris: Hermé.
Bontinck, François. 1966. "Aux origines de l'État Indépendant du Congo: Documents tirés d'Archives Américaines." *Publications de l'Université Lovanium de Léopoldville* 5(15).
Boulger, Demetrius C. 1898. *The Congo State, or the Growth of Civilisation in Central Africa*. London: W. Thacker and Co.

Boulger, Demetrius C. 1900. "The Congo State and Central-African Problems." *Harper's New Monthly Magazine* (February), pp. 373–88.
Boulger, Demetrius C. 1903. "The Attack on the Congo Free State." *North American Review* (15 December), pp. 825–36.
Bourne, H. R. Fox. 1903. *Civilisation in Congoland: A Story of International Wrong-Doing*. London: P.S. King and Son.
Bouvier, Paule. 1965. *L'accession du Congo belge à l'indépendance: Essai d'analyse sociologique*. Brussels: ULB.
Braeckman, Colette. 1992. *Le Dinosaur: Le Zaïre de Mobutu*. Pris: Fayard.
Braeckman, Colette. 1999. "Carve-up in the Congo." Trans. by Barbara Wilson. Mimeo in CEDAF archives, Brussels.
Brausch, George. 1961. *Belgian Administration in the Congo*. London: Oxford University Press.
Brown, Wendy. 1995. *States of Injury: Power and Freedom in Late Modernity*. Princeton: Princeton University Press.
Brubaker, Rogers and Frederick Cooper. 2000. "Beyond 'Identity.'" *Theory and Society* (February), pp. 1–47.
Brugailliere, Marie-Christine. 1993. "Un journal au service d'une conquête: *Le Mouvement Géographique* (1884–1908)." In Halen and Riesz, eds. *Images de l'Afrique et du Congo/Zaïre dans les lettres française de Belgique et alentour*. Brussels: Éditions du Trottoir.
Buchan, David. 1997. "France broadens African policy focus." *Financial Times*. 8 September.
Burrows, Capt. Guy. 1903. *The Curse of Central Africa*. London: R.A. Everett.
Burton, Richard Francis. 1877. *A Mission to Geleke, King of Dahomey*, 2 vols. London.
Bustin, Edouard. 1964. "After Stanleyville What?" *Africa Today* 11(10).
Bustin, Edouard. 1967. "Confrontation in the Congo." *Current History* (March).
Bustin, Edouard. 1968. "Consolidation in the Congo." *Current History* (February).
Bustin, Edouard. 1982. "The limits of French intervention in Africa: A study in applied neo-colonialism." Working paper no. 54. Boston University African Studies Center. Boston, MA.
Bustin, Edouard. 1999. "The Collapse of 'Congo/Zaïre' and its Regional Impact." In Bach, ed. *Regionalisation in Africa: Integration and Disintegration*. London/Bloomington: James Currey/Indiana University Press.
Butler, Judith. 1990. *Gender Trouble: Feminism and the Subversion of Identity*. New York: Routledge.
Buzan, Barry. 1998. "Conclusion: System Versus Units in Theorizing about the Third World." In Neuman, ed. *International Relations Theory and the Third World*. New York: St. Martin's Press.
Callaghy, Thomas M. 1979. "State Formation and Absolutism in Comparative Perspective: Seventeen Century France and Mobutu Sese Seko's Zaïre." Ph.D. Diss. University of California—Berkeley.
Callaghy, Thomas M. 1983. "External Actors and the Relative Autonomy of the Political Aristocracy in Zaïre." *Journal of Commonwealth and Comparative Politics* 21(3).
Callaghy, Thomas M. 1984. *The State-Society Struggle: Zaïre in Comparative Perspective*. New York: Columbia University Press.
Callaghy, Thomas M. 1986a. "The International Community and Zaïre's Debt Crisis." In Nzongola-Ntalaja, ed. *The Crisis in Zaïre: Myths and Realities*. Trenton: Africa World Press.
Callaghy, Thomas M. 1986b. "The Political Economy of African Debt: The Case of

Zaïre." In Ravenhill, ed. *Africa in Economic Crisis*. New York: Columbia University Press.

Callaghy, Thomas M. 1987. "The State as Lame Leviathan: The Patrimonial Administrative State in Africa." In Zaki Ergas, ed. *The African State in Transition*. New York: St. Martin's Press.

Campbell, David. 1992. *Writing Security: United States Foreign Policy and the Politics of Identity*. Minneapolis: University of Minnesota.

Canisius, Edgar. 1903. *A Campaign Amongst Cannibals*. Reprinted in Burrows, *The Curse of Central Africa*. London: R.A. Everett.

Chabal, Patrick and Jean-Pascal Daloz. 1999. *Africa Works: Disorder as Political Instrument*. Oxford: James Currey for the International African Institute.

Chatterjee, Partha. 1986. *Nationalist Thought and the Colonial World: A Derivative Discourse?* London: Zed Books.

Chatterjee, Partha. 1996. "Whose Imagined Community?" In Balakrishnan, ed. *Mapping the Nation*. London and New York: Verso.

Chomé, Jules. 1974. *L'Ascension de Mobutu: du Sergent Joseph Désiré au Général Sese Seko*. Brussels: Éditions Complexe.

Clapham, Christopher. 1996. *Africa and the International System: The Politics of State Survival*. Cambridge: Cambridge University Press.

Clapham, Christopher. 1999. "Boundaries and States in the New African Order." In Bach, ed. *Regionalisation in Africa: Integration and Disintegration*. London/Bloomington: James Currey/Indiana University Press.

Clark, John F. 1998. "Zaïre: The Bankruptcy of the Extractive State." In Villalón and Huxtable, eds. *The African State at a Critical Juncture: Between Disintegration and Reconfiguration*. Boulder: Lynne Rienner.

Close, William T. 2001. *A Doctor's Story*. New York: Ivy Books.

Cockx, A. and J. Lemmens. 1958. *Les Expositions Universelles et Internationales en Belgique de 1885 à 1958*. Brussels: SPRL.

Cohn, Bernard S. 1996. *Colonialism and Its Forms of Knowledge*. Princeton: Princeton University Press.

Collins, Carole J. L. 1997a. "The Congo Is Back!" *Review of African Political Economy* (72).

Collins, Carole J. L. 1997b. "Reconstructing the Congo." *Review of African Political Economy* (74).

Collins, Carole J. L. 1998. "Congo/Ex-Zaïre: Through the Looking Glass." *Review of African Political Economy* (75).

Comaroff, Jean and John Comaroff. 1991. *Of Revelation and Revolution: Christianity, Colonialism, and Consciousness in South Africa*. Vol. 1. Chicago/London: University of Chicago Press.

Commercial Appeal. (Memphis, TN).

Congressional Record. Various dates. U.S. Congress. Washington, D.C.

Congo belge et Ruanda et Ruanda-Urundi: Agriculture, Élevage, Forêt, Chasse, et Pêche. 1958. Brussels: Ministère des Colonies.

Connolly, William. 1991. *IdentityDifference: Democratic Negotiations of Political Paradox*. Ithaca: Cornell University Press.

Connolly, William. 1993. "Democracy and Territoriality." In Dolan and Dumm, eds. *Rhetorical Republic: Governing Representations in American Politics*. Amherst: University of Massachusetts Press.

Connolly, William. 1996. "Tocqueville, Territory, and Violence." In Shapiro and Alker, eds. *Challenging Boundaries*. Minneapolis: University of Minnesota Press.

Conrad, Joseph. 1975. "An Outpost of Progress." In *The Portable Conrad: Revised Edition*. New York: Penguin
Conrad, Joseph. 1988. *Heart of Darkness: Critical Edition*. New York: W.W. Norton and Co.
Cornell, Stephen. 2000. "That's the Story of Our Life." In Spickard and Burroughs, eds. *We Are a People: Narrative and Multiplicity in Constructing Ethnic Identity*. Philadelphia: Temple University Press.
Cox, Robert. 1993. "Gramsci, Hegemony and International Relations: An essay in method." In Gill, ed. *Gramsci, Historical Materialism and International Relations*. Cambridge: Cambridge University Press.
Crichton, Michael. 1980. *Congo*. New York: Ballentine Books.
Davidson, Basil. 1961. *Black Mother, Africa*. London: Victor Gollancz.
Davidson, Basil. 1992. *The Black Man's Burden: Africa and the Curse of the Nation-State*. New York: Times Books.
Dayal, Rajeshwar. 1976. *Mission for Hammarskjöld: The Congo Crisis*. Princeton: Princeton University Press.
De Baets, Antoon. 1991. "Le Congo dans les manuels d'histoire employés dans nos écoles." In *Decoder L'Image Du Noir: Brochure Éducative pour "Le Noir du Blanc."* Brussels: École sans Racisme.
De Boeck, Filip. 1996. "Postcolonialism, power and identity: Local and global perspectives from Zaïre." In Werbner and Ranger, eds. *Postcolonial Identities in Africa*. London: Zed Books.
De St. Moulin, L. 1990. "What is Known of the Demographic History of Zaire Since 1885?" In Fetter, ed. *Demography From Scanty Evidence: Central Africa in the Colonial Era*. Boulder: Lynne Rienner.
De Villers, Gauthier, ed. 1994. *Belgique/Zaire: Une histoire en quête d'avenir*. Paris: L'Harmattan.
De Villers, Gauthier. 1995. *De Mobutu à Mobutu: Trente ans de relations Belgique-Zaïre*. Brussels: DeBoeck Université.
De Witte, Ludo. 2001. *The Assassination of Lumumba*. New York: Verso.
Deleuze, Gilles and Félix Guattari. 1977. "Savages, Barbarians, Civilized Men." In *Anti-Oedipus: Capitalism and Schizophrenia*. Trans. by Robert Hurley et al. New York: Viking.
Denselow, Robin. 2001. "Quiet Spoken: UN Fears Cyprus-style Division in Congo." *The Guardian* (Manchester), 28 June, 1.
Diamond, Larry. 1987. "Class Formation in the Swollen African State." *Journal of Modern African Studies* 25(4).
Djungu-Simba K., Charles. 1997. "La figure de Patrice Lumumba dans les lettres du Congo-Zaïre." In Halen and Riesz, eds. *Patrice Lumumba entre Dieu et Diable: Un héros africain dans ses images*. Paris: L'Harmattan.
Donny, Albert. 1897–1901. *Manuel du Voyageur et du Résident au Congo*. 5 vols. Brussels: Hayez.
Doty, Roxanne Lynn. 1993. "The Bounds of 'Race' in International Relations." *Millennium* 22(3).
Doty, Roxanne Lynn. 1996. *Imperial Encounters: The Politics of Representation in North-South Relations*. Minneapolis: University of Minnesota.
Du Bois, Victor D. 1973. *Zaïre Under President Sese Seko Mobutu: Part I: The Return to Authenticity*. American University Field Staff Report. Central and Southern Africa Series 17(1).
Dunn, Kevin C. 2002. "A Survival Guide to Kinshasa: Lessons of the Father, Passed

Down to the Son." In John F. Clark, ed. *The African Stakes of the Congo's War*. New York: Palgrave.

Dunn, Kevin C. and Timothy M. Shaw, eds. 2001. *Africa's Challenge to International Relations Theory*. London: Macmillan.

East African, The. (Nairobi, Kenya).

Economist, The. (London).

Eisenhower, Dwight D. 1965. *The White House Years: Waging Peace 1956–1961*. Garden City: Doubleday.

Evans, Glynne. 1997. *Responding to Crises in the African Great Lakes*. Adelphi Paper 311. Oxford: Oxford University Press.

Fabian, Johannes. 1983. *Time and the Other: How Anthropology Makes Its Objects*. New York: Columbia University Press.

Ferguson, Kennan. 1996. "Unmapping and Remapping the World: Foreign Policy as Aesthetic Practice." In Shapiro and Alker, eds. *Challenging Boundaries*. Minneapolis: University of Minnesota Press.

Fieldhouse, D. K. 1981. *Colonialism 1870–1945: An Introduction*. London: Weidenfeld and Nicolson.

Fierlafyn, Luc. 1990. *Le Discours Nationaliste au Congo Belge durant la Période 1955–1960*. Brussels: CEDAF/ASDOC.

Financial Times. (London).

Fisher, Ian. 2001. "Heart of Greed." *New York Times*, 10 June, 16.

Fisiy, Cyprian F. 1998. "Of Journeys and Border Crossings: Return of Refugees, Identity and Reconstruction in Rwanda." *African Studies Review* 41(1).

Forbath, Peter. 1977. *The River Congo*. New York: E. P. Dutton.

Foucault, Michel. 1980. *Power/Knowledge: Selected Interviews and Other Writings, 1972–1977*. New York: Pantheon.

Fox, Renée C. 1984. *In the Belgian Château: The Spirit and Culture of a European Society in an Age of Change*. Chicago: Ivan R. Dee.

François, Albert. 1943. *Congo: Terre D'Héroisme*. 2d. Ed. Brussels: Office de Publicité.

French, Howard W. 1997. "The Great Gold Rush in Zaïre, Mining Concerns Court Rebels Even Before Mobutu's Ouster." *New York Times*, 18 April.

Gálvez, William. 1999. *Che in Africa: Che Guevara's Congo Diary*. Melbourne: Ocean Press.

Gann, L. H. and Peter Duigan. 1979. *The Rulers of Belgian African, 1884–1914*. Princeton: Princeton University Press.

Geller, Ernest. 1964. *Thought and Change*. London: Weidenfeld and Nicolson.

Gendarme, Fernard. 1942. *Croquis Congolais*. Brussels: Editions Wellens-Pay.

Gendebien, Paul-Henry. 1967. *L'Intervention des Nations Unites au Congo 1960–1964*. Paris: Mouton et Cie.

Gerard-Libios, J. and Benoit Verhaegen. 1961. *Congo 1960*. Brussels: CRISP.

Gibbs, David. 1991. *The Political Economy of Third World Intervention*. Chicago: University of Chicago.

Gill, Stephen. 1993. "Gramsci and Global Politics: Towards a post-hegemonic research agenda." In Gill, ed. *Gramsci, Historical Materialism and International Relations*. Cambridge: Cambridge University Press.

Gleijeses, Piero. 1994. "'Flee! The White Giants Are Coming!': The United States, the Mercenaries, and the Congo, 1964–65." *Diplomatic History* 18(2).

Gong, Gerrit W. 1984. *The Standard of "Civilization" in International Society*. Oxford: Oxford University Press.

Gould, Stephen Jay. 1981. *The Mismeasurement of Man*. New York: Norton.

Works Cited

Gourevitch, Philip. 1998. *We wish to inform you that tomorrow we will be killed with our families: Stories from Rwanda.* New York: Farrar Straus and Giroux.
Gramsci, Antonio. 1971. *Selections from the Prison Notebooks.* Trans. by Quintin Hoare and Geoffrey Nowell Smith. New York: International Publishers.
Gray, Christopher. 1998. "Multinational and Human Rights Promotion: A Role for Mining Companies in the Democratic Republic of Congo?" Paper presented at the African Studies Association Conference, Chicago, 31 October.
Greene, Graham. 1960. *A Burnt-Out Case.* New York: Viking.
Grimsley, Ronald. 1974. *From Montesquieu to Laclos: Studies on the French Enlightenment.* Geneva: Droz.
Grotius, Hugo. 1623 (1901). *The Rights of War and Peace.* London: Walter Dunne.
Grovogui, Siba. 1996. *Sovereigns, Quasi Sovereigns, and Africans.* Minneapolis: University of Minnesota Press.
Grovogui, Siba. 2000. "Sovereignty in Africa: Quasi-Statehood and Other Myths in International Theory." In Dunn and Shaw, eds. *Africa's Challenge to International Relations Theory.* London: Macmillan.
Gruesser, John Cullen. 1992. *White on Black: Contemporary Literature about Africa.* Urbana: University of Illinois Press.
Guardian, The. (London).
Halen, Pierre and János Riesz, eds. 1993. *Images de l'Afrique et du Congo/Zaïre dans les lettres française de Belgique et alentour.* Brussels: Textyles.
Halen, Pierre and János Riesz, eds. 1997. *Patrice Lumumba entre Dieu et Diable: Un héros africain dans ses images.* Paris: L'Harmattan.
Halen, Pierre. 1995. "L'Illustration du Congo et le Discours des 'Beaux-Livres.'" In Blanchard et al., eds. *L'Autre et Nous "Scènes et Types."* Paris: ACHAC.
Hall, John A. and G. John Ikenberry. 1989. *The State.* Minneapolis: University of Minnesota Press.
Hall, Stuart. 1980. "Encoding/decoding." In Hall et al., eds. *Culture, Media, Language.* London: Hutchinson.
Hall, Stuart. 1988. "The Toad in the Garden: Thatcherism among the Theorists." In C. Nelson and L. Grossberg, eds. *Marxism and the Interpretation of Culture.* Urbana/Chicago: University of Illinois Press.
Hall, Stuart. 1995. "Fantasy, Identity, Politics." In Carter, Donald and Squites, eds. *Cultural Remix: Theories of Politics and the Popular.* London: Lawrence and Wishart.
Hall, Stuart. 1996. "Who Needs 'Identity'?" in Hall and Du Gay, eds. *Questions of Cultural Identity.* London: Sage.
Hammond, Dorothy and Alta Jablow. 1970. *The Africa That Never Was.* Prospect Heights: Waveland Press.
Hannaford, Ivan. 1996. *Race: The History of an Idea in the West.* Washington: John Hopkins University Press.
Harbeson, John, Donald Rothchild, and Naomi Chazan, eds. 1994. *Civil Society and the State in Africa.* Boulder: Lynne Rienner.
Hawthorne, Peter. 1999. "Diamonds in the Rough." *Time.* 6 December.
Hettne, Björn and Frederik Söderbaum. 1998. *Politeia* 17(3) (special issue on the New Regionalism).
Hochschild, Adam. 1998. *King Leopold's Ghost.* Boston: Houghton Mifflin.
Hodgkin, Thomas. 1956. *Nationalism in Colonial Africa.* London: Frederick Muller.
Hoskyns, Catherine. 1965. *The Congo Since Independence.* London: Oxford University Press.

Hugon, Anne. 1993. *The Exploration of Africa: From Cairo to the Cape.* New York: Abrams.

Huliaras, Asteris C. 1998. "The 'Anglosaxon Conspiracy': French perceptions of the Great Lakes crisis." *Journal of Modern African Studies* 36(4).

Human Rights Watch. 1997. *Democratic Republic of the Congo: What Kabila Is Hiding.* New York: Human Rights Watch/Africa.

Inayatullah, Naeem. 1996. "Beyond the sovereignty dilemma: Quasi-states as social construct." In Biersteker and Weber, eds. *State Sovereignty as Social Construct.* Cambridge: Cambridge University Press.

Isaacman, Allan and Jan Vansina. 1985. "African Initiatives and Resistance in Central Africa, 1880–1914." In A. Adu Boahen, ed. *General History of Africa.* Vol. 7. Paris: UNESCO.

Jackson, Robert H. 1990. *Quasi-states: Sovereignty, international relations and the Third World.* Cambridge: Cambridge University Press.

Jackson, Robert H. and Carl G. Rosberg. 1982. "Why Africa's Weak States Persist: The Empirical and the Juridical in Statehood." *World Politics* 35(1).

Jacquemin, Jean-Pierre, ed. 1991. *Racisme Continent Obscur: Clichés, Stereotypes, Phantasmes à propos des noirs dans le Royaume de Belgique.* Brussels: CEC.

Jacquemin, Jean-Pierre, ed. 1985. *Zaïre 1885–1985: Cent ans de regards belges.* Brussels: CEC.

Jankowiak, Stanislaw. 1997. "Patrice Lumumba d'après la propagande à l'époque de la République Populaire Polonaise." In Halen and Riesz, eds. *Patrice Lumumba entre Dieu et Diable: Un héros africain dans ses images.* Paris: L'Harmattan.

Jeune Afrique. (Paris).

Jewsiewicki, Bogumil. 1979. "Zaire enters the World System: Its Colonial Incorporation as the Belgian Congo, 1885–1960." In Guy Gran, ed. *Zaire: The Political Economy of Underdevelopment.* New York: Praeger.

Jewsiewicki, Bogumil. 1980. "Political Consciousness among African Peasants in the Belgian Congo." *Review of African Political Economy* 19.

Kabila, Laurent-Désiré. 1998. "Hommage à Patrice Emery Lumumba: 19 January 1998 Speech." Available at http://rdcongo.org/frames/acp/archives/Official4.html.

Kabila, Laurent-Désiré. 1999. "Create Committees of the People's Power Everywhere: 21 January 1999 Speech." Available at http://194.78.3.66/congo.

Kabwit, Ghislain C. 1979. "Zaïre: The Roots of the Continuing Crisis." *Journal of Modern African Studies* 17(3).

Kalb, Madeleine. 1982. *The Congo Cables.* New York: Macmillan.

Kangafu-Kutumbagana. 1973. *Discours sur L'Authenticité.* Les Presse Africaines.

Kannyo, Edward. 1979. "Postcolonial Politics in Zaïre, 1960–79." In Guy Gran, ed. *Zaïre: The Political Economy of Underdevelopment.* New York: Praeger.

Kaplan, Amy and Donald E. Pease, eds. 1993. *Cultures of United States Imperialism.* Durham: Duke University Press.

Kaplan, Robert. 1994. "The Coming Anarchy." *The Atlantic Monthly* (February).

Kaplan, Robert. 1996. *The Ends of the Earth: A Journey at the Dawn of the 21st Century.* New York: Random House.

Karp, Ivan. 1991. "Culture and Representation." In *Exhibiting Cultures: The Poetics and Politics of Museum Display.* Washington, D.C.: Smithsonian Institution Press.

Katzenstein, Peter, ed. 1996. *The Culture of National Security: Norms and Identity in World Politics.* New York: Columbia University Press.

Keith, Arthur. 1919. *The Belgian Congo and the Berlin Act.* London: Oxford University Press.

Works Cited

Kelly, Sean. 1993. *America's Tyrant: The CIA and Mobutu of Zaïre*. Washington, D.C.: American University Press.
Kennan, George. 1946 (1993). "The Kennan 'Long Telegram.'" In Kenneth M. Jensen, ed. *Origins of the Cold War: The Novikov, Kennan, and Roberts "Long Telegrams" of 1946*. Rev. Ed. Washington, D.C.: United States Institute for Peace Press.
Kennedy, Pagan. 2002. *Black Livingstone: A True Tale of Adventure in the Nineteenth-Century Congo*. New York: Viking.
Kennes, Erik. 1999. *Essai Biographique sur Laurent-Désiré Kabila*. Brussels: Cahiers Africains.
Khrushchev, Nikita. 1974. *Khrushchev Remembers: The Last Testament*. Trans. and ed. by Strobe Talbot. Boston: Little, Brown.
Kingsolver, Barbara. 1998. *The Poisonwood Bible*. New York: Harper Flamingo.
Kitchen, Helen, ed. 1967. *Footnotes to the Congo Story*. New York: Walker and Co.
Kivilu, Sabakinu. 1990. "Population and Worker Mortality in Western Zaire." In Fetter, ed. *Demography From Scanty Evidence: Central Africa in the Colonial Era*. Boulder: Lynne Rienner.
Kopytoff, Igor. 1987. "The internal African frontier: The making of African political culture." In Kopytoff, ed. *The African Frontier: The Reproduction of Traditional African Societies*. Bloomington: Indiana University Press.
Lapid, Yosef and Friederich Kratochwil, eds. 1996. *The Return of Culture and Identity in IR Theory*. Boulder: Lynne Rienner.
Lefever, Ernest. 1965. *Crisis in the Congo: A United Nations Force in Action*. Washington: Brookings Institution.
Lemarchand, René. 1964. *Political Awakening in the Belgian Congo*. Berkeley: University of California.
Lemarchand, René. 1976. "The CIA in Africa: How Central? How Intelligent?" *Journal of Modern African Studies* 14(3).
Lemarchand, René. 1981. "Zaïre: The Unmanageable Client-State." In Lemarchand, ed. *American Policy in Southern Africa: The Stakes and the Stance*. 2d Ed. Washington, D.C.: University Press of America.
Lemarchand, René. 1994. *Burundi: Ethnocide as discourse and practice*. Washington: Woodrow Wilson Center Press.
Lemarchand, René. 1995. *Burundi: Ethnic Conflict and Genocide*. New York: Cambridge University Press.
Lemarchand, René. 1998a. "Genocide in the Great Lakes: Which Genocide? Whose Genocide?" *African Studies Review* 41(1).
Lemarchand, René. 1998b. "US Policy in the Great Lakes: A Critical Perspective." *Issue: A Journal of Opinion* 26(1).
Lemelin, Bernard. 1997. "De l'indifférence à l'effroi: le Congrès américain et Patrice Lumumba (1959–1961)." In Halen and Riesz, eds. *Patrice Lumumba entre Dieu et Diable: Un héros africain dans ses images*. Paris: L'Harmattan.
Lenin, V. I. 1939. *Imperialism: The Highest Stage of Capitalism*. New York: International Publishers.
Leopold II (a.k.a. "A Belgian"). 1903. *The Truth About the Civilisation in Congoland*. London: Sampson Low, Marston and Co.
Leslie, Winsome J. 1986. "The World Bank and Zaïre." In Nzongola-Ntalaja, ed. *The Crisis in Zaïre: Myths and Realities*. Trenton: Africa World Press.
Leslie, Winsome J. 1993. *Zaïre: Continuity and Political Change in an Oppressive State*. Boulder: Westview Press.

Leys, Colin. 1976. *Underdevelopment in Kenya: the Political Economy of neo-Colonialism 1964–71*. London: Heinemann.
Libre Belgique, La. (Brussels).
Lindqvist, Sven. 1992. *"Exterminate All the Brutes."* New York: New Press.
Longman, Timothy. 1998. "Rwanda: Chaos from Above." In Villalón and Huxtable, eds. *The African State at a Critical Juncture: Between Disintegration and Reconfiguration*. Boulder: Lynne Rienner.
Lorimer, Douglas. 1978. *Race, Class and the Victorians*. New York: Holmes and Meir.
Louis, W. R. and Jean Stengers, ed. 1968. *E. D. Morel's History of the Congo Reform Movement*. Oxford: Oxford University Press.
Lumumba, Patrice. 1962. *Congo, My Country*. New York: Praeger.
Lüsebrink, Hans-Jürgen. 1993. "Images de l'Afrique et Mise en Scéne du Congo Belge dans les Expositions Coloniales Française et Belges (1889–1937)." In Halen and Riesz, eds. *Images de l'Afrique et du Congo/Zaïre dans les lettres française de Belgique et alentour*. Brussels: Éditions du Trottoir.
Luwel, Marcel. 1967. *Tervuren 1897*. Tervuren: Musée Royal de l'Afrique Centrale.
MacGaffey, Janet, et al. 1991. *The Real Economy of Zaïre: The contribution of smuggling and other unofficial activities to national wealth*. London/Philadelphia: James Currey/University of Pennsylvania Press.
MacGaffey, Janet. 1987. *Entrepreneurs and Parasites: The struggle for indigenous capitalism in Zaïre*. Cambridge: Cambridge University Press.
MacGaffey, Wyatt. 1997. "Kongo Identity, 1483–1993." In Mudimbe, ed. *Nations, Identities, Cultures*. Durham: Duke University Press
Malaquias, Assis. 2000. "Reformulating International Relations Theory: African Insights and Challenges." In Dunn and Shaw, eds. *Africa's Challenge to International Relations Theory*. London: Macmillan.
Makau wa Mutua. 1994. "Redrawing the map along African lines." *The Boston Globe*, 22 September.
Malengreau, Guy. 1955. "Recent Developments in Belgian Africa." In C. Grove Haines, ed. *Africa Today*. Baltimore: John Hopkins Press.
Mamdani, Mahmood. 1998. "The Solution: Political Reform." *Mail & Guardian* (Johannesburg), 14 August. (Reprinted in *World Press Review*, November 1998).
Manwana-Mungongo. 1972. *Le Général Mobutu Sese Seko parle du Nationalisme Zaïrois Authentique*. Kinshasa: Éditions OKAPI.
Marchal, Jules. 1996. *L'Etat Libre du Congo: Paradis Perdu. L'Histoire du Congo 1876–1900*. 2 vols. Borgloon, Belgium: Editions Paula Bellings.
Marchal, Jules. 1999. *Travail Forcé pour le Cuivre et pour l'Or*. Vol. 1. Borgloon: Editions Paula Bellings.
Marchal, Roland. 1998. "France and Africa: The emergence of essential reforms?" *International Affairs* 74(2).
Marzorati, A. F. G. 1954. "The Political Organisation and the Evolution of African Society in the Belgian Congo." *African Affairs* 53(211).
Masuy, Christine. 1997. "Du Portrait au Personage: La diabolisation symbolique de Patrice Lumumba dans *La Libre Belgique*." In Halen and Riesz, eds. *Patrice Lumumba Entre Dieu et Diable*. Paris: L'Harmattan.
Mayall, James. 1990. *Nationalism and international society*. Cambridge: Cambridge University Press.
Mazrui, Ali. 1967. "African Diplomatic Thought and the Principle of Legitimacy." In Gappert and Thomas, eds. *The Congo, Africa and America*. Occasional Paper no. 15. Maxwell Graduate School, Syracuse University.

Works Cited

McClintock, Anne. 1995. *Imperial Leather: Race, Gender and Sexuality in the Colonial Contest*. London: Routledge.
McKinley, James C. Jr. 1997. "Zaïre's New Troops: Mining Executives Wielding Briefcases." *New York Times*. 17 April.
McLynn, Frank. 1989. *Stanley: The Making of an African Explorer*. London: Constable.
McNulty, Mel. 1997. "France's Rwanda débâcle." *War Studies Journal* 2(2) (spring).
McNulty, Mel. 1999. "The collapse of Zaïre: Implosion, revolution or external sabotage?" *Journal of Modern African Studies* 37(1).
McRobbie, Angela. 1994. *Postmodernism and Popular Culture*. New York: Routledge.
"Memorandum From the Director of the Bureau of Intelligence and Research to Secretary of State Herter, 25 July 1960." 1992. *Foreign Relations of the United States, 1958–1960*. Vol 14. *Africa*. Washington, D.C..
Merriam, Alan. 1961. *Congo: Background of Conflict*. Northwestern University Press.
Michel, Serge. 1962. *Uhuru Lumumba*. Paris: René Julliard.
Migdal, Joel. 1988. *Strong Societies and Weak States*. Princeton: Princeton University Press.
Miller, Christopher. 1985. *Blank Darkness: Africanist Discourse in French*. Chicago: University of Chicago Press.
Ministry of Justice (Belgium). 1960. *Congo July 1960 Evidence*. Antwerp: Excelsior.
Minneapolis Tribune. (Minneapolis).
Minter, William. 1986. "Candid Cables: Some Reflections on US Responses to the Congo Rebellions, 1964." In Nzongola-Ntalaja, ed. *The Crisis in Zaïre: Myths and Realities*. Trenton: Africa World Press.
Misser, François. 1998. "Kabila 'chosen by God.'" *New African*. March.
Mitchell, Timothy. 1988. *Colonizing Egypt*. London. Cambridge University Press.
Mobutu Sese Seko. 1975. *Discours, Allocutions et Messages, 1965–1975*. 2 Vols. Paris: Éditions J.A.
Mobutu Sese Seko. 1983. *Discours, Allocutions, Messages—1982: Une Grande Année Politique*. Kinshasa: Bureau du President.
Mobutu Sese Seko. 1989. *Dignité pour l'Afrique: Entretiens avec Jean-Louis Remilleux*. Paris: Éditions Albin Michel.
Mobutu, Joseph-Désiré. 1968. *De La Légalité à la Légitimité*. Kinshasa: Haut Commissariat à l'Information.
Mobutu, Joseph-Désiré. 1971. "Jeune Afrique Fait Parler Mobutu." *Jeune Afrique* (533/534), 30 March 1971.
Monde, Le. (Paris).
Monitor, The. (Kampala, Uganda).
Morel, E. D. 1904a. *King Leopold's Rule in Africa*. London: Heinemann.
Morel, E. D. 1904b. *The Treatment of Women and Children in the Congo State, 1895–1904. An appeal to the women of the British Empire, and of the United States of America*. Liverpool: John Richardson and Sons.
Morel, E. D. 1904c. *The Scandal of the Congo: Britain's Duty*. (Pamphlet in CEDAF archives, Brussels).
Morel, E. D. 1904d. "The 'Commercial' Aspect of the Congo Question." *Journal of the African Society*. (12).
Morel, E. D. 1908. *The Economic Aspect of the Congo Problem: The Kernel of the Question*. Liverpool: John Richardson and Sons.
Morel, E. D. 1909. *Great Britain and the Congo: The Pillage of the Congo Basin*. London: Smith, Elder and Co.
Morel, E. D. n.d. *The Belgian Curse in Africa*. Pamphlet in CEDAF archives, Brussels.

Morley, David and Kevin Robins, eds. 1995. *Spaces of Identity: Global media, electronic landscapes and cultural boundaries.* London: Routledge.
Morris, Richard and Richard Mauay. 1976. "Following the Scenario: Reflections on Five Case Histories in the Mode and Aftermath of CIA Intervention." In Robert Borosage and John Marks, eds. *The CIA File.* New York: Grossman.
Morue, Brigitte. 1980. *Lumumba a travers la presse belge: Jan. 1960-Nov. 1961.* Ph.D. Diss. Universite Libre de Bruxelles.
Mpinga Kasenda. 1975. "Le Mobutisme." *Remarques Africaines.* no. 454 (1 January).
MPR. 1967. "Manifeste du Mouvement Populaire de la Révolution (MPR)." *Etudes Congolaises* 10(3).
MRB: Southern Africa Monthly Regional Bulletin.
Mudimbe, V. Y., ed. 1997. *Nations, Identities, Cultures.* Durham: Duke University Press.
Mudimbe, V. Y. 1988. *The Invention of Africa.* Bloomington: Indiana University Press.
Mudimbe, V. Y. 1994. *The Idea of Africa.* Bloomington: Indiana University Press.
Mummendey, Dietrich. 1997. *Beyond the Reach of Reason: The Congo Story, 1960–1965.* Sora Mummendey.
Murphy, Craig N. 1997. "Book review of *Imperial Encounters* by Roxanne Lynn Doty." *American Political Science Review* 91(4).
Murphy, Craig. 1998. "Understanding IR: Understanding Gramsci." *Review of International Studies* 24.
Musambachime, Mwelwa C. 1987. "The Changing Political Personality of an African Politician: The case of Patrice Emery Lumumba, 1956–1961." *Genève-Afrique* 15(2).
Mutamba Makombo, Jean-Marie. 1993. *Patrice Lumumba correspondant de presse (1948–1956).* Brussels: CEDAF/ASDOC.
Naipaul, V. S. 1975. "A New King for the Congo." *The New York Review of Books.* 26 June.
Naipaul, V. S. 1979. *A Bend in the River.* New York: Vintage.
New Vision. (Kampala, Uganda).
New York Times. (New York).
Newbury, Catharine M. 1984. "Dead and Buried or Just Underground? The Privatisation of the State in Zaïre." In B. Jewsiewicki, ed. *L'Etat Independant du Congo, Congo Belge, Republique Democratique du Congo, Republique du Zaïre?* Ste-Foy, Quebec: Editions SAFI Press.
Newbury, David. 1998. "Understanding Genocide." *African Studies Review* 41(1).
Newsweek. (New York).
Ngandu Nkashama. 1972. "La litterature au Zaïre avant 1960." *Zaïre-Afrique* 68.
Ñgugi wa Thiong'o. 1981. *Decolonising the Mind: The Politics of Language in African Literature.* London: James Currey.
Nguza Karl-i-Bond. 1982. *Mobutu, ou l'incarnation du Mal Zairois.* London: Rex Collings.
Niemann, Michael. 2001. "Unstated Places—Rereading Southern Africa." In Vale, Swatuk, and Oden, eds. *Theory, Change and Southern Africa's Future.* London: Palgrave.
Nietzsche, Friedrich Wilhelm. 1982. *The Portable Nietzsche.* New York: Penguin Books.
Nkrumah, Kwame. 1960. *The Congo Situation.* Accra: Ghana Information Services.
Nugent, Paul and A. I. Asiwaju, eds. 1996. *African Boundaries: Barriers, Conduits and Opportunities.* London: Pinter.
Nyoto. (Kinshasa, Zaïre).
Nyunda ya Rubango. 1980. *Les principales tendances du discours politique zaïrois (1960–1965).* Brussels: CEDAF/ASDOC.

Nzongola-Ntalaja. 1977–78. "The Authenticity of Neocolonialism: Ideology and Class Struggle in Zaïre." *Berkeley Journal of Sociology* 22.
Nzongola-Ntalaja. 1982. *Class Struggles and National Liberation in Africa: Essays on the Political Economy of Neocolonialism*. Roxbury, MA: Omenana.
O'Brien, Connor Cruise. 1966. "The United Nations and the Congo." *Studies on the Left* 4.
Onishi, Norimitsu, 2001. "Congo: Ban Ends on Political Parties." *New York Times*, 18 May, 6.
Oppenheim, L. 1920. *International Law: A Treatise*. London: Longmans and Green.
Orwa, Katete. 1985. *The Congo Betrayal: The UN-US and Lumumba*. Nairobi: Kenya Literature Bureau.
Ó Tuathail, Gearóid and John Agnew. 1992. "Geopolitics and Discourse: Practical Geopolitical Reasoning in American Foreign Policy." *Political Geography Quarterly* 11.
Ó Tuathail, Gearóid and Simon Dalby, eds. 1998. *Rethinking Geopolitics*. London: Routledge.
Ó Tuathail, Gearóid, Simon Dalby, and Paul Routledge, eds. 1998. *The Geopolitics Reader*. London: Routledge.
Parry, Benita. 1983. *Conrad and Imperialism*. London: Macmillan.
Peemans, Jean-Philippe. 1975. "The Social and Economic Development of Zaïre Since Independence: An Historical Outline." *African Affairs* 74(295) (April).
Picard, Edmond. 1896. *En Congolie*. Brussels: Paul Lacomblez.
Pieterse, Jan Nederveen. 1992. *White on Black: Images of Africa and Blacks in Western Popular Culture*. New Haven: Yale University Press.
Pigafetta, Filippo. 1591 (1881). *History of the Kingdom of Congo*. Trans. by Margarite Hutchinson. London: John Murray.
Pile, Steve. 1997. "Introduction: Opposition, political identities and spaces of resistance." In Pile and Keith, eds. *Geographies of Resistance*. London: Routledge.
Pile, Steve and Michael Keith, eds. 1997. *Geographies of Resistance*. London: Routledge.
Piniau, Bernard. 1992. *Congo-Zaïre 1874–1981: La Perception du Lointain*. Paris: L'Harmattan.
Poulaine, Madeleine. 1931. *Une Blanche Chez Les Noirs*. Pris: Jules Tallandier.
Pratt, Mary Louise. 1992. *Imperial Eyes: Travel Writings and Transculturation*. London: Routledge.
Prunier, Gérard. 1995. *The Rwandan Crisis: History of a Genocide*. London: Hurst.
Prunier, Gérard. 1997. "The Great Lakes Crisis." *Current History* 96(610).
Quaghebeur, Marc et al., eds. 1992. *Papier Blanc, Encre Noire*. Brussels: Editions Labor.
Quinby, Lee. 1994. *Anti-Apocalypse: Exercise in Genealogical Criticism*. Minneapolis: University of Minnesota Press.
Ranger, Terrence. 1977. "The People in African Resistance." *Journal of Southern African Studies* 4(1).
Reed, David. 1966. *111 Days in Stanleyville*. London: Collins.
Reed, William Cyrus. 1998. "Protracted Patronage, Truncated Armed Struggle, and Political Consolidation in the Democratic Republic of the Congo." *Issue: A Journal of Opinion* 26(1).
Reed, William Cyrus. 1999. "Patronage, Reform, and Public Policy: The Role of Zaïre in the Great Lakes Crisis." Draft copy—mimeo in author's collection.
Reno, William. 1997. "Sovereignty and Personal Rule in Zaïre." *African Studies Quarterly* 1(3). Available at http://web.africa.ufl.edu/asq/v1/3/4.html.

Reno, William. 1998a. "Mines, Money, and the Problem of State-Building in Congo." *Issue: A Journal of Opinion* 26(1).
Reno, William. 1998b. *Warlord Politics and African States.* Boulder: Lynne Rienner.
Reyntjens, Filip. 1999. "Briefing: The Second Congo War: More than a Remake." *African Affairs* 98(391).
Rhodius, George. 1959. *Congo 1959, ou 50 ans de civilisation.* Brussels: Ministère de la Défense Nationale.
Richards, Paul. 1996. *Fighting for the Rain Forest.* Oxford: James Currey.
Richardson, Bill. 1997. "A Soft Landing in Zaïre?" *Newsweek,* 26 May.
Robinson, Ronald et al. 1968. *Africa and the Victorians: The Climax of Imperialism.* Garden City: Anchor Books.
Rom, Léon. 1900. *Le Nègre du Congo.* Brussels: Louis Vogels.
Rosenblum, Peter. 1997. "Endgame in Zaïre." *Current History* 96(610).
Rostow, W. W. 1960. *The Stages of Economic Growth: A Non-Communist Manifesto.* London: Cambridge University Press.
Rothchild, Donald and Naomi Chazan, eds. 1988. *Precarious Balance: State and Society in Africa.* Boulder: Westview.
Rothchild, Donald. 1987. "Hegemony and State Softness." In Ergas, ed. *The African State in Transition.* New York: St. Martin's Press.
Ryckmans, Pierre. 1948. *Dominer Pour Servir.* Brussels: L'Edition Universelle.
Rymenam, Jean. 1977. "Comment le régime Mobutu a sapé ses propres fondements." *Le Monde Diplomatique* (Mai).
Said, Edward. 1978. *Orientalism.* New York: Vintage.
Said, Edward. 1993. *Culture and Imperialism.* New York: Knopf.
Sakombi Inongo. 1997. "Interview: Sakombi, marabout de Kabila?" *L'Autre Afrique,* 17 December.
Sakombi Inongo. n.d. *Authenticité au Zaïre.* (pamphlet in CEDAF archives, Brussels).
Salongo. (Kinshasa, Zaïre).
Samarin, William J. 1989. "Language in the Colonization of Central Africa, 1880–1900." *Canadian Journal of African Studies* 23(2), pp. 232–49.
Sandbrook, Richard. 1985. *The Politics of Africa's Economic Stagnation.* Cambridge: Cambridge University Press.
Santoni, Ronald E. 1995. *Bad Faith, Good Faith and Authenticity in Sartre's Early Philosophy.* Philadelphia: Temple University Press.
Sartre, Jean-Paul. 1956. *Being and Nothingness.* Trans. by Hazel Barnes. New York: Philosophical Library.
Schatzberg, Michael G. 1978. "Fidélité au Guide: The JMPR in Zaïrian Schools." *Journal of Modern African Studies* 16(3).
Schatzberg, Michael G. 1980. "The State and the Economy: The 'Radicalization of the Revolution' in Mobutu's Zaïre." *Canadian Journal of African Studies* 14.
Schatzberg, Michael G. 1984. "Zaïre." In Shaw and Aluko, eds. *The Political Economy of African Foreign Policy.* Aldershot: Gower.
Schatzberg, Michael G. 1988. *The Dialectics of Oppression in Zaïre.* Bloomington: Indiana University Press.
Schatzberg, Michael G. 1991. *Mobutu or Chaos? The United States and Zaïre, 1960–1990.* Lanham, MD: University Press of America.
Scheyen, Raymond. 1956. *Et Le Congo?* Brussels: Van Ruys.
Schraeder, Peter J. 1994. *United States Foreign Policy toward Africa: Incrementalism, Crisis and Change.* Cambridge: Cambridge University Press.

Scott, Catherine V. 1995. *Gender and Development: Rethinking Modernization and Dependency Theory*. Boulder: Lynne Rienner.
Shapiro, Michael J. 1988. *The Politics of Representation: Writing Practices in Biography, Photography, and Policy Analysis*. Madison: University of Wisconsin Press.
Shapiro, Michael J. and Hayward R. Alker, eds. 1996. *Challenging Boundaries*. Minneapolis: University of Minnesota Press.
Shapiro, Michael J., G. Matthew Bonham, and Daniel Heradstveit. 1988. "A Discursive Practices Approach to Collective Decision-Making." *International Studies Quarterly* 32.
Sharpe, Jenny. 1995. "Figures of Colonial Resistance." In Ashcroft, Griffiths, and Tifin, eds. *The Post-Colonial Studies Reader*. London: Routledge.
Simons, Edwine, Roupen Boghossian, and Benoît Verhaegen. 1995. *Stanleyville 1959: Le procès de Patrice Lumumba et les émeutes d'octobre*. Brussels: CEDAF/ASDOC.
Singh, Frances B. 1988. "Racism and the *Heart of Darkness*." In Conrad. *Heart of Darkness: Critical Edition*. New York: W.W. Norton and Co.
Slade, Ruth. 1955. "English Missionaries and the Beginning of the Anti-Congolese Campaign in England." *Revue Belge de Philogie et d'Histoire* 33(1), pp. 37–73.
Slade, Ruth. 1957. "King Leopold II and the Attitude of English and American Catholics toward the anti-Congolese campaign." *Zaire: Revue Congolaise* 11(6), pp. 593–612.
Slade, Ruth. 1959. *English-Speaking Missions in the Congo Independent State (1878–1908)*. Brussels: Académie Royale des Sciences Coloniales.
Slade, Ruth. 1960. *The Belgian Congo: Some Recent Changes*. London: Oxford University Press.
Slade, Ruth. 1962. *King Leopold's Congo: Aspects of the Development of Race Relations in the Congo Independent State*. London: Oxford University Press.
Smith, Anthony D. 1991. *National Identity*. Reno: University of Nevada Press.
Smith, Stephen. 2001. "Ces Enfants-Soldats Qui Ont Tué Kabila." *Le Monde*, 10 February.
Smith, Stephen and Antoine Glaser. 1992. *Ces Messieurs Afrique: Le Paris-Village du continent noir*. Paris: Calmann-Levy.
Soir, Le. (Brussels).
Somers, Margaret R. 1994. "The Narrative Constitution of Identity: A relational and network approach." *Theory and Society* (23), 605–649.
Somers, Margaret R. and Gloria D. Gibson. 1994. "Reclaiming the Epistemological 'Other': Narrative and the Social Constitution of Identity." In Craig Calhoun, ed. *Social Theory and the Politics of Identity*. Oxford: Blackwell.
Speke, John. 1864. *Journey of the Discovery of the Source of the Nile*. New York.
Springfield Leader and Press. (Springfield, Missouri).
Spruyt, Hendrik. 1994. *The Sovereign State and Its Competitors: An Analysis of Systems Change*. Princeton: Princeton University Press.
Stanley, Henry M. 1872. *How I Found Livingstone*. New York: Harper and Brothers.
Stanley, Henry M. 1878. *Through the Dark Continent*. 2 vols. New York: Harper and Brothers.
Stanley, Henry M. 1885. *The Congo and the Founding of Its Free State*. 2 vols. New York: Harper and Brothers.
Starr, Frederick. 1907. *The Truth About the Congo: The Chicago Tribune Articles*. Chicago: Forbes and Co.
Stengers, Jean. 1972. "King Leopold's Imperialism." In Owen and Sutcliffe, eds. *Studies in the Theory of Imperialism*. London: Longman.
Stengers, Jean. 1989. *Congo Mythes et Réalités*. Paris: Éditions Duculot.

Stevenson, Adlai. 1960. "The New Africa." *Harper's* (May).
Stockwell, John. 1978. *In Search of Enemies: A CIA Story*. New York: WW Norton.
Strang, David. 1996. "Contested Sovereignty: The social construction of colonial imperialism." In Biersteker and Weber, eds. *State Sovereignty as Social Construct*. Cambridge: Cambridge University Press.
Taussig, Michael. 1993. *Mimesis and Alterity: A Particular History of the Senses*. New York/London: Routledge.
Tempels, Placide. 1948. *Bantu Philosophy*. Paris: Éditions Présence Africaine.
Tilly, Charles. 1975. *The Formation of the Nation-State in Western Europe*. Princeton: Princeton University Press.
Tilly, Charles. 1990. *Coercion, Capital, and European States, AD 900–1992*. Oxford: Basil Blackwell.
Time. (New York).
Todorov, Tzvetan. 1984. *The Conquest of America: The Question of the Other*. New York: Harper and Row.
Torfing, Jacob. 1999. *New Theories of Discourse: Laclau, Mouffe and Zizek*. Oxford: Blackwell.
Torgovnick, Marianna. 1990. *Gone Primitive: Savage Intellects, Modern Lives*. Chicago: University of Chicago Press.
Tousignant, Nathalie. 1995. *Les Manifestations Publiques du Lien Colonial entre la Belgique et le Congo Belge (1897–1988)*. Ph.D. Diss. Dept. d'Histoire, Université Laval, Québec.
Trefon, Theodore. 1989. "French Policy Toward Zaïre during the Giscard D'Estaing Presidency." *Les Cahiers du CEDAF*, 1.
Tully, Andrew. 1962. *CIA—The Inside Story*. New York: Morrow.
Turner, Thomas. 1997. "Kabila Returns, In a Cloud of Uncertainty." *African Studies Quarterly* 1(3). Available at http://web.africa.ufl.edu/asq/v1/3/4.html.
Turner, Thomas. 2001. "The Kabilas' Congo." *Current History* (May).
Twain, Mark. 1961. *King Leopold's Soliloquy*. New York: International Publishers
UN Security Council *Official Records*, 15th year, Supplement for July, August, and September, 1960, doc. S/4382, Add 11.
U.S. Department of State. 1978. "News Conferences, May 4 and 25 (Excerpts)." *Department of State Bulletin* 78(2016) (July).
U.S. Senate Report. 1976. *Alleged Assassination Plots Involving Foreign Leaders*. New York: W.W. Norton & Co.
Vance, Cyrus. 1983. *Hard Choices: Critical Years in America's Foreign Policy*. New York: Simon and Schuster.
Vangroenweghe, Daniel. 1986. *Du Sang sur les Lianes*. Brussels: Didier Hatier.
Vansina, Jan. 1966a. *Kingdoms of the Savanna*. Madison: University of Wisconsin Press.
Vansina, Jan. 1966b. *Introduction à l'Ethnologie du Congo*. Kinshasa: Editions Universitaires du Congo.
Vantieghem, Leen. 1996. "La Culture du Cacao au Mayombe (Congo belge) 1885–1914." In CGER, ed. *Chocolat: De la boisson elitaire au baton populaire*. Brussels: Marc Van Niewenhuize.
Vellut, Jean-Luc. 1987. "Résistances et espaces de liberté dans l'histoire coloniale du Zaïre: Avant la marche à l'Indépendance (1876–1945)." In Coquery-Vidrovitch, Forest, and Weiss, eds. *Rebellions-Révolution au Zaïre (1963–1965)*. Vol. 1. Paris: L'Harmattan.
Vellut, Jean-Luc. 1996. "Le cacao dans l'économie politique de l'ancien Congo belge." In

CGER, ed. *Chocolat: de la boisson elitaire au baton populaire.* Brussels: Marc Van Niewenhuize.
Verhaegen, Benoît. 1966/1969. *Rébellions au Congo.* Vols. 1 and 2. Brussels: CRISP.
Verhaegen, Benoît. 1992. "La Colonisation et la Décolonisation dans les manuels d'histoire en Belgique." In Quaghebeur et al., eds. *Papier Blanc, Encre Noire.* Brussels: Editions Labor.
Verwimp, Philip and Els Vanheusden. 1999. "The Foreign Policy of Belgium during the Zaïre/Congo Crisis: March 1996-March 1997." Paper presented at the International Studies Association Conference, Washington, D.C., 17 February.
Villalón, Leonardo A. and Phillip A. Huxtable, eds. 1998. *The African State at a Critical Juncture: Between Disintegration and Reconfiguration.* Boulder: Lynne Rienner.
Vincke, Edouard. 1993. "Discours sur le Noir: Images dans les espaces urbains de Bruxelles." In Halen and Riesz, eds. *Images de l'Afrique et du Congo/Zaïre dans les lettres fançaise de Belgique et alentour.* Brussels: Textyles.
Vints, Luc. 1984. *Kongo made in Belgium.* Leuven: Kritak.
Vitoria, F. 1917. "De Indis Recenter Inventis: De Iure Bello." In J. Brown Scott, ed. *The Classics of International Law.* Washington: Carnegie.
Von Horn, Carl. 1967. *Soldiering for Peace.* New York: David McKay.
Walker, R. B. J. 1991. "State Sovereignty and the Articulation of Political Space/Time." *Millennium.*
Walker, R. B. J. 1993. *Inside/Outside: International Relations as Political Theory.* Cambridge: Cambridge University Press.
Wallerstein, Immanuel. 1979. *The Capitalist World-Economy.* Cambridge: Cambridge University Press.
Wamba-dia-Wamba, Ernest. 1993. "Democracy, Multipartyism and Emancipative Politics in Africa: The Case of Zaïre." *Africa Development* 18(4).
Wamba-dia-Wamba, Ernest. 1999. "Interview: 'Kabila cannot be allowed to win a military victory.'" *New African* (February).
Ward, Herbert. 1891. *Five Years with the Congo Cannibals.* 3d ed. London: Chatto and Windus.
Watson, Adam. 1992. *The Evolution of International Society: A Comparative Historical Analysis.* London: Routledge.
Weber, Cynthia. 1995. *Simulating Sovereignty: Intervention, the State, and Symbolic Exchange.* Cambridge: Cambridge University Press.
Weber, Cynthia. 1998. "Performative States." *Millennium* 27(1).
Weber, Cynthia. 1999. *Faking It: U.S. Hegemony in a "Post-Phallic" Era.* Minneapolis: University of Minnesota Press.
Wechsler, Suruba Ibumando Georgette. 1999. *By the Grace of God: A true story of love, family, war and survival from the Congo.* New Horizon Press.
Weiss, Herbert. 1966. "Introduction." In CRISP, ed. *Congo 1964: Political Documents of a Developing Nation.* Princeton: Princeton University Press.
Weissman, Stephen R. 1974a. *American Foreign Policy in the Congo 1960–1964.* Ithaca: Cornell University Press.
Weissman, Stephen R. 1974b. "Zaïre: Fisticuffs For Mobutu." *The Nation,* 30 November.
Weissman, Stephen R. 1981. "The CIA and US Policy in Zaïre and Angola." In Lemarchand, ed. *American Policy in Southern Africa: The Stakes and the Stance.* 2d Ed. Washington, D.C.: University Press of America.
Willame, Jean-Claude. 1971. "Politics and power in Congo Kinshasa." *Africa Report* (January).

Willame, Jean-Claude. 1972. *Patrimonialism and Political Change in the Congo*. Stanford: Stanford University Press.
Willame, Jean-Claude. 1998. "The 'Friends of the Congo' and the Kabila System." *Issue: A Journal of Opinion* 26(1).
Willequet, Jacques. 1962. *Le Congo Belge et la Weltpolitik (1894–1914)*. Brussels: Presses Universitaires de Bruxelles.
Williams, G. Mennen. 1967. "U.S. Objectives in the Congo, 1960–65." In Kitchen, ed. *Footnotes to the Congo Story*. New York: Walker and Co.
Wilungula B. Cosma. 1997. *Fizi 1967–1986: Le Maquis Kabila*. Brussels: CEDAF.
Winter, Roger P. 1996. "Lancing the Boil: Rwanda's Agenda in Zaïre 1996." Paper presented at the International Studies Association Conference, Washington, D.C., 17 February.
Wood, Denis. 1992. *The Power of Maps*. New York: Guilford Press.
World Press Review. (New York).
Wrong, Michela. 2001. *In the Footsteps of Mr. Kurtz*. New York: HarperCollins.
Wyvekens, Pierre. 1989. *The Many Faces of Brussels*. Liège: Editions du Perron.
Young, Crawford. 1965. *Politics in the Congo: Decolonization and Independence*. Princeton: Princeton University Press.
Young, Crawford. 1967a. "Congo-Kinshasa Situation Report." *Africa Report*. (October).
Young, Crawford. 1967b. "Violence and Rebellion in the Congo." In Gary Gappert and Garry Thomas, eds. *The Congo, Africa and America*. Occasional Paper no. 15. Maxwell Graduate School, Syracuse University.
Young, Crawford. 1978. "Zaïre: The Unending Crisis." *Foreign Affairs* 57(1).
Young, Crawford. 1994. *The African Colonial State in Comparative Perspective*. New Haven: Yale University Press.
Young, Crawford and Thomas Turner. 1985. *The Rise and Decline of the Zaïrian State*. Madison: University of Wisconsin Press.
Zalewski, Marysia and Cynthia Enloe. 1995. "Questions about Identity in International Relations." In Booth and Smith, eds. *International Relations Theory Today*. University Park: Pennsylvania University Press.
Zartman, I. William, ed. 1995. *Collapsed States: The Disintegration and Restoration of Legitimate Authority*. Boulder: Lynne Rienner.

Index

abacos, 113–115, 117
ABC News, 4–6, 15–16
Adelman, Kenneth, 111–112, 117
Adorno, Theodor, 192–193
"Africa War One," 167–170
AIDS, 5, 165
Albright, Madeline, 165, 167
Ali, Muhammad, 105–106, 121, 124–125, 132, 179, 191
Allen, Chris, 159, 160
Alliance des Bakongo (ABAKO), 73
Alliance des Forces Démocratiques pour la Libération du Congo (AFDL), 3, 144, 153–155
Allied Democratic Front (ADF), 152–153, 156
American Mineral Fields, 167
Anderson, Benedict, 72
Angola, 1, 111, 122, 129–130, 159–160, 177
   Congo war, 2–4, 141, 145, 157, 168
   invasion by Zaïre, 128–129, 153, 193
   looting Congo resources, 2, 157
   overthrow of Mobutu, 144–145, 153–154
animation, 113
Arendt, Hannah, 94,
authenticité, 106, 107, 109–118, 120, 129, 155
   emulation of, 125–126
   relation to Western philosophy, 119–120, 192–193

Ball, George, 85–86, 89–91
Banyamulenge, 3, 143–144, 150, 155
Banyarwanda, 143
Baudouin, King, 62, 63, 66, 67, 73, 82, 84–85, 89, 125
   Independence day speech, 66–67, 76, 77, 102
Bederman, Gail, 186
Belgique Coloniale, La, 24, 184
Belgium
   annexation of Congo, 8, 15, 22, 25, 37, 58–59, 67, 187

   colonial policies, 15, 59, 68–74, 90, 110, 111, 114, 119, 124, 137, 148–149, 172, *see also* Paternalism
   independence of Congo, 63, 66–73
   Katangan secession, 81, 100–101
   military intervention, 6, 63–64, 79–85, 172
   national identity, 28, 29, 35, 37, 50–52, 56, 68–70
   relations with Joseph Kabila, 177
   relations with Laurent-Désiré Kabila, 163, 167–170
   relations with Lumumba, 83–85, 96, 174–175, 179
   relations with Mobutu, 118–119, 121–134, 141, 146, 154–155, 159–161, 163, 172
   see also Baudouin, King *and* Leopold II
Bemba, Jean Pierre, 156, 158, 195
Berkeley, Bill, 179, 180
Berlin Conference, 8, 22, 41, 42, 51, 55
Boma, 63
Boulger, Demetrius C., 56
Braeckman, Colette, 195
Britain, 22, 24, 29, 51–54, 73, 99, 125
Bronx Zoo, 179
Brown, Wendy, 195
Brussels Independence Roundtable Conference, 62, 75
Brussels Universal Exhibition (1958), 61–62, 67–68, 73, 78, 187
Bukavu, 144, 151–152
Bula Matari, 70–71
Burrows, Guy, 187
Burundi, 140, 149, 150–152
   Congo war, 1–4, 141, 155–158, 168
   Kabila, Laurent-Désiré, 144, 145, 153, 155–158
Bush, George, 131–132, 163–164
Bustin, Edouard, 154, 194–195
Butler, Judith, 12

Callaghy, Thomas, 136, 192
Campbell, David, 7, 86, 189

Camus, Albert, 119
Canisius, Edgar, 52
cannibalism, 29, 34, 48, 52, 53, 54–56, 87, 109, 123, 133
Cão, Diego, 7
Carte de Mérite Civique, 72, 74
Carter, Jimmy, 130–131, 193
Casement, Roger, 51–53
Catholic Church, 59, 62, 71, 81, 143, 187–188
  see also Christianity and Christian missionaries
Central Intelligence Agency (CIA), 64, 86, 91, 93–97, 116–118, 121, 128, 174, 190, 193
Césaire, Aimé, 117
Chad, 3, 126, 145, 168
Chatterjee, Partha, 77–78
chieftancy, 71, 113, 114–116, 118
China, 117, 127, 128, 130
chocolate, 69
Chomé, Jules, 131
Christian missionaries, 5, 14, 24, 28, 46, 50, 51, 52, 56, 62, 71, 178, 180, 186
  see also Catholic Church and Christianity
Christianity, 27, 28, 30, 37–38, 48, 81, 143, 184
  see also Catholic Church and Christian missionaries
civil society, 28, 143, 155
Clapham, Christopher, 147, 169
Clinton, Bill, 164–165
Close, William T., 179, 180
clothing, 67, 76, 133
  as national identity markers, 113–115, 117, 118–119
  as social markers, 32–33, 88
cold war, 9, 13, 65, 86–103, 106–108, 121, 122, 126–134, 141, 164
  end of, 141, 159–161
Colonial Exhibition for 1897 World's Fair, 34–36
Comaroff, Jean and John, 14, 26
Commité d'Etudes du Haut-Congo (CEHC), 21
communism
  fear of, 6, 13, 74, 85–103, 106, 122, 128–132, 159
Congo, Illustré, Le, 24, 47, 48, 184
Congo Reform Association, 50, 51, 56
Congo Reform movement, 25, 50–59, 87, 109
Congorama, 67, 187

Congress, American, 16, 73, 93, 96, 165
Connolly, William E., 27, 185
Conrad, Joseph, 4, 15, 16, 47, 52–53, 87, 133, 166
corruption, 9, 96, 116, 133, 140, 163, 172
counterhegemony, 107, 120–123
Crichton, Michael, 133–134
Cuba, 129–130

de Schrijver, Auguste, 68
de St. Moulin, Léon, 45
de Vattel, Emerich, 37–38
De Witte, Ludo, 179, 180
DeBeers, 154
democratization, 139–140, 160, 164–165
Dequae, André, 62
d'Estaing, Giscard, 131, 193
Devlin, Lawrence, 93–94, 96
diamonds, 153–154, 167
discourse
  power defined, 6, 10–16, 106–107, 173, 183
Doty, Roxanne, 12, 14, 16, 135, 174, 191, 193
Dulles, Allen, 94–95, 96, 190

Eisenhower, Dwight, 86–88, 90–91, 96, 99, 101–103
Elisabethville, 96,110
Emin Pasha, 23, 183, 186
ethnicity, 27, 37, 39, 42, 73, 76, 77, 143, 147–152, 155, 158, 194–195
évolués, 71–73,74
Existentialism, 119, 192–193
Expo (1958), see Brussels Universal Exhibition (1958)

Ferguson, Kennan, 17, 86, 185
Fisiy, Cyprian F., 151–152
Force Publique, 54–55, 62, 78–79
  mutiny of, 63, 78–80, 83, 88
Forces Armées Rwandaises (FAR), 2, 144, 149–151, 156
Forces Armées Zaïroises (FAZ), 144
Foreman, George, 105–106, 124–125, 132, 179, 191–192
Foucault, Michel, 6–7, 119, 121, 183
Fox, Renée, 37
Fox Bourne, H. R., 52, 187
France, 22, 24, 29, 51, 54, 73, 81, 84, 99, 141
  chasse gardée, 159, 161–162

Index 217

competition with United States, 162–163
Fashoda Syndrome, 162–163, 195–196
Operation Turquoise, 161–162
relations with Joseph Kabila, 177
relations with Laurent-Désiré Kabila, 162–163, 167–170
relations with Mobutu, 120, 122, 126–134, 139, 146, 154–155, 159–164, 172
French-Sheldon, May, 56
Frente Nacional de Libertaçao de Angola (FNLA), 128
Front for the Defense of Democracy (FDD), 150–151, 156
Front Démocratique du Burundi (FRODEBU), 150–151

Garang, John, 152
Geller, Ernest, 112
gender, 27, 30, 35–36, 68, 158, 185, 186
genealogical approach, 6–7, 17, 171, 173–176
genocide, 156
  under Leopold II, 45, 55–56
  Rwandan, 2, 4, 13, 142–144, 148–152, 155, 160, 161–164, 180
Germany, 29, 51, 54, 187
Ghana, 75, 97–98, 101
Gibbs, David, 11
Gizenga, Antoine, 99
gold, 126, 167
Goma, 144, 148, 151–152, 157
Gourevitch, Philip, 158–159, 164, 169
Gramsci, Antonio, 14, 120–121, 174, 176–177, 183
Greene, Graham, 87, 133
Grovogui, Siba, 135
Guevara, Ché, 2

Habyarimana, Juvénal, 2, 143, 149, 161
Hall, Stuart, 10, 13, 107, 123, 183
Hammarskjöld, Dag, 63, 99, 100, 103, 125
"heart of darkness," 4, 5–6, 9, 15, 16, 52–53, 87, 109, 122, 133, 165, 166, 173, 178–180, 186
hegemony, 14, 106–107, 120–121
Heidegger, Martin, 119
Hochschild, Adam, 11, 178–180
Hodgkin, Thomas, 187
Hoskyns, Catherine, 84

Huliaras, Asteris, 162–163
Hutu, 148–152, 161

Ilunga, Emile, 157, 158
Inayatullah, Naeem, 135
Interahamwe, 2, 143–144, 149–150, 151, 156, 161–162, 169
International African Association (IAA), 21
International Association of the Congo (IAC), 21, 41, 42
International Geographic Conference, 21, 49
International Monetary Fund (IMF), 132, 160
Israel, 125, 127
ivory, 7, 34, 51

Jackson, Robert H., 134–135
Japan, 126

Kabila, Joseph, 4, 177–178
Kabila, Laurent-Désiré
  assassination, 1, 2, 4, 171, 177
  as President, 2, 3, 145, 154–158, 165
  as rebel leader, 2, 3, 140, 144, 146, 148, 150, 154
  authoring Congo's national identity, 154–155, 158
  relations with Belgium 163, 167–170
  relations with France, 162–163, 167–170
  relations with Rwanda, 3–4, 144, 145, 153, 155–158, 165
  relations with Uganda, 3–4, 144, 145, 153, 155–158
  relations with United States, 3, 144, 164–170
Kabwit, Ghislain, 113
Kagame, Paul, 2, 143, 149–150, 156, 157, 158
Kangafu-Kutumbagana, 111, 119
Kaplan, Robert, 166, 169
Kappend, Eddy, 1
Kasai, 144
Kasavubu, Joseph, 62, 75, 83, 94, 99, 189
  conflict with Patrice Lumumba, 63–64, 93–94, 102
Kasereka, Rachidi, 1
Katanga, 2, 70, 81, 129–131, 188–189
  secession from Congo, 63–64, 83–85, 91, 99, 100–101
  see also Shaba

Kennan, George, 86–87
Kennedy, John F., 89, 96–97
Kennedy, Pagan, 178–180
Khrushchev, Nikita, 98–100
Kigali, 3, 144, 164
Kimba, Évariste, 116
Kingsolver, Barbara, 5, 178, 180
Kinshasa, 3, 14, 106, 110, 114, 122, 123, 125, 131, 132, 137, 140, 142, 144, 145, 153, 164
  see also Leopoldville
Kisangani, 110, 133, 144, 157
  see also Stanleyville
Kivilu, Sabakinu, 45
Kivu provinces, 2, 3, 143, 144, 147, 150, 163
Kongo Kingdom, 7, 26, 39, 110–111, 192

labor, 32–33, 40–41, 46, 76
  forced labor, 22, 41, 44, 45, 51, 55, 59, 66, 76, 122
language, 26, 37, 49, 72, 74, 76, 77, 110–111, 117, 119–120, 147, 148, 158
Lemarchand, René, 126, 149, 150, 152
Leopold II, 62, 69, 70, 110, 183–184
  authoring Congo's identity, 14, 15, 23–25, 28–42, 44–50, 55–59, 67, 86, 87, 109, 170, 174
  colonization of Congo, 5, 8, 21–59, 66, 67–68, 172, 178
  greed and resource extraction from Congo, 11, 45, 52–55, 74, 178, 186
Leopoldville, 62, 64, 73, 75, 94–95, 102, 106, 110, 174
  see also Kinshasa
Libre Belgique, La, 78, 79, 80, 81, 83–84, 102
Livingstone, David, 23
Lord's Resistance Movement, 152
Lumumba, Patrice, 107, 127, 144
  assassination, 1, 5, 64, 96, 114, 117, 172, 174–175, 178–179
  authoring of Congo's national identity, 74–79, 83, 120
  branded as a communist, 6, 13, 87, 90–97, 190
  early political career, 74–75
  goatee and physical appearance, 91–93
  independence, 62–63, 66–70, 83–85
  Independence Day speech, 66, 76–77, 84, 91, 102
  legacy, 114, 117, 155, 178, 192
  relations with Belgium, 83–85, 96, 174–175, 179
  relations with United States, 6, 13, 14, 64–65, 84–103, 174–175
  visit to United States, 84, 103
  visit to UN, 14, 102–103, 174

Malengreau, Guy, 70
Mandela, Nelson, 154, 158
Matadi, 63
Mau Mau, 87, 188
McClintock, Anne, 24, 40, 44, 68, 185
McNulty, Mel, 142
mercenaries, 81, 135, 144
mimicry, 24, 33, 34, 121–123, 175
Mobutisme, 109, 129
Mobutu, Joseph-Désiré, 63, 64, 93–94, 99, 100, 102, 142, 158
  authenticité, 106, 107, 109–120, 125–126, 129, 155, 192–193
  authoring Congo's national identity, 107–134, 142–143, 147–148
  cancer, 139–141
  coup (1965), 106, 109
  death, 140
  Mobutisme, 109, 129
  name change, 106, 110, 192
  personal fortune, 116, 125, 140, 172
  opposition to, 2, 15, 128–138, 140–141, 144–145
  overthrow, 3, 144–145, 146, 152–155, 160, 162, 166
  relations with Belgium, 118–119, 121–134, 141, 146, 154–155, 159–161, 163, 172
  relations with France, 120, 122, 126–134, 139, 146, 154–155, 159–164, 172
  relations with Rwanda, 140, 143, 147–154
  relations with Uganda, 140, 143, 147–148, 152–154
  relations with United States, 6, 11, 107–108, 116–117, 122–138, 141, 146, 153–155, 159–161, 163–170, 172, 189
  supported by the West, 6, 11, 13, 93–94, 100, 107–108, 116–117, 121–134, 154, 159–165, 172
  Zaïrianisation, 109, 117, 127, 192
Modernization theory, 97
Morel, E. D., 22, 25, 50–59
Mouvement pour la Libération du Congo (MLC), 156–157

Mouvement Géographique, Le,
  24, 47, 184
Mouvement National Congolais
  (MNC), 74–75
Mouvement Populaire de Révolution
  (MPR), 109–111, 113, 114–116
Movimento Popular de Libertação de
  Angola (MPLA), 128, 153,
  157, 159–160
Mudimbe, V. Y., 71, 184
Mugabe, Robert, 157–158
Mulele, Pierre, 155
Mummendey, Dietrich, 109
museums, 16, 35–36, 187
Museveni, Yoweri, 2, 146, 147, 148,
  152–153, 156–157

Naipaul, V. S., 133–134, 193–194
Namibia, 2–4, 145, 157, 168
National Conference,
  139–140, 143, 160
National Council for the Defense of
  Democracy (CNDD), 150–151
Nationality Act (1981), 143
Ndadaye, Melchior, 149–150
"New Barbarism" thesis, 166–170
New York Herald, 23, 38, 43
New York Times, 4, 102, 123,
  124, 129–130, 132–133, 175,
  179, 190, 193
Newbury, David, 4, 16, 142, 148, 165
Newsweek, 166, 167, 193, 196
Nixon, Richard, 125
Nkrumah, Kwame, 75, 98, 100–101
North Atlantic Treaty Organization
  (NATO), 90, 102, 160
North Korea, 117
Notre Congo, 18, 65, 66, 68–69, 80,
  81, 86, 97
N'Sele Manifesto, 114–115
Nyangoma, Leonard, 150
Nyerere, Julius, 2, 113–114, 125, 193
Nyoto, 114

Opération Turquoise, 161–162
Organization of African Unity (OAU)
  15, 120, 125, 135, 191

Paternalism, 65, 68–74, 75, 77, 79–83,
  85, 86, 97, 116, 119, 124, 187–188
Peck, Raoul, 179, 180
Penfield, James K., 93
Portugal, 7–8, 22, 27, 37,
  111, 122, 128

Pratt, Mary Louise, 38, 40, 49, 185

railroad, 33, 67, 69, 70
Rassemblement Congolais pour la
  Démocratie (RCD), 156–157
Reagan, Ronald, 131–132
rebellions, 83, 106
  under Belgian rule, 15, 33–34, 71
  under Kabila, 1–5, 142–145,
    155–158, 161, 162, 167–170
  under Mobutu, 15, 140–141,
    147–150, 152–154, 160,
    161, 164–165
"Red Rubber," 22, 25, 51, 55, 56, 59
  see also rubber
Reed, William Cyrus, 142
refugees, 2–4, 143–144, 145, 149–150,
  151–152, 160, 164, 194
Reno, William, 135–136
resistance, 14, 15, 24, 33–34, 62–63,
  71, 175–176
  see also rebellions *and* riots
Rhodesia, 81, 122
  see also Zimbabwe
Richards, Thomas, 34
riots, 62, 73, 74
Roberto, Holden, 128
Rom, Léon, 43
Rosberg, Carl G., 134–135
Rosenblum, Peter, 142, 143
Rostow, W. W., 97, 190–191
Rothchild, Donald, 136
Ruanda-Urundi, 61, 148–149, 187
rubber, 22, 35, 45, 51, 52, 109, 186
  see also "Red Rubber"
"Rumble in the Jungle," 105–106,
  124–125, 132, 179, 191
Rwanda, 161, 162, 176, 177
  Congo war, 1–4, 141, 155–158, 168
  genocide, 2, 4, 13, 142–144,
    148–152, 155, 160, 161–164, 180
  looting Congo's resources, 2, 157
  relations with Kabila, 3–4, 144, 145,
    153, 155–158, 165
  relations with Mobutu, 140,
    143, 147–154
Rwandan Patriotic Front (RPF), 2, 3,
  143–144, 150, 161, 165
Ryckmans, Pierre, 68, 188
Rymenam, Jean (Benoît
  Verhaegan), 131

Said, Edward, 174
Sakombi Inongo, Dominique, 112,
  119, 155, 195

Sandbrook, Richard, 136
Sartre, Jean Paul, 119
Savimbi, Jonas, 128
Schatzberg, Michael, 117, 126, 193
Senegal, 117
Senghor, Léopold Sédar, 117
Shaba, 144
    see also Katanga
Shaba I, 128–130, 132, 135
Shaba II, 128, 130–132, 135, 192
Shaft in Africa, 193
Sheppard, William, 178, 180
slave trade, 102
    Atlantic slave trade, 7, 27–28, 30
    East African/"Arab" slave trade, 30, 36, 42–44, 46, 48, 55, 66, 67
Smith, Anthony, 112
Société Générale Congolaise des Carrières et Mines, 124
Soir, Le, 85, 102, 193
Somalia, 163–165
Somers, Margaret, 64
South Africa, 81, 122, 128, 153–154, 157–158, 168
Southern African Development Community, 157
Soviet Union, 15, 63, 85–87, 89–90, 98–100, 121, 128–130
    collapse of, 141, 159–160
    spatial constructions, 25, 26, 32, 36–42, 44, 46, 47, 49, 53, 59, 70, 71, 75–76, 79–83, 91, 97, 134–138, 141–142, 153–154, 175–177
Stanley, Henry Morton, 110, 186
    authoring Congo's identity, 14, 15, 23–24, 26–34, 37–45, 55, 59, 66, 67, 70, 86–88, 109, 122, 170, 172, 174
    exploration of the Congo River basin, 5, 21–34, 37–42, 172, 183
    violence, 5, 43–45
Stanleyville, 64, 74, 75
    see also Kisangani
Starr, Frederick, 56
State Department, U.S., 89, 93, 94, 96, 100, 127, 164
Stevenson, Adlai, 191
Sudan, 3, 140, 145, 152, 156, 168, 183
Sudan People's Liberation Army (SPLA), 152

Tanzania, 113, 117, 125
Tarzan, 5, 123, 193
Taussig, Michael, 30–31, 43

Tempels, Placide, 118
Tervuren, 34–36, 62, 78, 185, 187
Time, 86, 88, 91–94, 102, 124, 125, 169, 190
Tintin in the Congo (*Tintin au Congo*), 16, 69
trade, 7, 8, 21, 41, 42, 46–48, 50–51, 55–57, 122, 140, 161
Tshombe, Moïse, 63, 75, 81, 84–85, 91, 101, 123
Tutsi, 147–152, 155, 156
Twain, Mark, 55–56

Uganda, 162, 169, 176
    Congo's war, 1–4, 141, 155–158, 168
    looting Congo's resources, 2, 156, 157
    relations with Kabila, 3–4, 144, 145, 153, 155–158
    relations with Mobutu, 140, 143, 147–148, 152–154
Uniao Nacional para a Independência Total de Angola (UNITA), 128, 145, 153, 157
Union Minière, 70, 71, 124, 131
United Nations, 15, 120, 125, 135, 161, 164, 175
    Congo Crisis, 63–64, 81, 85, 98–103, 191
    Congo's civil war, 163, 177
    relations with Lumumba, 14, 94, 99, 102–103, 174
United States, 15, 22, 41, 48, 51, 52, 56, 86
    Congo Crisis, 6, 13, 63–65, 85–97, 99–103
    relations with Joseph Kabila, 177–178
    relations with Laurent-Désiré Kabila, 3, 144, 164–170
    relations with Lumumba, 6, 13, 14, 64–65, 84–103, 174–175
    relations with Mobutu, 6, 11, 107–108, 116–117, 122–138, 141, 146, 153–155, 159–161, 163–170, 172, 189
    see also Central Intelligence Agency (CIA) and State Department
Uvira, 144

Vance, Cyrus, 130
Vansina, Jan, 112, 118, 184
"Viagra" war, 195

Voix du Congolais, La, 72

Wamba-dia-Wamba, Ernest, 145, 146, 156–158, 194
Ward, Henry, 46, 186
Washington Post, 96, 124, 126, 132
Weber, Cynthia, 9, 52, 175, 186–187
Weissman, Stephen, 98–99, 100, 193
West Nile Bank Front, 152
Westphalian state system, 39–41, 42, 134–138, 171, 175–177
Willame, Jean-Claude, 162, 196
Williams, G. Mennen, 91
women, 36, 68, 113, 189
World Bank, 132, 160
Wrong, Michela, 179, 180

Young, Crawford, 69, 70–71, 83, 188, 194

Zaïre
etymology, 110–111, 192
name change, 106, 110–111, 141, 145
Zaïrianisation, 109, 117, 127, 192
Zambia, 125, 130
Zimbabwe, 1
Congo's war, 2–4, 141, 145, 157–158, 177
looting Congo's resources, 2, 157–158

CPSIA information can be obtained at www.ICGtesting.com
Printed in the USA
LVOW07s1918010715
444622LV00004B/177/P